PARDON AND ASSURANCE

OTHER TITLES FROM SGCB

In addition to the book in your hand Solid Ground is delighted and honored to offer the following titles:

The Sufferings of the Church of Scotland by Robert Wodrow
The Scottish Pulpit by William Taylor
The Life and Letters of James Renwick by W.H. Carslaw
Precious Seed: Discourses of Scots Worthies
The Doctrine of Justification by James Buchanan
Paul the Preacher by John Eadie
Greek Text Commentary on Galatians by John Eadie
Greek Text Commentary on Ephesians by John Eadie
Greek Text Commentary on Philippians by John Eadie
Greek Text Commentary on Colossians by John Eadie
Greek Text Commentary on Thessalonians by John Eadie
Divine Love: A Series of Discourses by John Eadie
Lectures on the Bible for the Young by John Eadie
Opening Scripture: Hermeneutical Manual by Patrick Fairbairn
Martyrland: A Tale of Persecution by Robert Simpson
The Preacher and His Models by James Stalker
Imago Christi: The Example of Jesus Christ by James Stalker
Sabbath Scripture Readings from the OT by Thomas Chalmers
Sabbath Scripture Readings from the NT by Thomas Chalmers
Lectures on the Book of Esther by Thomas M'Crie
The Psalms in History and Biography by John Ker
A Pathway into the Psalter by William Binnie
Heroes of Israel: Abraham – Moses by William G. Blaikie
Expository Lectures on Joshua by William G. Blaikie
Expository Lectures on 1 Samuel by William G. Blaikie
Expository Lectures on 2 Samuel by William G. Blaikie
Luther's Scottish Connection by James McGoldrick

PARDON AND ASSURANCE

How to Know for Certain
That Your Sins are Forgiven
And You are Bound for Heaven

WILLIAM J. PATTON
Edited by John M'Ilveen

SOLID GROUND CHRISTIAN BOOKS
BIRMINGHAM, ALABAMA USA

Solid Ground Christian Books
PO Box 660132
Vestavia Hills AL 35266
205-443-0311
sgcb@charter.net
solid-ground-books.com

Pardon and Assurance
by William John Patton (1829 – 1895)

First Solid Ground Paperback Edition June 2009

Taken from the 1902 edition published by
Oliphants LTD., London & Edinburgh

Cover design by Borgo Design, Tuscaloosa, AL

Cover image from Ric Ergenbright.
View his images at **ricergenbright.com**

ISBN: 978-159925-209-4

CONTENTS

BIOGRAPHICAL SKETCH OF
THE AUTHOR

T HE REVEREND WILLIAM JOHN PATTON was a
great winner of souls. He aimed directly at the
conversion of sinners, and sinners in large numbers
were converted. Having passed through a great crisis
in his own spiritual history, the lines of his gospel-
teaching were, in consequence, boldly drawn and distinctly marked, and few inquiring ones could listen
to his discourses without discovering the way of peace
with God. Possessing special evangelistic gifts, his
services were in constant demand, and everything from
his pen was eagerly read, in all parts of the Church of
which he was a minister ; and hence it has come to pass
that, to-day, there are multitudes all over the north of
Ireland who fondly think of him as their spiritual father.

He was born on 26th May 1829, near Donaghadee,
a small seaside town in the county of Down. His
father, Mr. Robert Patton, was a farmer of independent
means, much respected by all the people of the town
and district. His mother, Miss Jane Corry, was a
daughter of Mr. John Corry of Turnagardy, near Newtownards in the same county, and sister of Mr. Robert
Corry, founder of the well-known Belfast firm of Messrs.
J. P. Corry & Co., whose eldest son, Mr. James Porter
Corry, successively represented the borough of Belfast
and a division of County Armagh in the House of
Commons, and was created a baronet by Her Majesty
the Queen. Both parents were persons of decidedly
religious character. For many years his father was an
honoured eld   of the Church, and for forty years was

not known to be absent once from public worship on the Lord's day. The children of this worthy couple consisted of one daughter and four sons, the daughter being tne eldest of the family, and the subject of this sketch the eldest of the sons.

It was the wish of the parents that William John, their eldest boy, should devote himself to the ministry of the Church, and for this they often prayed. His mother was a woman who abounded in prayer, often joining with others in intercessions for their friends. He himself has told that when he was a little lad, a distant relative frequently visited at his father's house, and that when his mother and she went upstairs, he sometimes slipped up after them, and, listening, heard them praying for all their friends by name, himself among the number. After his conversion took place, he often thought that it might have been in answer to those prayers.

His father, who had married late in life, was removed by death in 1848, at the advanced age of eighty-four years, when all the children were still comparatively young; while his mother survived her husband nearly forty years, her death taking place only a few years before that of her son.

At first he attended a public school in the neighbourhood of his father's residence, but his early education was conducted principally by private tutors. Among those who were thus concerned in his instruction were Mr. Irvine, afterwards Rev. Dr. Irvine of Toronto; Mr. Cairnduff, who afterwards obtained a Government appointment in Tasmania; and Mr. Thomas Blain, afterwards the celebrated Dr. Blain, Headmaster of the English School in the Royal Belfast Academical Institution. Subsequently he was sent to the Royal Academical Institution in Belfast, then by far the best school in Ulster, where he completed his preparation for College. During his attendance at the Institution, he resided in the house of his uncle, Mr. John Arnold, one of the most godly elders ever connected with the Irish Presbyterian Church.

His collegiate studies, during his undergraduate course, were prosecuted at the Old Belfast College, where he gained first place in more than one of the classes, and where, in addition to the usual subjects of study, he attended the "Irish Class" conducted by Mr. M'Devitt. In 1849 he proceeded to New College, Edinburgh, where he took the whole of his theological course. While attending New College, he was a regular worshipper in Free St. John's under the ministry of the celebrated Dr. Thomas Guthrie, and was in the habit of taking very copious notes of the sermons of that renowned preacher.

From what has now been stated, it will be seen that he possessed ample opportunities for the acquisition of a thoroughly sound education. And of these he took full advantage. As a student he was most diligent, persevering, and energetic. And these qualities, well developed in student days, became characteristic of his entire subsequent career. "Whatsoever his hand found to do, he did it with his might." Nor were his labours in school and college days confined to class-rooms. As a specimen of how he was in the habit of spending most of his summer holidays, I shall here give his programme of study for each day, during six weeks immediately succeeding his return from Edinburgh after his second session there.

"Rise at five o'clock, and dress till 5.30, taking a shower-bath for the sake of health and comfort. From 5.30 till 6.30 read Dick's *Lectures on Theology*—not rapidly, but slowly, so as to digest it thoroughly as I go along. From 6.30 till 7.30 write letters, or select some useful subject, and make whatever observations occur to my own mind on it, taking care that there shall be no book before me while writing. This will gradually train me to Independent thinking, and enable me likewise to express my ideas with ease and accuracy without that plagiarism which is so very common among students, and, indeed, in the literary world generally. At 7.30, having first used the dumb-bells for expanding the chest, go out and walk along the Millisle shore, taking care to be always home for breakfast at 8.30. During this walk I should reflect on, and endeavour to digest, what I had read in Dick before going out. This would impress upon my mind, so as not to be forgotten, the truths which I had learned. After breakfast, read a chapter in the Bible, going regularly through some book, and then pray. Let family worship by no means be neglected, for God has said that He will 'pour out His fury on them that call not on His name.' In order to obtain a more minute knowledge of the Bible, it would be well, before commencing study, to write down in a few words the subjects embraced in the chapter just read. An analysis of the Bible thus formed would be found exceedingly useful, and the exercise profitable in after life. These exercises would likely occupy three-quarters of an hour, so that all things would be ready for commencing study at 9.15. Spend the first quarter of an hour till 9.30 in reading over the notes of Dr. Cunningham's Lectures, so as not to let them slip out of my memory, and occupy the remaining two hours of this sitting till 11.30 in reading *Shaw on the Confession*, or some other book on theology. This, with the time spent on Dick in the morning, making upwards of three hours each day, should in a short time give a respectable knowledge of the chief subjects of divinity. At 11.30, after using the dumb-bells, go out and take exercise till 1.30. This should give an appetite for dinner, which will be over at furthest at 2, when study should again commence. From 2 till 2.15 read some portion of the Bible through regularly, and analyse each chapter as it is read, and occupy the remaining two hours of this sitting, till 4.15, in reading Mosheim, Neander, M'Crie, or some other book on Church History. Then go out for a walk till tea-time at 5.30. After tea, read the day's portion in Kitto's *Illustrations* ; and, having done so, spend the next hour in studying Romans or Hebrews, using the assistance of some good commentary— Hodge or Haldane on the former, and Stuart or Barnes on the latter. The remaining three hours till 10 cannot be so exactly apportioned, but may be profitably spent in writing essays, sermons, or lectures, reading poetry, or acquiring a further knowledge of the Bible. I must be in bed every night at 10, since seven hours is little enough time for sleep, and 5 in the morning is the hour at which I must rise, according to Todd's *Student's Guide.*"

Having so carefully prepared himself, he had no difficulty in passing the examination of his Church as a candidate for licence to preach. This he did with special distinction on 28th October 1852, having been under examination for only eighteen minutes, while each of the other candidates on the occasion was examined for more than an hour.

On 10th November following, he was licensed to preach the gospel by the Presbytery of Ards, and immediately after was invited by Rev. David Hamilton,

Convener of the General Assembly's Jewish Mission, to become a missionary to the Jews. This invitation he declined, as he thought he did not possess the special qualifications necessary for such a position. "None," he said, "but those whom God has gifted with a larger share than usual of tact, talent, and acuteness are qualified for such a work."

The first vacant church in which he preached as a candidate was that of Dromara, a village situated almost in the centre of his own county of Down. From this church he received a call, and, having accepted it, was ordained as their pastor by the Presbytery of Down on 29th June 1853; and there he continued to labour till his death.

On the occasion of his removing to Dromara, a public and largely attended meeting of the inhabitants of his native town was held in his honour, at which a most complimentary address, with a large collection of books, was presented to him. The Rev. John M'Aulay, under whose pastoral care he had been brought up, presided, and spoke in very warm terms of his young friend. In the course of his remarks, referring to an illness through which he himself had recently passed, and as showing the esteem in which Mr. Patton was held by those who had known him from his youth, he said, "Of one thing I am certain, that if, in the providence of God, my late sickness had proved fatal, Mr. Patton would not have gone far from home." Dr. Stuart, addressing Mr. Patton, and speaking in the name of the meeting, said, "Always maintaining an unblemished character, by your labours in the Sabbath school, and by your willingness to assist in every work of faith and labour of love, you have endeared yourself to all who have known you."

From all that has now been stated, it is manifest that his youth had been blameless in the eyes of all who knew him; that his College course had been one of distinction; that he had been a diligent student of the Bible, and a willing worker in every good cause; and that he entered on his ministry well prepared by education and reputation for his life-work. But, sad to say, he seems to have been yet much in the dark about spiritual things, and without any clear perception of his personal interest in Christ. According to the view which he himself afterwards took of his case, he was when ordained, and for fully six years after, an unconverted man. One thing, however, is certain: he was not all that time without a deep and real concern about his salvation. When in after life he looked back on the past, one of the occasions most distinctly impressed on his memory was when, at eighteen years of age, he read, for the first time, the Memoir of the Rev. Robert Murray M'Cheyne. After reading that book, he was for three weeks in a state of great spiritual anxiety, and one day, when walking in a field in the neighbourhood of Donaghadee, he prayed very earnestly, and wept bitterly for his sins. If there had been any one to speak to him at that time, and to put before him clearly God's method of justifying the sinner, he would very likely have been then led to put his trust in Christ. But, as he himself said, he resisted the Holy Spirit, and his anxiety having left him, did not again return for seven years. Not, however, that during all those years he was without any thought concerning his salvation ; but ideas resembling a sort of fatalism seem to have taken possession of his mind. He seemed to argue that if he were elected he would be saved ; if not, he must be damned ; and that, therefore, he would just have to take his chance.

At a later period, the Holy Spirit again strove with him mightily, and he was led to put forth great efforts to secure his salvation. He prayed much, sometimes spending nearly a whole day on his knees. He seemed to think that such diligence would greatly please God and procure His favour. He believed that a Christian ought to have deep sorrow for sin and intense love for the Saviour, and he tried hard to have these feelings, but in vain. He fancied that he himself was very willing to be saved in God's way, but that God was not willing to give him His Spirit ; and he thought that if he were at last damned, the fault would not be his, but

God's. "This," he afterwards declared, "was horrible profanity." He did not then see that it was he who, in the pride and stubbornness of his heart, was standing out in rebellion against God and His method of salvation by free grace. He did not perceive that, being ignorant of God's righteousness, he was going about to establish a righteousness of his own, and would not submit himself to the righteousness of God.

At length the year 1859 came, with its great religious awakening. "This," he was wont to say, "was the greatest year the north of Ireland ever saw." More people, perhaps, were converted in that year than in any half-dozen years before or since. Dromara shared largely in the blessing. For a whole fortnight no work whatever was done in the parish, the entire time being taken up with prayer and religious conversation. Hundreds were converted in a few months. On some occasions the church could not accommodate one-fourth of the people who came together, and the service had to be held in the open air. Throughout this awakening Mr. Patton was intensely in earnest, and took a prominent part in promoting it. And yet his views regarding the way of life were not clear. His position seemed very much to resemble that of John Wesley about the time of his mission to Georgia, when, as he afterwards expressed it, "he was in a state of salvation as a *servant*, but not as a *child*, of God."

At this time various means were employed by God to keep him in earnest. The chief of these was intercourse with his cousin, Mr. John Alexander Arnold of Belfast. "I saw him very often," Mr. Patton said, "and his conversation was nearly always about Christ, and seldom did I leave him without being stimulated." On Hallowe'en Day, 1859, the two cousins went to Newtownards, to pay a visit to their Aunt Milliken, who resided near that town. This aunt was a remarkably good woman, but remarkable especially for her prayerfulness. For forty or fifty years she had been in the habit of rising every night, putting a cloak about her, and spending a considerable time in praying for herself and others. Mr. Arnold thought it very likely that it was in answer to her prayers that he himself had been converted; and so he had suggested to Mr. Patton that they should visit her at Hallowe'en, and ask her to continue her prayers for them. " We went," said Mr. Patton, " by train. We spent a pleasant day, asked our aunt to be sure and continue her prayers for us, and came away. We expected to be in time for the last train to Belfast, but were just in time to see it move off from the station without us. What was to be done? Go back? No. Walk the eight miles to Belfast? Yes. So we started. That was a walk to be remembered. We felt and said that Jesus was with us as we went along, and talked about Him. By and by we knelt down on the roadside, and both prayed. A little after we came to a glen, and there, on the side of a road, we saw, through the window of a poor cottage, a party of friends met to spend Hallowe'en. Mr. Arnold stopped, looked in, and suggested that we should go in and talk to them. I asked what excuse we could make. 'Oh,' said he, 'ask for a drink, of course.' I said, if he went first, I would follow. So in he went, and asked for a drink, and in a minute or two the whole party were in a state of earnest excitement. He seemed to be literally 'full of the Holy Ghost.' He talked to them about Jesus and His love, and His death, and their death, and asked, were they prepared to die? He prayed, and I prayed, and off we came, the master and mistress of the house coming to the door and asking us to be sure and call again if we were passing. The whole interview did not last more than six or eight minutes. I have sometimes thought how strange it must have seemed to the people assembled, and that some of them might possibly yet turn up in heaven as converted through that unceremonious visit on Hallowe'en, 1859. We shall see. If so, they will forgive the want of ceremony on our part." These incidents serve to show what sort of a man Mr. Arnold was, and what a powerful influence he must have exercised on the mind of one in the condition in which Mr. Patton then was.

His religious concern was also deepened by an observation addressed to him by an old man at Spurgeon's Tabernacle in London. He was coming out from hearing Mr. Spurgeon preach, when the old man by his side asked him how he liked the sermon. Mr. Patton replied that he liked it pretty well, but that he thought he had often heard a much better one. "Are you a judge?" inquired the old man. "Only a man," said he, "who has been born again could be a judge of a sermon like that." This remark was the means of awakening very serious thoughts in his mind.

The date when the light of the gospel broke in clearness upon his mind was the 22nd of August 1860. The description of how it happened may be best given in his own words :—

"I knew a young man who was well acquainted with his Bible, as far as head knowledge is concerned. He had been anxious by fits and starts for years ; he had tried to get peace by resolutions, and by struggling, and by praying, and by making efforts to feel sorry for sin and love to God, and by looking inside to see if he had got faith ; and now, had he been asked, he would have said he was waiting for feelings. 'What feelings?' 'Why, the feelings that people have just before they are converted.' He had been looking for something like an electric thrill from head to foot before he would find peace. There are no such feelings at all. It is a pure delusion of the devil to keep anxious ones from looking to Christ at once. All right feelings come after we have believed in Jesus. We must trust the word of Jesus without any feelings at all, and depend on Him. We shall never be saved if we do not take a step in advance of our feelings. This young man was waiting for the feelings.

"One day he had been thinking over John iii. 16, and he lay down in bed at night, but not to sleep. The Spirit of God was working in his heart. He thought, 'God loved the world.' That is wonderful—He loved the world—the wicked world that defied Him and dishonoured Him, and laughed His mercies to scorn. And He 'so loved the world, that He gave His only-begotten Son.' He gave His Son, His only-begotten Son, to die for His enemies, 'that whosoever believeth on Him should not perish, but have everlasting life.' Why, he thought, that is the very thing I want— I want not to perish, but to have everlasting life. And 'whosoever' —why, that means me as well as any other person. And so I shall not perish, but have everlasting life, if I only believe on Christ.

"And then and there he was enabled to believe it, and to rest on Christ. He leaped from his bed. Could this be conversion?

So simple a thing as this ? Was it just believing that God loved the world, and sent His Son ; and just resting on Christ ? 'Yes,' whispered God's Spirit. 'Why, I have been waiting for months for feelings. How foolish I have been !' And down he got on his knees, and thanked God for converting him, and asked Him to enable him to live like a Christian. And he looks back on that night as the night of his conversion."

For a short time his joy was great, but by and by his feelings became less intense, and this change in his feelings led him sometimes to doubt whether after all he was born of God. He was not yet wholly delivered from dependence on feeling, and to some extent there was a falling away from first earnestness. But in November of the following year he experienced a great reviving of his soul and strengthening of his faith. This was brought about by reading Boardman's *Higher Christian Life.* The reading of that book marked a new epoch in his spiritual history. From that time he never again doubted his interest in Christ. And from that time till the day of his death he ever, as he himself expressed it, " tried honestly to hold up Christ." The village of Dromara became a centre of blessing, and the influence of his preaching was felt for many miles round. Perhaps there was no place in all the north of Ireland where more real good was done. Not only were souls converted in his own congregation, but hundreds also in neighbouring congregations and wherever he went to preach. For more than thirty years he never refused an invitation to preach when it was in his power to accept it ; and everywhere his theme was the same— Christ : Christ dying, rising, ascending, interceding, and coming again ; justification, sanctification, heaven, hell. And if all the members of his congregation, and multitudes besides, were not saved, it was not because the way was not clearly stated, nor because they were not urged with burning earnestness to yield themselves to the Saviour.

Considering what his own experience had been, it was little wonder that he had a holy horror of an unconverted ministry. This feeling he often expressed. "There are persons," he said, " who do not profess to be Christians, but are honest and truthful and noble enough not to tell a lie. With all their faults, they say, 'We won't tell a lie.' How they put to shame persons who go to the Lord's Table, and take the bread and wine, and thereby declare that they take Christ, when they know very well that it is a lie! And how they put to shame ministers who not merely go to the Lord's Table, but presume to preside at it, and get into the pulpit, and profess to teach others the way to heaven, when they know very well that they have never travelled it themselves, and know nothing about it!" He thought churches should take more effectual means than they often do of guarding against this great danger. He felt that if he himself had been more faithfully dealt with regarding his personal salvation, while passing through College, he might have been led to the knowledge of the truth as it is in Jesus, at least before entering on the work of preaching the gospel. And so, when a new edition of *The Constitution and Government* of his Church was about to be published, he wrote to the committee in charge of the matter, very strongly urging that stringent rules should be inserted on the subject. He said:

"I know very well that, no matter what care is taken, some unworthy men will get into the ministry. There was a Judas even among the apostles. But surely we are responsible for using all lawful means. And is not this of all matters the most important? What is the use of learning and talent in a minister if he has not grace? He is only a learned hater of God, a talented servant of the devil, an accomplished child of wrath, an amiable heir of hell. *An unconverted minister!* What a lifelong hypocrisy! Pretending to tell others the road to heaven, and not knowing it himself! Oh, the meanness of it, the shabbiness of it, the dishonesty of it! It would be nobler far to break stones on the roadside. Surely in this case the proverb holds true that 'A living dog is better than a dead lion.' Is not this a matter of a hundred-fold more importance than the bits of routine that some will be sending forward to you? By all means attend to their bits of routine. Put the pieces of green baize on the third class carriages, and make them as comfortable as you can. But see to it that the carriages are hooked on to the engine, otherwise the engine will be off, and the green-baized carriages left behind at the station."

2

This letter was not without the desired effect. Its suggestions were largely embodied in the Church's procedure, and have in many quarters borne good fruit. And as showing how deep were his convictions on the subject with which it dealt, it may be mentioned that when recording in his diary the completion of the very tasteful manse which he himself had been mainly instrumental in having erected for the minister of Second Dromara, he added this prayer: "O Lord, grant that no unconverted man may ever reside in it as minister of Second Dromara. For Jesus' sake. Amen."

It was about seven months previous to his conversion that Mr. Patton was united in marriage with Miss Mary Heron, daughter of the Rev. Alexander Heron, the very excellent minister of the neighbouring parish of Ballyroney. In her he found one who had the deepest sympathy with him in all his spiritual conflicts, and who, after his entrance into the liberty of the gospel, was one with him in all his aspirations and hopes. After thirty-four years of married life, and when her body lay cold in the coffin, her husband's testimony was, "Mary Patton walked with God."

Mrs. Patton early knew the Lord ; in fact, she could not remember a time when she did not more or less love Him. She was always distinguished by her grave, sweet earnestness of purpose. And all through life she was remarkable for her truthfulness, prayerfulness, love of the Bible, and trying to do every little thing so as to please the Lord. As evidence of her truthfulness, it may be mentioned that when attending a boarding-school in Dublin she was known in the school as "Little Truth." And as showing her love of the Bible, it will be enough to state that throughout the whole of her married life she was in the habit of reading the Old Testament through once every year, the New Testament twice, the Psalms four times, and the fifty-third chapter of Isaiah every morning. She was in the habit of marking her Bible very carefully, and of entering important notes on the margin. Here is a note, entered very neatly, in the beautiful copy of the Scriptures which she was using at the time of her death: "*All your peace is to be found in believing God's Word about His Son.*" The Rev. Wm. Romaine, in presenting a Bible to a young minister, wrote, "You cannot read it too much. *Wear it out in reading.*" This was exactly what Mrs. Patton did with three or four copies of the Scriptures. She read them, and marked them, until they were "in leaves."

And not only did she read the Bible; she read it with much prayer. Her habit was to spend an hour and a half in prayer each morning before breakfast, and to spend in prayer and reading the Bible not less than three hours each day. On the afternoon of each Lord's day she occupied two additional hours in intercession—praying for the members of her husband's congregation, and for those persons whose names were entered on her "prayer list."

She prayed about everything, about every little circumstance of her life. For some years she kept a book in which she recorded "a few of many answers" which she had received from God to her prayers. In it I have found more than two hundred such records.

She was never strong, and had several severe illnesses. As a consequence, she was not able to engage in much active Christian service. But no one can tell how much better the world may be for her having lived in it; nor how much blessing her continuous prayers may have been the means of bringing down upon the parish of Dromara.

While sometimes mirthful, and not without a vein of humour, she was, as a rule, of a sorrowful spirit. When in tolerably good health, she was a rejoicing and assured Christian; but when nervous or ill, she was disposed to take a gloomy view of her spiritual state. That she was a true Christian, no one ever doubted but herself.

About two years after his entrance into the possession of the "larger life" of the gospel, we find Mr. Patton, in order to promote still more his growth in grace, writing out a solemn dedication of himself to God.

"COVENANT WITH GOD.

1864.

"I, William John Patton, feeling myself to be a poor sinner, lost and undone by nature, but having learned the good news that 'Christ Jesus came into the world to save sinners,' do hereby take Him as my Saviour — my 'righteousness and strength.' Constrained by His love, I present MYSELF a living sacrifice to Him—my time, and talents, and influence; my bodily strength and worldly substance; and *Resolve* that henceforth, by His grace, the great object of my life shall be to glorify God by a life of holiness and of usefulness in the salvation of sinners.

"Taught by His Word that of myself I 'can do nothing,' but that 'I can do all things through Christ, who strengtheneth me,' I hereby cast myself into Thine arms, O Jesus, and beseech Thee to fill me with Thy Holy Spirit, so that I may die unto sins, especially my besetting sins, and live unto righteousness, and each day 'grow in grace and in the knowledge of my Lord and Saviour.' And now, Lord, I am Thy child, having Thy Spirit in me. Oh, fill me with the fulness of God, and use me for Thy glory.

"This Covenant I hereby promise before God that I will strive to keep, battling with all my might against the world, the flesh, and the devil, as long as I shall live; not trusting, however, in my own strength, for I have none, but in Him who has said, 'All power is given unto *Me* in heaven and in earth; and lo, I am with you alway, even unto the end of the world.'

"I adopt the language of Jonathan Edwards as mine, praying *his* God to keep me : 'I have been before God, and have given myself, all that I am and have, to God, so that I am not, in any respect, my own. I can challenge no right in this understanding, this will, these affections, which are in me. Neither have I any right to this body, or any of its members ; no right to this tongue, these hands, these feet ; no right to these senses, these eyes, these ears, this smell, or this taste. I have given myself clean away, and have not retained anything as my own.'

"'Now, unto Him that is able to do exceeding abundantly above all that we ask or think, *according to the power that worketh in us*, unto Him be glory.' Into Thine arms, O Jesus, I cast myself as a helpless child, for time and for eternity. So help me, God.

"Signed at Dromara, this twenty-ninth day of February 1864.
"WILLIAM JOHN PATTON."

As a part of this covenant he engaged to rise each morning at five o'clock, and proposed to spend four

hours at least each day in reading the Bible, meditation, and prayer, for his own growth in grace—"little
enough," he said, "for one whose duty it is to give
himself continually to prayer and the ministry of the
Word." He signed the whole on his knees, and
appended the prayer: "Lord, I cannot keep it, but
I trust in Thee. Enable me. Increase my faith.
Amen."

This prayer was needed, for he soon found that
while the spirit was willing, the flesh was weak. And
it is noteworthy that what in 1864 he recorded as a
promise, in 1868 he expressed entirely in the form of
a prayer. He felt that he came far short of his ideal.
And on his birthday in 1868 we find him writing:

"This day I am thirty-nine years old. Alas, Lord! how my
time has been wasted! Thirty years living without God! And
ever since I have been converted, how little I have done compared
with what I might, had I looked up more to Jesus for grace, read
my Bible more prayed more, and risen earlier! Lord, forgive me.
Especially for the last three years I have not been as prayerful,
and as active for the salvation of souls, as for the previous years
since my conversion. Lord, save me from bringing disgrace on
Thy cause. May I be enabled to expect to be made by Thee very
holy and very useful."

From this time onward his thoughts, and even conversation, were greatly taken up with the subject of
holiness. He attended conferences for the deepening
of spiritual life almost every summer. He went to
Oxford, Brighton, London, Dublin, Keswick, and other
places, and almost always obtained stimulus, but never
attained the fulness of blessing which he desired. I
imagine he often misunderstood the speakers, supposing
that they were describing what they themselves had
experienced, and not merely what every Christian *ought*
to be. And so, very frequently, on these occasions, his
lament was, "I have not attained." I remember well
how, about a year before his death, when the Life of
Dr. Andrew Bonnar, for whom he had a great regard,
was published, he said it was a relief to learn that even
he was very much like one's self, often feeling a great

mixture of motives in the doing of his work, and having cause to bewail that fact.

Mr. Patton himself sometimes spoke on the subject of the Christian life in a way which led some to suppose he was claiming a sort of sinless perfection. Nothing, however, was further from his intention. In a sermon to his people on the twenty-fifth anniversary of his ordination, he said: " My shortcomings have been many, as no one knows better than myself. And I ask God to forgive me."

His spiritual life was marked by distinct stages of advance. There was first the time when he got rid of all difficulty about *feelings*, and when he saw clearly that the one ground of hope before God is " the finished work " of Christ,—when, in fact, he saw the meaning of 2 Cor. v. 21 : " He hath made Him to be sin for us, who knew no sin, that we might be made the righteousness of God in Him."

Then there was the time when he obtained clearer views as to the *freeness* of the gospel offer, and as to God's being delighted to bestow the benefits of Christ's death on every one who will receive them—when he came to see that Christ and His death are as free to sinners as the air they breathe.

Next, there was the time when he came to realise more fully his *oneness* with Christ, and consequently God's great delight in all who are in Christ.

Then, again, just as at an earlier stage he had seen the value of Christ's obedience and death, he came to see more clearly the value of His *resurrection life:* the doctrine set forth in Rom. v. 10: " If, when we were enemies, we were reconciled to God by the death of His Son, much more, *being reconciled, we shall be saved by His life."*

And, lastly, he came to realise more fully the great *power of prayer.* The believer comes to God, who loves him as He loves His own Son; he comes to God as one with Him who has all power in heaven and in earth; what, therefore, may he not ask and obtain ?

Thus his life was a growth, a progress from grace to grace, an advance from glory to glory, until, at the hour of his departure from this world, he reached the excellent glory. Not, however, that the progress was uniform. There were times when he seemed to decline in grace ; and others again, when he seemed to get a great lift in the divine life. But, on the whole, it was with him as with the incoming tide : one wave may fall short of the one which immediately preceded it ; but, as time passes, it is clearly seen that the flow is inward, and that the tide is becoming fuller and fuller.

As has been already stated, a period very distinctly marked, as one of advance, was that which immediately followed his attainment of the full assurance of his salvation. This was in 1861 ; and so, the years from 1861 till 1864 he always regarded as a "little garden" in the field of his Christian experience. During those years his joy was most exuberant, and his activity in proclaiming the gospel by both voice and pen almost boundless. For seven miles all round his church, wherever an opening was presented, he preached Christ —in schoolhouse, barn, parlour, and highway. At this time also he began to write for the periodical press of Ireland and Scotland ; and soon he was found regularly contributing articles on practical godliness to such publications as *The British Messenger, The British Herald, The Family Treasury, The Evangelical Witness, The Monthly Messenger,* and *Plain Words.* Many of these articles attracted the attention of other editors, who asked to be allowed to reproduce them, and who at the same time invited the author to become one of their contributors. Accordingly, we find him writing : "What reason I have to be thankful for this means of usefulness ! Lord, give me an unction to write scripturally, plainly, pointedly, and affectionately ; and bless this means of making Jesus known."

In 1869 he wrote a New Year's Address, entitled *A Gold Chain for Children.* Its seven links were : CHRIST, PARDON, A NEW HEART, A HOLY LIFE, A

HAPPY LIFE, A HAPPY DEATH, HEAVEN. It had a wide circulation, and soon he began to hear of persons in various places having been converted by the reading of it, many of those who had received blessing conveying their thanks to him for having written it. So greatly was he encouraged, that he resolved that, so long as God was pleased to spare him and give him health, he would write an address for each New Year. To this resolution he faithfully adhered, and during the next twenty-six years, twenty-six such addresses proceeded from his pen, the last one being sent forth from his dying bed, and appearing only a few weeks before his decease. Some of these booklets reached a circulation of 20,000 copies, and, as the years passed, bundles of letters were received from those who had derived spiritual benefit. A little girl, the daughter of a brother minister, only expressed the truth when she wrote: "Your New Year's Address is very nice. It ought to do good, and I know it will. Father says that your addresses always do. He never heard of one that didn't do more or less good." This very youthful correspondent added: "I do love your addresses so much. They are so earnest, and seem to reach down into one's heart—at least, they did reach into mine once, and I never can be thankful enough for *that*."

Nor was it children alone who appreciated these annual addresses ; older people, perhaps, were benefited by them still more. Mr. Patton himself greatly valued the testimony borne to their worth in a letter which he received from the late Rev. Professor Witherow, of Londonderry, just a short time before that distinguished servant of God died. It was the last letter which Dr. Witherow wrote, and was as follows :—

"DERRY, 17*th December* 1889.

"DEAR MR. PATTON,—Thanks for your excellent New Year's Address on ' Putting away Sin.' When deprived of the services of the sanctuary last Sabbath, I read it through, and it gave me comfort and peace and joy. Oh that all our ministers had the clear views of the divine plan of salvation that you have ! These blessed tractates are very dear to me. I have cherished them all through life; and it is my desire to die with the belief and love of them in my heart. I am still able to walk through the grounds here, but I feel my work is done.—Farewell, and God bless you.

"THOMAS WITHEROW."

This letter was read at Dr. Witherow's grave on the day of his funeral, in presence of a great concourse of ministers, students, and others, many of whom were in tears.

Mr. Patton performed a service for the cause of God, in connection with the great work of Foreign Missions, which must not be overlooked here, though he never received much credit for it when living. The Foreign Mission of the Irish Presbyterian Church was established in 1840, and its sphere of operations was India; but in 1867 a forward step was taken, and a branch of the mission established in China. This latter event was mainly brought about through the exertions of Mr. Patton. It was he who, through the press and by other means, first brought the subject before the members of the Church. The impulse leading him to do this had its origin in a thought which seized his mind one morning when conducting family worship in his manse at Dromara. As was his wont, he was praying for the conversion of the heathen, and was led to make special mention of China, with its hundreds of millions of people, most of whom had never heard the name of Jesus, when suddenly there flashed into his mind as distinctly as if he had heard the words spoken—"You hypocrite! *You* praying the Lord to send the gospel to China, when you never gave anything toward it!" At once he became a subscriber to a Society having for its object the Christianisation of that land; and his interest in the subject increasing, he was soon led to ask why his own Church should not have a China mission. Accordingly, he wrote articles for the magazines, and addressed communications to the newspapers, urging that the Church could and should do something for the evangelisation of the great heathen country of China, whose many millions had lately become accessible to the gospel; other Protestant Churches had entered in to possess the land for Christ, and the Church in Ireland should not stand idly by. India, he admitted, had not too many missionaries, but China was in a much worse position, with only about a hundred missionaries for its four hundred millions of people. He marshalled his facts and arguments with great skill, and urged the cause with great enthusiasm, and as a result the Church was stirred. He corresponded largely with Mr. Donald Matheson, an active member of the Foreign Mission Committee of the Presbyterian Church of England, from whom he obtained most valuable help. And from many of his brethren in the ministry, notably from the Rev. S. J. Moore of Ballymena, he received much encouragement and assistance. The task he had undertaken, however, was not an easy one, as the leaders of the Church, who were mainly responsible for the management of the Foreign Mission, were not in favour of the new departure, fearing that it might draw to itself the money so much needed for the mission in India. Mr. Patton argued that it was a shame for the Church to do so little for the conversion of the heathen; that, in addition to what was given for India, she could easily support at least half a dozen missionaries in China; that, in fact, there were six congregations, each of which could easily support one itself; that there were rich members who might be expected to come forward with large donations for such an object; and that, if they asked God in faith, all they needed would be supplied. A conference of those in favour of the project was held in Belfast; two overtures to the General Assembly asking for the establishment of the mission were adopted, one by the Presbytery of Down, with which Mr. Patton was connected, and the other by the Presbytery of Ballymena, of which Mr. Moore was a member; and these were supported by one afterwards adopted by the Synod of Belfast. Enthusiasm carried the day. The General Assembly unanimously agreed to undertake the mission, some of the members who had been unfavourable even going the length of speaking on its behalf. Mr. Patton was greatly rejoiced, and in the amount of support which was soon forthcoming, he was not altogether disappointed. Many gave largely. His own uncle, Mr. Robert Corry of Belfast, came forward with a proposal to charge his property with a contribution of £100 a year, so long as the Church should maintain a mission in China ; and this offer was immediately afterwards carried into effect.

Thus there sprang into existence that mission in Manchuria which is now carried on in conjunction with the United Presbyterian Church of Scotland, and which is one of the most prosperous in connection with the Irish Presbyterian Church. That Mr. Patton was regarded by the Christian public as the principal instrument in its origination, was made abundantly manifest on the occasion of the ordination of the two first missionaries who were sent forth. The arrangements for the ordination having been announced, and his name not being mentioned in connection with them, more than one communication immediately appeared in the public press, expressing indignation that "the founder of the mission" should not have been invited to take part in the services. In reply to these communications, Mr. Patton wrote : " I am indeed thankful to have been in some degree the means, with my friend Mr. Moore of Ballymena, of turning the attention of our Church to China. I am thankful, also, that in God's gracious providence the mission has been firmly established, not only by the unanimous resolution of the General Assembly, but in the hearts of our people. I am sorry that it was not in my power to offer myself as one of the first missionaries. Nothing but a supposed inability to learn the language prevented my doing so. But it was easy work when God was working, and guiding, and blessing, and raising up friends on every side. Perhaps I may say that it did occur to me some time ago, though I never mentioned it to any one, that the Board of Missions might possibly ask Mr. Moore and myself to take part in the ordination services ; but there is no ground for 'indignation' because they did not. We can be present on the occasion, which I hope to be."

This mission, as was to be expected, was always dear to his heart, and was often the subject of his prayers. With many of its missionaries he was on most intimate terms of friendship, regularly corresponding with them, rejoicing with them in their successes, and sympathising with them in their difficulties. But throughout almost his entire ministry he was an ardent advocate of all forms of missionary effort, and was instrumental in leading his own people to largely increase their givings for such objects.

From the time of the great spiritual movement under Messrs. Moody and Sankey in 1874, it became very common for ministers to have a series of special evangelistic services in connection with their congregations each year. In these services Mr. Patton was very frequently asked to assist. During the winter months especially, he was away from home, engaged in such work, two or three nights almost every week. For almost fifteen years, it may be said, he was the unpaid evangelist of the Church. And greatly were his labours blessed. Hundreds of people look back to such services conducted by him, as the time when they passed from death to life.

Such visits to various parts of the Church often proved to be times of refreshing to ministers as well as to their congregations. His buoyancy of spirit, great hopefulness regarding the conversion of sinners, and exceedingly clear statements of gospel truth, often greatly encouraged them in their work. The godly wife of a minister, since also gone home, wrote him after one of his visits: "My husband preached yesterday with more power and loving earnestness, and fuller offers of free grace, than I ever remember. Oh, how I thank God for sending dear Mr. Patton among us. The Holy Spirit is teaching me something of the beauty and fulness and power of those grand and gracious words, 'Yet not I, but Christ liveth in me.' Our loving God is as delighted to bless *His people* as to convert sinners."

His manner in addressing his audiences on these
occasions, and indeed on all occasions, was all his own.
It was not faultless, and it could not in all respects be
profitably copied.   But it possessed four characteristics
well worthy of imitation—clearness, brightness, earnestness, and urgency.   The good points of his style could
not be better summed up than in words which he himself addressed to a young man on the occasion of
his being licensed to preach the gospel.   He said:
"Cultivate a manner of loving earnestness—like the
Apostle Paul *beseech* people, and *pray* them.   Dr. James
Hamilton of London speaks of ministers who 'offer
the gospel with clenched fists.'   Then, remember, you
must arrest the attention of your hearers, and keep
them awake.   It is quite possible to do this without
what is called 'eloquence.'   There are few people
naturally eloquent.   But there is a kind of eloquence
which we all may have.   Some one has said that
'perspicuity and earnestness combined always make
eloquence'; and this is the very best kind of eloquence.
Seek, then, to have clear ideas on your subject, and a
clear order in your mind; and if you are in earnest,
there is no fear of your arresting the attention of the
people.   But, remember, you must be really in earnest,
and not merely seeming to be.   People see through us
far better than we imagine.   Then, again, urge immediate
decision, and expect results at once.   I have often
thought of the Philippian jailor, who knew scarcely
anything about Christ and Christianity, and yet was
brought to Christ that night.   I wonder if that ignorant
heathen had asked some of us what he must do to be
saved, what we would have told him.   Might it not have
been something like this: 'I am glad to see you in earnest:
now give up your wicked ways and your bad company;
keep good company; come to our meetings regularly;
here is a Bible for you to read; pray earnestly; commence
family worship; and continue to seek God, and some
day He will convert you'?   Would we really have
told him, 'Believe on the Lord Jesus Christ, and thou
shalt be saved,' and have expected him to be saved

that night? I hope we would." The point pressed
with great earnestness at the close of all his discourses
was immediate submission to God, and immediate
acceptance of Jesus Christ and His finished work. He
would conclude with such words as these: "And now,
dear friend, do you accept Christ? Yes or No? Yes
or No? He died to save sinners, even the chief, and
He is here at this moment, offering to take all your
sins, and to come into your heart, and make you holy.
You are bound to accept His offer, and to rest on His
atonement. And the Holy Spirit is here to enable
you. Just speak to Jesus, and say, 'Lord Jesus, *here*
and *now*, I do take Thee to be my Saviour, and Thy
death to be an atonement for my sins.' If you honestly
mean this, salvation is already begun. May God
enable you to do so, for Christ's sake."

It was not alone his sermons and addresses, spoken or
written, which were used by God to the conversion of
sinners. A great means of blessing to very many was
his conversations with individuals. Wherever he went,
when he met with a person for the first time, if a suitable
opportunity were presented, he was almost sure to say,
"I hope you sometimes think about Christ?" By this
means he was generally able to discover whether or not
the individual was a Christian. And if it appeared that
there was ignorance of the one thing needful, a very
kind and encouraging explanation of how pardon was
to be obtained was sure to follow. From the time that
he himself obtained a clear view of his interest in Christ,
he always set it before him as one great object of his
life to seize opportunities for leading individuals to the
Saviour. The rule which he laid down for himself was:
"*I should make a business of religion, and aim, like
Christ, to be instant not only in season, but out of season.
I should therefore be ever on the watch for opportunities
of directing sinners to Christ, and stimulating saints—
not ashamed, wherever I am, at home or abroad, among
the godly or the ungodly, to confess Christ, that I may be
confessed by Him before His Father and the holy angels.*"
In harmony with this rule is the following entry in his

diary:—"Going along from Newry to Ballyroney, I was very prayerful. I spoke to a good many about Christ, and found it quite easy and natural. And so it is *when one has been with God.*"

One evening, when conducting an evangelistic service in the neighbourhood of Belfast, he met a very clever young man, a student, who was studying with a view to the ministry. In course of conversation with him, he asked him, did he think he had accepted Christ as his Saviour. The young man admitted that he was much perplexed on the subject, and did not see his way clearly. But as the result of the conversation which followed he soon became a happy Christian, and ultimately an earnest missionary in India. On another occasion, when preaching in a city church, after coming down from the pulpit, he found a young man, a son of the minister of the church, standing in one of the passages ; and, putting his hand on his shoulder, he said, "*Young friend, did you ever really thank Christ for dying for you ?*" The young man, taken aback by the unexpected question, hesitated for a little, and then replied, " Perhaps not in the right way." " Then," said Mr. Patton, leading him aside into one of the pews, "just do it now." What followed proved the means of his conversion, and he is now studying with a view to becoming a minister of the gospel. These are specimens of the way in which God used His servant.

This sketch would be very incomplete did it not emphasise what was undoubtedly the secret of Mr. Patton's success in the service of God. It was not his intellectual abilities, though these were respectable ; nor his natural eloquence, of which he possessed but a moderate degree ; nor even his earnestness of manner, in which he greatly excelled. It was his sanctity ; his constant fellowship with God ; his habit, as he himself would have expressed it, of " looking up to Jesus hour by hour." And the means by which this condition was maintained was twofold — constant prayer, and daily devotional reading of the Scriptures. For more than thirty years there was, perhaps, no house in all Ireland where there were more prayer and devout meditation on the Word of God than in the Dromara manse. I have already described Mrs. Patton's habits in reference to these subjects. And Mr. Patton was only recommending his own practice in the following advice which he gave to a young friend about to enter on the public ministry of the Word :—" You must read the Bible regularly and slowly with prayer for your own personal benefit. You will never be worth anything as a minister if you do not. Your faith in Christ will be in proportion to your prayerful study of the Bible. We are all desirous of feelings, and look for lightning flashes from God to come down on us and make us holier and better. Really, it is not lightning flashes we need expect so much as a steady fire kept up by means of fuel ; and the fuel is the Word of God read with prayer. This will last, and will give us stability and power. Did you ever know a man very useful who did not study the Scriptures much with prayer? This was the secret of the success of Luther, and Calvin, and Knox, and Baxter, and Bunyan, and M'Cheyne. Romaine wrote to a friend : ' Oh, sir, what are you doing that other books are so much read, and the Bible so neglected? I saw my folly twenty-two years ago, and have since studied little else.' And George Müller, of Bristol, scarcely ever gives an address without dwelling on this point—that we must read the Bible early in the morning for our growth in grace; that this will be the means of keeping us looking up to Christ all day long; and that if we do not thus read the Bible much with prayer, we shall be 'spiritual dwarfs.'

" Yes; this reading of the Bible with prayer will be the means of keeping us looking up to Jesus. I take for granted you are depending on Jesus for your personal salvation. But it is quite possible to do so, and to be utterly useless. You must be looking up to Him day by day for larger measures of His Spirit, and for power to overcome besetting sin. Do ask Him to keep you from besetting sin, as nothing hinders usefulness like cherishing some such sin. And one of the most besetting sins of ministers is self-seeking. Oh, beware of getting

up on the shoulders of the Lord Jesus to show off yourself! What a sin and shame! And alas! how common!
Luther said he had an enemy in himself worse than
either the pope or the devil—THIS SELF. And so have
you and I. It is said that after an oration of Cicero, the
people would go home saying, 'Oh, what an orator!' but
after an oration of Demosthenes, they would go home
saying, 'Up! let us fight against Philip.' Never seek
to send the people away saying, 'What a popular
preacher!' but send them away saying, 'I must read
my Bible more, and pray more, and love God more, and
love my fellow-men more.'"

Early in 1894, Mrs. Patton, who had been very ill for
several months, departed to be with Christ. She had
come to Belfast for special medical treatment; and
though very weak, she earnestly urged the doctor to
allow her, on the first Sabbath of February, to attend
the Crescent Church, where the Lord's Supper was to
be observed, and where her husband had agreed to
preach on the occasion. Having obtained his consent,
she attended, and, though suffering a good deal of pain,
remained to the close of the service, and partook for the
last time of the sacred emblems of her Saviour's body
and blood. On the following Friday night, after
worship, and just after she herself had prayed aloud
that God would not ask her to suffer long nor severely,
an attack of hæmorrhage came on. She said, "Carry
me to bed." As they laid her on the bed, she whispered
to her husband, "Is this death?" In another moment
she had the answer, for without a struggle or a sigh she
was where, beyond the sufferings of earth, there is rest.

The three or four months of his wife's last illness
were a time of great anxiety to Mr. Patton, and, not
long after she was laid in the grave, it became manifest
that his own health was beginning to fail. He had
resumed his pastoral work, but did not feel strong.
Toward the end of August I received from him a letter,
in which he said that he was feeling unwell, and that
his physician had told him he had got some heart
affection, and must, for a time, cease all work. At the

time he wrote, however, he said he was much better, and hoped, in a short time, to be able to preach at least once a day. But he added, "No one can tell ; God only knows. Any heart affection is dangerous at sixty-five years of age. But I was tenfold worse, apparently, six years ago ; and God raised me up, and gave me six years since of fair health and work. It will be an easy thing to get my pulpit supplied for six or eight weeks. I hope that will be enough. But God knows. There may be more danger than I think. If so, thank God ' I know whom I have believed, and am persuaded that He is able to keep that which I have committed to Him against that day.' "

Having recovered somewhat, he went to Harrogate for a few weeks, but returned no better ; and about the end of October he wrote : " I am as ill as I can be, and am just waiting every day till the Master sends for me. This is probably my last letter to you." For three months longer he suffered greatly, and, on 31st January 1895, fell asleep in Jesus. Of him truly we may say, " Blessed are the dead which die in the Lord from henceforth : yea, saith the Spirit, that they may rest from their labours ; and their works do follow them."

Over his grave at Dromara there has been erected a square monument of dark Aberdeen granite, surmounted by a draped urn, and with the four sides finely polished. On the front face have been inscribed the following words :—

In Memory of

Rev. WILLIAM JOHN PATTON,

Minister of Second Dromara Presbyterian Church.

Born, May 26, 1829.
Ordained, June 29, 1853.
Died, January 31, 1895.

He was a devout Christian ; a faithful minister of Jesus Christ ; an earnest Evangelist ; a valued writer ; and through his instrumentality multitudes were added to the Lord.

On one of the other sides is an inscription composed by himself in memory of Mrs. Patton :—

In Memory of

MARY PATTON,

The beloved wife of Rev. W. J. Patton, who fell asleep in Jesus on 9th February 1894.

"An example of the believers, in word, in conversation, in charity, in spirit, in faith, in purity."

On the third side have been engraved, by his own instruction, six texts of Scripture, from which he derived much blessing :—

TEXTS OF GOD'S WORD,

From which he often received great good :

1. "Christ died for the ungodly."—ROM. v. 6.
2. "It is finished."—JOHN xix. 30.
3. "Him that cometh to Me I will in no wise cast out."—JOHN vi. 37.

———

4. "Lo! I am with you alway."—MATT. xxviii. 20.
5. "The blood of Jesus Christ His Son cleanseth us from all sin."—1 JOHN i. 7.
6. "If we confess our sins, He is faithful and just to forgive us our sins, and to cleanse us from all unrighteousness."—1 JOHN i. 9.

On the fourth side has been inscribed :—

HIS DYING TESTIMONY :

I THANK GOD,

"For I know whom I have believed, and am persuaded that He is able to keep that which I have committed unto Him against that day."

PREFACE

M Y DEAR READER,—What I aim at in this book, is that, by the blessing of God, you may be brought to accept Christ as your Saviour, or, if you have already accepted Christ, that you may know surely that you have eternal life.

Not long ago I was walking along a beautiful road with a young man whom God has used much in His service. He talked so beautifully and scripturally, that I was led to ask him how he was led to Christ, and he told me. I think a short account of it will be a very fitting introduction to this book.

"I was quiet and thoughtful," he said. "I had read my Bible regularly, and prided myself that I knew it pretty well. In fact, I was proud of my Bible knowledge and my orthodoxy. At the same time I was very well aware that I was not a real Christian. At length God made me anxious. For two long years I wrought as hard as any galley slave; and I see now that it was all in order to do something that would lay God under an obligation to pardon me. That was my real motive. I did not see, with all my orthodoxy, that God was so satisfied with the death of Christ in the room of sinners, that He was delighted to pardon me any moment for Christ's sake."

"You do not mean," I remarked, "that you were anxious all those two years? You were anxious by fits and starts, and at other times you were careless?" "No; I was downrightly anxious all the time during those two years." "And what did you do?" "I read my Bible each day, at regular, stated times, and I thought there was something dreadfully wrong if I was in any way prevented from reading the full time. I prayed in the same way, at stated times, and I fasted also. I tried my best to keep from sinning, and scarce lifted my head or looked up, and spoke little to any one, for fear of saying something that would grieve God." "It must have been an awful time," I said. "It was the most awful drudgery I ever had. I was resolved to lay God under an obligation to pardon me—that He could not get over pardoning me. And yet I prided myself on my Bible knowledge; and if any one had asked me, Can you do anything to atone for your sins? I would have answered, Decidedly not. How are you to be saved? By Christ alone."

"How were you brought to Christ at last?" "Well, I had a cousin, to whom I had spoken at the beginning of the two years. I said something like this to him— that we had souls to be saved, and that we might soon die, and that we should be prepared to meet God. He said it was all true; but that we were not going to die yet; and seemed to pay no attention to it, and to be quite careless. At the end of the two years, I got a letter from him one morning, saying that he had been attending some meetings in Belfast, and that many present there had been converted, and that he had been converted, and that his sins were forgiven, and that God was his friend, and how happy it was to know that you were a Christian. When I got his letter, my heart rose in rebellion against God. I thought it was not fair in God to convert him, who had been careless all along, and to leave me, who had sought so diligently to please Him, without pardon and peace. I really believed it was not fair."

"Please tell me how you were led to Christ at last?" "This young man had a sister, a cousin of mine, and she wrote after they returned from Belfast, asking me to come over; and I went. But still I was priding myself on my Bible knowledge, and thought I was far superior to them in this. My cousin dealt with me very wisely. She did not talk directly to me about my soul ; but she told me how another person—a young woman—had been brought to Christ in Belfast. 'Tom,' she said (we will call him Tom, though that is not his name), 'this young woman was really anxious, and she saw she could not save herself by all her doings and efforts, but she saw that "*Jesus was wounded for her transgressions, and bruised for her iniquities*" ; and that "*He had borne her sins in His own body on the tree*" ; and that she would not have to bear the punishment of her sins herself if she was willing to let the Lord bear it for her. She saw also that Jesus had finished the work, and had suffered enough to atone for her sins, and had left nothing for her to do in the way of making atonement, and that she had only to say, meaning it, "Thank Thee, Lord Jesus; I do take Thy death to atone for my sins, and I do take Thee to be my Saviour." She just rested on Christ and His death for pardon ; and if you had seen how happy she was !'

"After telling me this in the forenoon, we talked about everything else all the day long till near ten o'clock at night. I am sure she was praying for me, and I was downrightly in earnest to be saved. About ten o'clock she returned to the subject, and said, 'Now, Tom, are you not in earnest about what we were talking about this morning? Would you not like to know that your sins were forgiven?' I just listened to her, and said nothing. She went on to tell me that there was nothing whatever we could do to atone for our sins, or prepare ourselves; and that Christ had done all, and suffered all; and that His work was finished, and free to us; and that Jesus was here just now, willing to take our sins and save us; and that we need not wait a moment. Then she said we would kneel down and pray.

"We got down upon our knees in the room alone; and she prayed on, and on, and on. Soon after she began, I became more in earnest, and really believed that I was resting upon Christ, and felt almost impelled to rise from my knees and say, *I believe—I believe—I believe.* I can see now that God's Spirit was working mightily in me. But the devil—I see clearly that it was the devil—kept whispering, Don't make a fool of yourself—it is all a delusion—a mere emotion—a passing excitement. If you would rise now and afterwards fall away, what a fool you would make of yourself! And so I did not rise, but continued kneeling, and my cousin continued praying. Not long after, the devil suggested, Now your day of grace is gone—you had your opportunity. If you had taken it, and risen, you would have been saved. But now it is gone for ever. You will never have another chance. Oh, what agony I had in my heart! My cousin still prayed on; and I resolved that if the Spirit would only strive with me in the same way again, I would rise and confess that I did believe in Christ.

"It was not long before the Spirit of God began to work in my heart again, and to show me that Christ was willing to take my sins, and save me ; and I sprang to my feet, and said, *I believe—I believe—I believe.* My cousin rose also, and said how glad she was ; and then she began to tell me of the devices of the devil, and how he would try to deceive me. I have scarce had a temptation during the years since that my cousin did not warn me of between ten o'clock that night and two o'clock next morning."

"Please tell me some of the warnings she gave you?" "'Tom,' she said, 'to-morrow morning, when you awake, the devil will be sure to tell you that it was all a delusion—a mere emotion ; and you must have a text of Scripture to meet him with — something substantial to stand on. There is nothing like a text of Scripture when fighting with the devil. Tell him —"*Christ, His own self, bare our sins in His own body on the tree*" (1 Pet. ii. 24); or—"*Him that cometh to Me I will in no wise cast out*" (John vi. 37). Tell him that you *do* rely on Christ, and that you *will* rely on Christ.'"

"What other things did she tell you?" "That the devil would be sure to suggest wicked thoughts to my mind, and put them into my heart, and then tell me I

was just as bad as ever. He would ask me—Could
I be converted when I had these wicked thoughts?
Then I was to run at once to Jesus, and tell Him how
the devil was tempting me, and that I could not
overcome him myself; but that He had promised—
'*My grace is sufficient for thee ; for My strength is made
perfect in weakness*' (2 Cor. xii. 9); and tell Him that
I relied on Him to keep me."

"What more did she say to you?" "That the devil
would surely tell me that I could not stand, that I
would certainly fall. And I was to tell him that it
was quite true that I could not stand of myself, but
that my Saviour Jesus had promised that *He would
keep me from falling* (Jude 24), and that '*His name was
called Jesus, because He shall save His people from their
sins*' (Matt. i. 21). I shall never forget that night!

"I remained at my cousin's house for a few days,
and then returned home. I told my brother all I had
heard and been taught about Jesus; and it was not
long till he was converted, and we have been a great
comfort to each other ever since. A young sister, who
has since died, was soon brought to Christ also."

Such is the substance of the young man's story. I
do not guarantee the very words, but this is the
substance. Now, my dear reader! what do you know
about this matter? Do you see that God is so satisfied
with the death of Christ upon the Cross for sinners,
that He is willing to pardon you this moment for
Christ's sake? Do you see that you have not to wait
two years, nor two hours, nor two minutes, to make
God willing to pardon you; that God is this moment
beseeching you to be willing that Christ should be your
Substitute and Saviour?

Do you see that you could not do a thing that
would atone for your sins if you lived to the age of
Methuselah ; and that you don't need to do a thing to
atone for your sins, if you are willing to accept Christ?
Do you see that Christ is just now beside you, *praying*
you to let Him take your sins and carry them for you?
Oh, do what He bids you!—"*Come unto Me, all ye that*

labour and are heavy laden, and I will give you rest"
(Matt. xi. 28).

A part of this book has been printed already in the
form of New Year Addresses, some of which have had
a circulation of twenty thousand copies, chiefly in
Ulster, and have been blessed by God to the conversion
of not a few. But the larger part of it has not been
printed before.

I am very anxious about the way in which you read
it, that you may really profit by it.

> *1st,* Read it when you are alone with God, and not
> when others are bustling round about you.

> *2nd,* Read it slowly. There is no use in hurrying
> over a book like this.

> *3rd,* Read it prayerfully, asking God, as you turn
> over each page, to make it the means of leading
> you to Christ.

> *4th,* Read it for yourself, and not for others. Apply
> it to yourself.

And ere you have finished it, may you be able to
say, " *I know whom I have believed, and am persuaded
that He is able to keep that which I have committed unto
Him against that day* " (2 Tim. i. 12).

PARDON AND ASSURANCE

I

The Happiness of Being a Christian

SOME time ago I said to a godly young woman, "If there was a thoughtless young girl in the room with you whom you loved, and whom you wished to lead to Christ, what would you say to her first?" After a pause, she replied, "I think I should begin by telling her the happiness of being a Christian."

The devil tries to persuade people, and especially young people, that if they were Christians they must give up all pleasure and enjoyment, and always wear a long face; and that, while this might do well enough for old people of seventy or eighty years of age, it would never do for young people who were just entering life, and wishing to enjoy it. But ask any earnest Christian, and he will tell you that he never had any real, enduring happiness till he became a Christian, and that "*wisdom's ways are ways of pleasantness, and all her paths are peace.*" M'Cheyne writes: "I can assure you, from all I have ever felt of it, the pleasures of being forgiven are as superior to the pleasures of an unforgiven man, as heaven is higher than hell."

Are people happy who are living in sin? There is, no doubt, a kind of pleasure and excitement in it; there is a "*laughter that is like the crackling of thorns under a pot.*" But how short-lived and unsatisfactory it is! Tell me, reader! have you not followed hard after some pleasure, and when you got it, found it no better than a soap-bubble that bursts in your hand? Have you not tried to appear very merry when you were very miserable? Colonel Gardiner tells us that, when living a wicked and profligate life, and when pleasure seemed to follow pleasure, so that he was called "the happy rake," he was all the while most miserable, envying his very dog, and wishing to be, as the brute was, void of a conscience that could neither be bribed nor laid to sleep.

Lord Chesterfield, the famous "Man of the World," wrote, towards the close of his life: "I have run the silly rounds of business and pleasure, and have done with them all. I have enjoyed all the pleasures of the world, and, consequently, know their futility, and do not regret their loss. I estimate them at their real value, which is, in truth, very low; whereas those who have not experienced them always overrate them. They see only the gay outside, and are dazzled with their glare; but I have been behind the scenes, and have seen all the coarse pulleys and dirty ropes which exhibit and move the gaudy machine. I have been as wicked and as vain as Solomon, and am now at last able to feel and attest the truth of his reflection, that all is vanity and vexation of spirit. I bear my situation because I must, whether I will or no. I think of nothing but killing time the best way I can, now that it has become my enemy."

Lord Byron, the great genius and poet, who had entrance into every society, and who gratified every wicked passion of his nature to the full, wrote, without any immediate prospect of death the following lines:—

"Though gay companions o'er the bowl
Dispel awhile the sense of ill,
Though pleasure fills the maddening soul,
The heart—the heart is lonely still.

Count o'er the joys thine hours have seen;
Count o'er the days from anguish free;
And know, whatever thou hast been,
'Twere something better not to be."

" *There is no peace, saith my God, to the wicked.*" The fact is, we are so made that we cannot possibly be happy while living in sin. God has joined together sin and misery; He has also joined together holiness and happiness; and no one can put them asunder.

Jesus wants us to be happy—happy in doing His will. Not one of us is as happy as He wishes us to be. He said, "*These things have I spoken unto you, that My joy might remain in you, and that your joy might be full.*" David prayed, "*Restore unto me the joy of Thy salvation,*" and said, "*Happy is that people whose God is the Lord.*" The Apostle Paul tells us that "*The kingdom of God is not meat and drink, but righteousness, and peace, and joy in the Holy Ghost.*" And again he says, "*The fruit of the Spirit is love, joy, peace,*" etc. And, writing to the Christians of Philippi, his language is, "*Rejoice in the Lord alway: and again I say, Rejoice*" (Phil. iv. 4).

It is not grace that makes people unhappy, but the want of it; and Christians should rejoice, and let the world see them rejoice. It does great injury to God's cause when the world sees them morose and melancholy. There is a "*foolish talking or jesting which is not befitting,*" which is too common, even among Christians; but God's people should be joyful and happy.   .

WHY SHOULD CHRISTIANS BE HAPPY?

1. *They are pardoned and safe.* When a man sees that he has sinned against God thousands of times, and that his sins deserve hell; and when he sees that Christ has loved him and died for him, and borne the punishment of all these sins in his room, and that they are now forgiven and forgotten—will he not rejoice? Does not the sailor rejoice when he is snatched from a watery grave? Bunyan, when converted, wished to tell his joy to the very crows that sat upon the ploughed land before him. "Tongue cannot express the sweet comfort and peace of a soul in its earliest love." And not merely in its earliest love, but all his life long will

a Christian rejoice that his sins are forgiven. A
missionary friend wrote to me from his home in a
heathen land, that one day he began to think of God's
goodness to him in pardoning all his sins against God,
and against his neighbour, and against himself, and
that he had to go away alone and weep for very joy.
The world says, " Happy is the man who rolls in wealth,
who lives in splendour, who is adding field to field,
whose family are prospering in the world"; but God
says, " *Blessed is the man whose transgression is forgiven,
whose sin is covered.*"

Reader! would you not be far happier if you knew
that your sins were forgiven? At present you dare not
think of death, or judgment, or hell; and when the Spirit
of God brings these things to your remembrance, you try
to drive them away. And do you call that happiness?
Happiness, indeed! A strange kind of happiness! Would
you not sleep more soundly, and work more pleasantly,
and eat your food with more gladness of heart, if you
knew that when you died you would get to heaven?
And why should you not, when " *Christ Jesus came into
the world to save sinners*"—even the chief?

2. *God loves them, and they love Him.* Reader! do
you remember that time when you were very, very
happy? Now, look back and think what it was that
made you so happy. Was it not that some one loved
you, or that you loved some one? *You were happy in
your love.* Perhaps the greatest happiness on earth is
when the love of God is shed abroad in the heart by the
Holy Ghost given to us. My Christian reader will never
forget that night when, on his bed, he began to think
what a kind, loving, forgiving, gracious, good Heavenly
Father he had, and when he saw much more of His love
than he had ever seen before. Perhaps he will remember
talking to Him as one talks to a friend, and saying,
" My loving Father, Thou didst love me, and give Thy
Son to die for me; and now Thou lovest me as Thou
lovest Thy Son, and wilt give me everything that is
good for me. Father, Thou knowest that I love Thee;
but oh, forgive me that I love Thee so little, and give

me grace to love Thee more." That was a night to be remembered.

Nor will he forget that day when he began to think of Jesus and His love. He saw that Jesus had loved him, and died for him, and did love him now as His own Father loved Christ. He saw also that Jesus had united him to Himself, and that he was really married to the greatest, and richest, and mightiest, and wisest, and loveliest Being in heaven or earth; and that though he was poor, yet he had a rich Husband to supply all his need; and the tears ran down his cheeks for joy as he cried, " *My Beloved is mine, and I am His.*" What a joy to the believer to know that he has Jesus, this loving Friend, with him every day and every hour, to guide and keep him, and to supply all his need! Reader! would it not give you happiness to know that you had a loving friend ever near you, who was very wise, and had promised to guide you continually, and was very rich and powerful, and had promised to supply all your need? Such a Friend is Jesus. David Livingstone found Him such in Africa; and wherever he went he believed this verse, which he called Christ's "word of honour": " *Lo, I am with you alway, even unto the end of the world.*" Harriet Beecher Stowe found Him such. When she was a little girl some fourteen years old, she went one Sabbath to her father's church. That Sabbath Dr. Lyman Beecher tried to show his hearers that Jesus offered Himself to be a lifelong Friend to every human being. His little daughter saw what a blessing it would be to have such a Friend; and then and there she was enabled to accept Jesus as her Friend, and she found Him to be so during her long life; and this is one of her leading ideas in all her writings—*Jesus, a lifelong Friend, ever beside me.* When our hearts see this, we can understand that verse of the Apostle Peter: " *Whom having not seen, ye love; in whom, though now ye see Him not, yet believing, ye rejoice with joy unspeakable and full of glory.*"

And how it delights the Christian to know that the Holy Spirit loves him, and dwells in him for the very

purpose of enabling him to live a holy life, and that his
"*body is the temple of the Holy Ghost*" ! Oh, the blessedness of knowing this "*power which worketh in us,*" able
to overcome every sin, and fit us for every duty ! We
happen to know a person, who, walking one day along a
road, began to think over this promise of Christ : "*I will
pray the Father, and He shall give you another Comforter,
that He may abide with you for ever ; even the Spirit of
truth ; whom the world cannot receive, because it seeth
Him not, neither knoweth Him : but ye know Him ; for
He dwelleth with you, and shall be in you*" (John xiv. 16,
17). And as he walked along and meditated, the Holy
Spirit brought home to him that He was with him, and
in him, and would abide with him for ever, and would
fit him for his work on earth ; and before he was aware,
he burst into a ringing laugh of joy. Then was "his
mouth filled with laughter, and his tongue with melody,"
and he went on his way rejoicing. What a joy to know
that God loves us !

3. *They hold communion with God—talking to God, and
listening to God talking to them.* There is a pleasure in
knowing that a loving friend is present, even though we
do not talk to him. But the pleasure is greatly increased
by communion with him. What pleasure has the
Christian often in opening his Bible, and saying, "*Speak,
Lord, for Thy servant heareth,*" and listening to God talking
to him ! And what pleasure in discovering new mean-
ings in God's Word ! When Archimedes found out the
mathematical problem on which his thoughts had been
so long engaged, he rushed out of the bath and ran
through the streets, crying " I have found it—I have found
it !" And when God opens the eyes of the Christian to
see new beauties in the Bible, he can say with Jonathan
Edwards : "The sweetest joys and delights I have
experienced have not been those that have arisen from
a hope of my own good estate, but in a direct view of
the glorious things of the gospel."

And what delight in pouring out the heart to God, and
telling Him what we would not tell to the nearest friend
on earth ! The wife of Jonathan Edwards was one of the

most godly women who ever lived. During her married life she had often visions of the divine love and glory that kept her in raptures for hours. But even when she was a young girl of thirteen, her future husband wrote the following about her: "They say there is a young girl in —— who is beloved of that Great Being who moves and rules the world, and that there are certain seasons in which this Great Being, in some way or other invisible, comes to her, and fills her mind with exceeding sweet delights. She is of a wonderful sweetness, calmness, and benevolence of mind. She will sometimes go about from place to place singing devoutly, and seems to be always full of joy and pleasure, and no one knows for what. She loves to be alone, walking in the fields and groves, and seems to have some one invisible always conversing with her."

Hedley Vicars, that Christian young officer, wrote to his younger sister: "My dear sister, I tell you honestly, I would willingly part with every earthly pleasure in life for one hour's communion with Jesus every day." And then what a rapture there sometimes is in the great congregation, praising and adoring our Father in heaven, or sitting at the table of His Son with great delight!

4. *They are happy in overcoming sin, in pleasing God, and in doing good to their fellow-men.* "*In keeping God's commands there is great reward.*" Yes — "*in keeping them.*" Sydney Smith said that if you want to be happy yourself, try to make some one else happy each day; that very little would do it—a kind word to one, a kind letter to another, a penny or sixpence or a cast-off garment to another; and thus you would make 365 persons happy each year, and this would make yourself happy. There is much truth in this. Try it, my reader! and see. But when the Christian does these things to please Jesus, how much more joy they give! Every word spoken for Jesus pleases Him, every cup of cold water given because you think He wants you to do it, pleases Him. "*I was hungry, and ye gave Me meat; I was thirsty, and ye gave Me drink; I was a stranger, and ye took Me in.*"

4

What happiness there is in overcoming sin by the power of the Holy Spirit! Old Brooks says truly, " There is a thousand times more pleasure in denying ourselves than in gratifying our wicked passions." David Brainerd, on his death-bed, said, " I have had more pleasure this morning than all the drunkards in the world enjoy, if it were all extracted." The last words of Matthew Henry were: " You have been used to take notice of the sayings of dying men, this is mine—that a life spent in the service of God, and communion with Him, is the most comfortable and pleasant life that any one can live in the present world." And when God makes a Christian the means of leading a soul to Jesus, and thus " *converting a sinner from the error of his ways, and saving a soul from death*," it gives an hundred-fold more pleasure than the gratifying of any wicked desire. " How sweet," says M'Cheyne, " to work all day for God, and then lie down beneath His smile ! "

5. *They are happy in looking forward to heaven as their home.* Does the miser rejoice not only in the gold he has in hand, but in his bank cheques and promises to pay, reckoning them as good as cash? So does the Christian believe God's promises, and rejoice in prospect of being soon in heaven. To be for ever in that *Better Paradise*, and walk along the river which runs through it, and eat its twelve manner of fruits ; to be for ever in that *New Jerusalem*, with its streets of gold, and its gates of pearl ; to be for ever in that *Father's house*, where are many mansions, and to feel its freedom from care, and to enjoy his Father's love, and to know that he is at home at last !

To be for ever where there is no sorrow, nor sighing, nor pain ; where there is no temptation nor sin, and nothing to hurt or destroy in God's Holy Temple ; where we shall be making new discoveries continually about God and His works and ways, and learning the truth of His promise: " *What I do, thou knowest not now, but thou shalt know hereafter* " ! To look forward to all this is happiness.

To be for ever with that Father who loved us, and gave His only-begotten Son to die for us; for ever with that Son who loved us, and died for us, and now lives to watch over us; for ever with that Holy Spirit who strove with us, and when we resisted, strove on till He brought us to the foot of the Cross, and enabled us to lay down our load there, and who now dwells within us to make us holy!

To be for ever with the holy angels who encamped round us on earth, and watched over us lest we should dash our foot against a stone ; for ever with our dear friends who fell asleep in Jesus, talking to them about the way the Lord led us on earth, and the blessedness of heaven, and taking sweet counsel again together; for ever making new acquaintance with those we had often heard of, but never known on earth—perhaps speaking face to face with Paul or John, Luther or Knox, Henry Martyn or Robert M'Cheyne! To look forward to all this is happiness.

6. *They are happy even in affliction.* Others are happy when they have no affliction ; the Christian alone is happy in it. He knows that it comes from the hand of a kind Father who has promised—*"All things work together for good to them that love God."* He knows that it comes through the hand of Him who was nailed for him to the tree, and he draws near to Him who handles the rod, and this lightens the stroke. The Apostle Paul had more afflictions than most people, yet he could say, " *We glory in tribulations also, knowing that tribulation worketh patience ; and patience, experience ; and experience, hope."* He reckoned that "*these light afflictions which were but for a moment"* were "*not worthy to be compared with the glory that shall be revealed in us."* Indeed they are not. Five minutes in heaven will make amends for all. And when the Lord does lay on the rod, He gives grace to bear it. What a lovely promise this is : "*God is faithful, who will not suffer you to be tempted above that ye are able, but will with the temptation also make a way of escape that ye may be able to bear it"* (1 Cor. x. 13)!

I know no better illustration of this truth than Richard Williams, medical missionary to Patagonia, cooped up in his little boat, and dying of scurvy and starvation, yet exquisitely happy. A night or two before he died, he wrote in his journal: " Should any- thing prevent my ever adding to this, let all my beloved ones at home rest assured that I was happy, beyond all expression, the night I wrote these lines, and would not have exchanged situations with any man living. Let them also be assured that my hopes were full and blooming with immortality ; that *Heaven*, and *Love*, and *Christ*, which mean one and the same divine thing, were in my heart ; that the hope of glory filled my whole heart with joy and gladness ; and that to me to live is Christ, and to die is gain. I am in a strait betwixt two, to abide in the body, or to depart and be with Christ, which is far better. Let them know that I loved them, and prayed for every one of them. God bless them all."

7. *They are happy in death.* What is death to those who are Christians? It is the Lord Jesus coming and tak- ing them away home to Himself, that where He is, there they may be also. It is no pity of them, though often it is a pity of those left behind. We have seen not a few Christians die, and nearly all died in peace, willing " to depart and to be with Christ, which is far better." Even those who may have had doubts and fears during their life had them cleared away before they died, and were ready to cry out, " *O death, where is thy sting ? O grave, where is thy victory ? Thanks be to God, who giveth us the victory through our Lord Jesus Christ.*"

Some have had not only *peace*, but *rapture*. We will give two well-known cases of rapture on a dying bed. Payson, near his last days, wrote to his sister : " Were I to adopt the figurative language of Bunyan, I might date this letter from the land of Beulah, of which I have been for some weeks a happy inhabitant. The Celestial City is full in my view. Its glories beam upon me, its breezes fan me, its odours are wafted to me, its sounds strike upon my ears, and its spirit is breathed into my heart. Nothing separates me from it but the river of death, which now appears but an insignificant rill that may be crossed at a single step whenever God shall give permission."

Toplady seemed, during his last illness, to be in the vestibule of heaven. With sparkling eyes he exclaimed to a friend, "Oh, my dear sir, I cannot tell the comforts I feel in my soul,—they are past expression. My prayers are all converted into praise. I enjoy heaven already in my soul." When he was told, about an hour before his death, that they were made willing to part with him, tears of joy ran down his cheeks as he added, "Oh, what a blessing that you are made willing to part with me; for no mortal can live after the glories which God hath manifested to my soul."

Yes, dear reader! there is real happiness in being a Christian. God gives him joys that the unconverted know nothing about. They fancy that they would have to cross every desire of their nature, and live a life of constant restraint and pain, if they became Christians. So Satan tries to persuade them. But nothing of the kind. "*A new heart also will I give you, and a new spirit will I put within you*" (Ezek. xxxvi. 26). God takes away no pleasures but sinful pleasures, and gives new pleasures that swallow up the old ones. He has put no desires into us that He has not given legitimate means of gratifying.

Suppose that a man had got a love for some poison, there are two ways in which he might be put from taking it. *First,* his hands might be tied behind his back, and his friends might prevent him by force from going near it; or, *second,* some other drink might be provided, so sweet and pleasant and wholesome, that all love for the poison would be taken away. Now, it is not in the first way of restraint that God keeps us from sinning, but in the second way of giving a new heart, and new desires, and new pleasures, making it sweet and pleasant to serve God. Look at a mother with her babe. To an onlooker it might seem a toil and hardship for her to take such trouble with her child.

But in reality it is an exquisite pleasure, such is the love that God has given her for her babe. A little boy has a rattle, and rattles away, and you could not force it out of his hand. But he grows up, and one day his father gives him a pony and saddle. At once he drops the rattle, and leaps into the saddle, and rides away. What does he care for the rattle when he has got a pony and saddle!

Augustine, in his *Confessions*, telling of his conversion, and of certain sinful pleasures he had long indulged, and without which he thought that life would scarce be worth living, breaks forth thus: "How sweet did it at once become to me to want the sweetness of those toys, and what I feared to be parted from was now a joy to part with! For Thou didst cast them forth from me, Thou true and highest sweetness. Thou castedst them forth, and for them, enteredst in Thyself, sweeter than all pleasure."

Andrew Fuller also tells that from the time of his conversion "my former wicked courses were forsaken. I had no manner of desire after them. They lost their influence over me. To those evils, a glance at which, before, would have set my passions in a flame, I now felt no inclination. With joy and triumph I said, My soul is as a weaned child."

Oh, my reader! that you knew the joy of being a Christian!

II

Sin—What It Is

UNCONVERTED reader, I wish to write to you now about sin, and its sinfulness, and its consequences. I know that this is not a pleasant subject. Sinners do not like it, for the same reason that Ahab did not like Micaiah; it does not speak good concerning them, but only evil. Nevertheless it is a most useful subject. If you saw your *danger*, you could not be careless and unconcerned about your soul. If you saw your *sinfulness*, you would see that you could not do anything that would atone for your sins, and you would cease putting off your salvation till you would make yourself better. If you saw you were utterly *helpless*, you would not be far from the kingdom of God. May God's Spirit open your eyes to see these things!

1. *What is sin?* The Apostle John says: "*Sin is the transgression of the law*" (1 John iii. 4). The Apostle Paul says: "*Cursed is every one that continueth not in all things which are written in the book of the law to do them*" (Gal. iii. 10). And again: "*By the law is the knowledge of sin*" (Rom. iii. 20). God, who made us, has given us a law; and when we obey it, we are obedient children, and when we disobey it, we are sinners, and must be punished. "*The Lord is our Judge, the Lord is our Lawgiver, the Lord is our King.*" What a great God He is! He is "the King eternal, immortal, invisible, the only God" (1 Tim. i. 17). He made the sun, moon, and stars, Pleiades and Orion, and all the host of them, and He keeps them in their courses. He made us, and

has as much right to take away our lives any moment
as he Has to take away the lives of those numberless
little animals that are on the leaves of the trees, and
that fall into the river every autumn and are drowned.
He is our righteous Governor, and has given us His
law.

This law was written on the heart of Adam in Paradise.
It is written on the hearts of the heathen, and they are
bound to keep it. " *Which show the work of the law written
in their hearts, their conscience also bearing witness, and
their thoughts the meanwhile accusing or else excusing one
another*" (Rom. ii. 15). But God has given us the
Bible, and His law is written in the Old and New
Testaments. The sum of it is in the Ten Commandments, which He gave by His own voice from Sinai, and
which are binding on every one as a rule of life. Christ
gave a summary of this law, and it is this: " *Thou shalt
love the Lord thy God with all thy heart, and with all thy
soul, and with all thy mind, and with all thy strength:
this is the first commandment. And the second is like,
namely this, Thou shalt love thy neighbour as thyself*"
(Mark xii. 30, 31).

This is the law we are bound to obey. It is a copy
of God's own nature, and is holy and just and good.
There is not a command too many, nor one too few. It
is perfect, like God Himself. This law Jehovah must
insist on.

We may have sinned, and be unable to keep the law
as we ought; but shall our sinfulness and enmity to
God rob Him of His right to our perfect obedience?

What is the nature of our inability to keep God's law?
Is it want of hands, or feet, or intellect, or affections?
Not at all. It is simply this—we hate God, and love
sin, and have no will to do the will of God. If our
hearts loved God and His will, it would be easy. In
Gen. xxxvii. 4, we are told that Joseph's brethren "*hated
him, and could not speak peaceably unto him.*" Why could
they not speak peaceably to him? Simply because they
hated him so much. Was this inability of theirs any
excuse? No; in this consisted the greatness of their

sin. Peter tells us in 2 Pet. ii. 14, of men *"having eyes full of adultery, and that cannot cease from sin."* Why could they not cease from sin? Because their eyes were full of adultery. Was this inability any excuse? No; in this consisted the greatness of their sin. It was a real fact that they could not cease from sin; yet this did not excuse them, it made their sin the greater.

Did ever a drunkard plead as an excuse, before a magistrate, that he had such a love for drink that he could not pass a public-house without going in and getting drunk? Did ever a murderer plead, at the bar of justice, that he hated his victim so much that he could not go near him without killing him? Would not this show *malice prepense*, and make his crime the greater? The only reason why you cannot keep God's law is because you love sin so much, and hate God so much. *" The carnal mind is enmity against God; for it is not subject to the law of God, neither indeed can be."*

Your own conscience tells you that you are a free agent, and that you are responsible for your actions. God has written these two facts upon the hearts of men, and we can no more doubt them than we can doubt our existence. These are ultimate facts of which we are conscious. We are debtors, then, to do the whole law. God demands it of us, and He only demands what is just, and what He must demand if He would not surrender His glory as God. Were He to retreat from this demand, and wink at sin in any form, He would cease to be God. His law is binding on us.

2. *God's law extends to the thoughts and desires of the heart as well as to outward actions.* It is exceeding broad. Listen to what Christ says in His Sermon on the Mount. This is what He says about the Sixth Commandment: *" Ye have heard that it was said by them of old time, Thou shalt not kill; and whosoever shall kill shall be in danger of the judgment: but I say unto you, That whosoever is angry with his brother without a cause shall be in danger of the judgment: and whosoever shall say to his brother, Raca, shall be in danger of the council; but whosoever shall say, Thou fool, shall be in*

danger of hell fire" (Matt. v. 21, 22). With this agree the words of the Apostle John: "*Whosoever hateth his brother is a murderer, and ye know that no murderer hath eternal life abiding in him*" (1 John iii. 15).

Again, this is what Christ says about the Seventh Commandment: "*Ye have heard that it was said by them of old time, Thou shalt not commit adultery: but I say unto you, That whosoever looketh on a woman to lust after her hath committed adultery with her already in his heart*" (Matt. v. 27, 28). Some thoughtless readers seem to think that the Sermon on the Mount is a very lovely address, so nice and easy for sinners. It is a lovely address, but not so lovely for sinners as for saints. " God save me from the Sermon on the Mount when I am judged in the last day," said a person who knew what was in that Sermon, and what was in the human heart. It is *the law* that is chiefly preached in the Sermon on the Mount. " *Think not that I am come to destroy the law or the prophets: I am not come to destroy, but to fulfil. For verily I say unto you, Till heaven and earth pass, one jot or one tittle shall in no wise pass from the law, till all be fulfilled*" (Matt. v. 18).

Paul tells us that he would not have known sin if he had not read the Tenth Commandment: "*Thou shalt not covet.*" He had not seen before that the mere inward desire was evil. But when God showed him this, how changed his thoughts were about sin! "*I was alive without the law once; but when the commandment came, sin revived, and I died*"—died to all hope of saving myself.

3 *God's law extends to sins of omission as well as of transgression.* What are the sins to be mentioned by Christ in the Day of Judgment, as given in the 25th chapter of Matthew? " *Then shall He say unto them on the left hand, Depart from Me, ye cursed, into everlasting fire, prepared for the devil and his angels: for I was an hungered, and ye gave Me no meat: I was thirsty, and ye gave Me no drink: I was a stranger, and ye took Me not in: naked, and ye clothed Me not: sick and in prison, and ye visited Me not. Inasmuch as ye did it not to one of the*

least of these, ye did it not to Me." These are all sins of omission.

In this same chapter we read what the Lord said to the man who had got the one talent. He had got only one, and he did not squander it, but he made no good use of it, and kept it hid in the earth. Perhaps he thought because he had got only one, that little or nothing would be required of him. But his Lord calls him " *Thou wicked and slothful servant,*" and says to the attendants, " *Take therefore the talent from him, and give it unto him that hath ten talents, and cast ye the unprofitable servant into outer darkness :* THERE *shall be weeping and gnashing of teeth.*"

Read also what God said about the inhabitants of Meroz—a town which had sent no one to fight with Deborah and Barak against the enemies of the Lord. " *Curse ye Meroz, said the angel of the Lord, curse ye bitterly the inhabitants thereof.*" And why? What was the sin of which they had been guilty? Was it murder? No. Or theft? No. Or blasphemy? No. But the sin was, Doing nothing for God. " *Because they came not to the help of the Lord, to the help of the Lord against the mighty*" (Judg. v. 23).

God's word is: " *Cursed is every one that continueth not in all things which are written in the book of the law to do them.*" Mark! we must *continue* in all things written in the law to do them to the end, otherwise we are under the curse. And the Apostle James says : " *Whosoever shall keep the whole law, and yet offend in one point, he is guilty of all* " (ii. 10). He is a sinner, and can never do anything himself that will blot out his sins. One murder makes a man a murderer, and he is hung for it. One theft makes a man a thief, and he is imprisoned for it. And one sin makes a man a sinner, so that he must die for it. Nothing that he can do can blot out that one sin. He cannot get to heaven without resting upon Christ, and upon what He has done. You may think this hard, but it is what God's law demands. You look upon God as such an one as yourself, who thinks sin a trifle. But sin is no trifle.

and God is not such an one as yourself. He is "*the Holy, Holy, Holy Lord God Almighty,*" who cannot let sin go unpunished. The thief, when caught, thinks the law hard; but that does not change it; and your thoughts about the law of God will not alter it any more than the crying of an infant will stop a storm. Who of us, then, does not need to pray the prayer that good Archbishop Usher prayed in his last moments: "Lord, forgive me all my sins, but in special, Lord, forgive me my sins of omission"?

4. Reader! you are a sinner. Take a glance first at your *Deeds*, then at your *Words*, then at your *Thoughts;* and in reference to each of these look at what you have *omitted* to do as well as at what you have done, which you should not have done.

(1) *Look at your Deeds.* Have you read your Bible as much as you ought? and practised it as you ought? Have you prayed as much as you ought? as earnestly? and as believingly? and in the name of Jesus? Have you gone to the house of God as regularly as you ought? and when you did go, was it to meet God and get His blessing? or was it to see and to be seen? Have you sought to train your children for God? and have you been kind and Christlike to your servants? Children! have you honoured your father and mother, and obeyed them? Servants! have you sought to work fairly and honestly, not with eye-service as men-pleasers, but in singleness of heart, fearing God? Then what about your everyday business in the world? Do you ask God to guide you in it? Do you bring the details of it to Him, and seek to do it for His glory? And what about your neighbours? Are you kind to them? And do you seek to do them good as far as is in your power? Or are you not intensely selfish, and just mind *Number One?* Do you ever speak to your neighbours about Christ when you have an opportunity? or give a tract to them? or lend a book to them with prayer? Have you ever written a letter to any one to seek to bring him to Christ? Have you given as much as you could to send the gospel to the heathen? Have

you not spent more last year on drink or on a party than you have given to God altogether? What have you done for God, or for the Church of God?

Then about sins of *transgression*. Have you not broken God's Sabbath again and again? What company do you keep? Of course you ought to be kind and courteous to all, but have you not loved the company of the wicked rather than of God's children? Perhaps you have cheated your neighbour in buying or selling, in a shop, or in a market, and prided yourself on getting an unfair advantage of him. Perhaps you have got drunk once, twice, many times. Perhaps you have committed adultery, not merely in thought, but in act. And have you not resisted the Holy Ghost again and again when He strove with you? Remember that these are sins against God; and that unless you have gone to Jesus with them, and put them upon His head, they are all marked down against you this moment in God's Book, and you cannot possibly get to heaven without their being forgiven.

(2) *Look at your Words.* "*I say unto you, That every idle word that men shall speak, they shall give account thereof in the day of judgment. For by thy words thou shalt be justified, and by thy words thou shalt be condemned.*" These are the words of Jesus. Have you spoken to your children and to your servants about Jesus, as you ought? Have you sought to reprove sin in a kind and Christlike way? Or have you not rather laughed at it, and encouraged it? "*Thou shalt not hate thy brother in thine heart: thou shalt surely rebuke thy neighbour, and not bear sin because of him*" (Lev. xix. 17, R.V.). Have you not been ashamed of Jesus, and refused to stand up for Him, when not to stand up for Him was almost to deny Him? Have you not?

Then, again, how many idle, wicked words have you spoken since you were born? Perhaps you have used filthy words, or words of double meaning, seeking to excite obscene thoughts in others. How filthy the heart must be when the words are so filthy! And how many backbiting words you have spoken, speaking evil of others behind their backs. Remember God says: "*Let all bitterness, and wrath, and anger, and clamour, and evil speaking be put away from you, with all malice; and be ye kind one to another*" (Eph. iv. 31). Pascal says that if all our friends only knew what we have said about them behind their back, we would not have four friends in all the world. Is this true of you? Then have you not exaggerated and told downright lies, knowing them to be lies? forgetting that "*all liars shall have their part in the lake which burneth with fire and brimstone.*"

Perhaps you have cursed and sworn, and asked God to damn you, or to damn others. What a sin to pray such awful prayers! I tell you that if you were five minutes in hell, you would never ask God to damn you or anybody again: it would put an end to your damning.

How true is God's word!—"*There is none righteous, no, not one. They are all gone out of the way, they are together become unprofitable; there is none that doeth good, no, not one. Their throat is an open sepulchre; with their tongues they have used deceit; the poison of asps is under their lips: whose mouth is full of cursing and bitterness*" (Rom. iii. 10–14).

And remember, these sins of your words are all marked down in God's Book against you, and you cannot possibly get to heaven till they are washed out in Christ's blood.

(3) *Look at your Thoughts.* Some people say they have good hearts. It is because they neither know their hearts nor the Bible. God says: "*The heart is deceitful above all things, and desperately wicked: who can know it? I, the Lord, search the heart*" (Jer. xvii. 9).

Unconverted reader! there is no love to God in your heart. The great sin is not to love the Lord with your heart. But you never did a thing in your life from real love to God. If you loved a person, you would think about that person, and try to please him. Now, do you think about God, and try to please Him? He has watched over you with an eye that never slept, and guarded you with an arm that never wearied, and yet He has not been in all your thoughts. You have forgotten Him and all His kindness to you, and you have lived very much as you would have if there had been no God. You never did a thing in your life with a view to please Him. "*The ox knoweth his owner, and the ass his master's crib; but Israel doth not know, My people doth not consider.*"

And how thankless you have been! You never once since you were born heartily thanked God for sending His Son to seek and save you. Did you? Jesus has been with you every day and hour of your life. If I asked you, you would tell me you believe He came from heaven and died for you; and yet you never thanked Him—never once really meaning it. Now, did you? Could you imagine a more ungrateful man or woman or child? Is not this the height of iniquity? Is not this the depth of depravity? You never had a higher motive for your conduct than the fear of hell, or the fear of jail, or self-interest, or to be seen of men. This is the "good heart" you have!

Nay, more! *Your heart is full of all manner of wickedness.* It is full of pride, and vanity, and conceit, and self-seeking—of envy, and jealousy, and malice, and hatred, and revenge. Oh, the meanness and shabbiness of your motives if they were but known! Here is what God says about your heart, and He knows it: "*Out of the heart proceed evil thoughts, murders, adulteries, fornications, thefts, false witness, blasphemies*" (Matt. xv. 19).

These are what He sees in your heart. If there were a glass door into it, and we could see it, these are what would be seen crawling all round it. What did Paul say to Titus about Titus and himself before they were Christians? "*Speak evil of no man, for we ourselves also were once foolish, disobedient, deceived, serving divers lusts and pleasures, living in malice and envy, hateful and hating one another*" (Tit. iii. 3). This is what God says about our hearts by nature. We do not like to think it is true about ourselves; but the more we know ourselves, the more clearly we shall see that it is all true.

Your heart hates God. So God says. I think I hear you say, "No, I do not feel hatred to God in my heart." Your feelings are not the best judge in this matter. You like to be in company with your parents, or your children, or that man whom you love. But you do not like to be alone with that other man whom you hate. Now tell me, do you like to be alone with God, talking to Him? Would you not rather spend an hour on the roadside breaking stones, if no one saw you, than an hour alone with God talking to Him? Yes, you would.

Again, you have heard that God hates your wicked ways, and yet you would like to go on in them without restraint. Is not that a fact? Would you not be really glad to think that there was no God at all? Listen to what God says: " *The carnal mind is enmity against God,*"—not merely hates God, but is hatred of God,—"*for it is not subject to the law of God, neither indeed can be. So then they that are in the flesh cannot please God*" (Rom. viii. 7, 8). How can God be pleased with anything done by a heart that hates Him? The first thing a man does that pleases God is accepting His Son. M'Cheyne says, in one of his sermons: " I venture to say there is not an unconverted man present who has the most distant idea of the monstrous wickedness that is now within his breast. Stop till you are in hell, and it will break out unrestrained. But still, let me tell you what it is: You have a heart that would kill God if you could. If the bosom of God were now within your reach, and one blow would rid the universe of God, you have a heart fit to do the deed."

This hatred of God is the reason why, up till the present, you have rejected Christ. You have the same heart exactly that the Jews had who put Christ to death. Do not imagine, I beseech you, that you are any better than they. Had the Son of God been incarnate in your town or parish, and been crucified on some hill in your neigh-

bourhood, you, who up till to-day have rejected Him
and said, No, no, I will not have Thy death as the
atonement for my sins, nor have Thee as my Saviour,
would have joined in the cry, "Away with Him, away
with Him, crucify Him." Your hearts hate Him, though
you may not think so.

Surely, dear reader, you must see that you have
sinned against God hundreds of times in thought and
word and deed. How often have you sinned against
Him in a day? How many days are there in the year?
365. How many years old are you? Ten, twenty,
forty, seventy. Are you not ready to cry out with
Ezra, "*O my God, I am ashamed, and blush to lift up my
face to Thee, for our iniquities are increased over our
head, and our trespass is grown up unto the heavens*"?
You are a sinner, "*guilty before God.*" Nothing that
you can do in the future can ever blot out your past
sin. Do you see this?

5. *Therefore by the deeds of the law there shall no flesh
be justified in His sight* (Rom. iii. 20). You can never
earn heaven by your works. If you lived to the age of
Methuselah, you could not do a thing that would blot out
even one of your past sins. You may be a good neighbour, and sober, and honest, and accomplished, and the
delight of every society in which you move. And yet,
in one respect, there is no difference between you and
that poor thief lying in jail, or that lost one who has
left her father's house, and whose name is never mentioned there but in sobbing prayer to God. *You are a
sinner*, and can never get to heaven unless you have the
blood of Christ sprinkled on your heart. In other
respects you differ greatly from that thief and that
harlot; and thank God every day for His restraining
grace that has made you to differ. "There goes John
Bradford, but for the grace of God," that good man used
to say when he saw criminals passing his house for
the gallows. Yes, be thankful. But remember what
Paul says, speaking on this very point: "*There is no
difference, for all have sinned and come short of the glory
of God*" (Rom. iii. 23).

5

Look at those two men standing at the barrack gate. The one is five feet three inches high, the other is five feet eleven. But there is no difference in this respect— they both come short of being six feet high, and cannot, therefore, get enlisting in the Life Guards. Look at those two women at the door of the physician. The one is standing, and in rags; the other rides in a carriage, and is clothed in velvet. But there is no difference in this respect — they have both got the cancer. Look at those two boys drowning in that sinking ship. The one is rich, the other poor ; the one is learned, the other ignorant. But there is no difference in this respect — they are both drowning. So, dear fellow-sinner, there is no difference between you and that drunkard, or that thief, or that harlot in this respect : *You have sinned, and cannot get to heaven unless you trust Christ.* Nay, it may be that in the eyes of God you are more sinful than they are; that your temptations were less than theirs, and your advantages greater than theirs. It may be that they made greater efforts to resist sin, and strove more against temptation, though they fell, than you did who never fell so far, simply because you were never tempted so much. There is far less difference in the eyes of God than there is in the eyes of men between one sinner and another, when both are out of Christ. When God looks down from heaven, He sees that both hate Him ; the one as certainly as the other.

Think not, then, that because you are amiable and moral and accomplished, you will get to heaven without Christ. There were amiable and moral and accomplished persons at the time of the Flood, but all perished except those who were inside the ark. There were amiable and moral and accomplished persons among the Egyptians that night when the destroying angel passed by, but the firstborn was slain in every family where God did not see the blood upon the door-post. Thank God if you are amiable and moral and accomplished, but cry out, " God be merciful to me, a sinner, for Christ's sake," and depend for salvation only on Christ and His finished work. Nothing else can save you.

"Not the labour of my hands
Can fulfil Thy law's demands:
Could my zeal no respite know,
Could my tears for ever flow,
All for sin could not atone:
Thou must save, and Thou alone."

"None but Christ! none but Christ!" said John Lambert the martyr, as he lifted up the stumps of his arms all flaming with fire—"None but Christ!" And to the same effect were the dying words of David Dickson of Irvine: "I have taken all my good deeds and all my bad deeds, and have cast them together in a heap before the Lord, and have fled from both to Jesus Christ: and in Him *I have sweet peace.*"

May this peace be yours, my reader!

III

The Sinfulness of Sin

THE Apostle Paul speaks of sin as being "exceeding sinful" (Rom. vii. 13). Few people think that it is so. Many seem to think that it is a mere trifle —a matter of no importance; that they have only to cry, "Lord, bless me," when they are dying, and that sin will be put away from them. I know a minister who had in his congregation a farmer and his wife, who were clever and prospering in the world. One day the minister, when visiting, found the farmer's wife in the parlour alone, and God gave him grace to speak plainly to her, and to say he was afraid she thought too much about this world, and too little about the next one. She turned on him angrily, and said, "Surely the Lord will give me five minutes to make my peace with Him before I die!" Some months afterwards that minister was sent for hurriedly to go to that house. When he arrived, he found the wife lying in bed, having got a paralytic stroke. God had not given her even five minutes. Are there not many like her who make little of sin? They judge of sin—

By the opinion of the world. What does the world, which lieth in wickedness, know about God's hatred of sin? The natural man cannot understand "*the things of the Spirit of God, for they are foolishness unto him; neither can he know them, because they are spiritually discerned.*" It matters not what the world thinks, but what God thinks. Amiable and accomplished and learned people of the world are just amiable children of wrath,

accomplished servants of the devil, learned heirs of hell.
When Paul preached to the accomplished and learned
Athenians, he yearned over them just as much as over
the most barbarous, knowing that they needed the salvation of their souls just as much as the others did. Others
judge of sin—

By natural conscience. Conscience is God's vicegerent
in the soul, and must be listened to. But it needs to
be instructed by the Bible. The Hindoos and Chinese
kill their female children, and put to death their old
men and women ; and their consciences chide them
not. There are many, even in Bible lands, whose consciences have been drugged by sin. The Bible speaks
of persons "*having their conscience seared with a hot
iron.*" What do they know about God's thought of
sin ? William C. Burns, the great evangelist of Scotland
and China, writes: "The conscience may give you no
uneasiness, and yet you may be on the very brink of
hell. A dead conscience leads many to damnation
without a warning. They dream that they are to escape
until they awake under the scorchings of the fire that
is never quenched, and the gnawings of the worm that
never dies." But, on the other hand, see conscience
quickened by the Holy Spirit, and you will hear anxious
inquirers asking, "Can I be saved at all? Surely my
iniquities are too great to be forgiven?"

In order that we may see sin somewhat in the light
of God's countenance, let us look at it in six Bible
lights :—

1. *Look at sin in the light of God's holiness.* "When
we say that God is holy, we mean two things—*First,*
that He is perfectly and unchangeably free from all
iniquity Himself; and *second,* that His blessed nature
recoils, with an essential and infinite abhorrence, from
the very sight of iniquity in any of His creatures"
(William C. Burns). Hear what the Bible says about
God's holiness: "*They rest not day and night, saying,
Holy, Holy, Holy, Lord God Almighty*" (Rev. iv. 8).
"*Thou lovest righteousness, and hatest wickedness*" (Ps.
xlv. 7). "*Thou art of purer eyes than to behold evil, and*

canst not look on iniquity" (Hab. i. 13). God says in Jer.
xliv. 4 : "*Oh, do not this abominable thing that I hate.*"
When Job saw God's holiness, he exclaimed, "*I have
heard of Thee by the hearing of the ear, but now mine eye
seeth Thee : wherefore I abhor myself, and repent in dust
and ashes*" (xlii. 5, 6). And we would do the same if
we saw how holy God is. When Isaiah saw His holiness, he exclaimed, "*Woe is me! for I am undone ;
because I am a man of unclean lips, and I dwell in the
midst of a people of unclean lips : for mine eyes have seen
the King, the Lord of Hosts*" (vi. 5).

God is a *loving* God, a thousand times more loving
than any of us imagine, but His love is the love of a
holy God ; and He has told us of a way through Christ
in which He can pardon the guiltiest and yet be holy.
But He cannot pardon except through Christ. Some
people seem to "think that God is so kind, so indulgent,
so lenient, so imbecile, that men may do what they like
against Him, and break His every law, and put the
pry of their impertinence and rebellion under His
throne ; that while they are spitting in His face and
stabbing at His heart, He takes them up in His arms
and kisses their infuriated brow and cheek, saying, 'Of
such is the kingdom of heaven.'" Now the God of the
Bible is not like that.

How striking are His own words proclaimed to Moses
at Sinai ! They are often quoted, but with the sterner
parts left out. "*And the Lord passed by before him,
and proclaimed, The Lord, the Lord God, merciful and
gracious, long-suffering, and abundant in goodness and
truth, keeping mercy for thousands, forgiving iniquity
and transgression and sin, and that will by no means
clear the guilty ; visiting the iniquity of the fathers upon
the children, and upon the children's children, unto the third
and to the fourth generation*" (Ex. xxxiv. 6, 7). Take
these solemn words, "That will by no means clear the
guilty," and ponder over them in your heart.

2. *Look at sin in the light of God's judgments on it
upon earth.* Glance over the Bible, and see how much
God hates sin. He hurled the angels that fell out of

heaven—*because He hates sin.* He drove His first son and daughter out of Eden, and sent them wanderers over the world—*because He hates sin.* He held down the whole world under the flood till every soul was drowned—*because He hates sin.* He rained fire and brimstone upon the cities that are now in Sodom's Sea —*because He hates sin.* He drowned Pharaoh and his chariots in the Red Sea—*because He hates sin.*

Perhaps His hatred of sin is seen even more in the way in which He laid the rod upon His own people of Israel when they sinned. After they had crossed the Red Sea, and were on the border of the Promised Land, because they did not believe His promises, and reckon upon His giving them the land, "*He sware in His wrath that they should not enter into His rest,*" and He made them wander forty years in the wilderness, till every one above twenty years old had died, except Caleb and Joshua. Why? *Because He hates sin.* After they were settled in their own land, when they fell into sin, He raised up enemies who afflicted them, and at last He sent them away captives to Babylon. Why? *Because He hates sin.* When His only-begotten Son came, and His chosen people, the Jews, did not receive Him as their Saviour, He destroyed that city of Jerusalem which He loved, and sent such sufferings on its inhabitants as had never been before in the world, and never shall be again. Their blood flowed down its streets in streams, and so many were crucified that no more wood could be got to make crosses, and the rest were sent away wanderers over the world. Why? *Because He hates sin.* And this earth, which has been so polluted with sin, is yet to be burned up. Why? *Because He hates sin.*

Look again at His judgments on particular individuals when they sinned. *Moses,* "the servant of the Lord," was not permitted to enter the Promised Land, because he lost his temper, striking the rock twice, and saying, "*Hear now, ye rebels; must we fetch you water out of this rock?*" *Achan the son of Carmi* was stoned to death, with his wife and children, because, amid the rich spoil of Jericho, he took the wedge of gold and the Babylonish garment. *Eli* lost the priesthood, and his sons and daughters were slain, because "his sons made themselves vile, and he restrained them not." *Uzzah* was struck dead, because he touched the ark, which no one but a priest was permitted to touch. *That noble prophet of Judah*, who rebuked Jeroboam to his face, was slain by a lion, because he disobeyed God by eating and drinking at Bethel, though God took him straight to heaven. *Jonah* was swallowed by a whale, because he shirked an unpleasant duty, and fled to Joppa when God ordered him to Nineveh.

And does not my reader know some godly man or woman of his acquaintance who has been greatly afflicted? The case of Job shows that this may not be as a chastisement of sin. But does God ever lay more afflictions on any one than his sins deserve? And if such afflictions are sent upon the best of Christians to keep them from falling, and to make them look to Christ, what must the godless deserve? *If the righteous scarcely be saved, where shall the ungodly and the sinner appear?*" "We must begin by believing the horror that sin ought to inspire before we are capable of feeling it," said Adolphe Monod.

3. *Look at sin in the light of a place of eternal punishment.* I cannot understand how any one can read his Bible, honestly seeking to find out what it teaches, without seeing that it teaches the doctrine of eternal punishment. "*These shall go out into eternal punishment; but the righteous into eternal life*" (Matt. xxv. 46, R.V.). The same word is used both for the punishment and the life—the word *eternal.* If the one is not for ever, neither is the other. Read Mark ix. 43-48, and see how Jesus spoke about hell: "*Where their worm dieth not, and the fire is not quenched.*" Read also Rev. xiv. 11: "*The smoke of their torment ascendeth up for ever and ever, and they have no rest day nor night.*" It is the loving Jesus, and John, the disciple whom Jesus loved, who speak more about hell than any others do.

I will quote a few sentences spoken by Principal

Edwards, D.D., of Wales, author of Commentaries on *First Corinthians* and on *Hebrews*. This learned and loving man says: "There are great and good people in these days who deny hell. They do this because they are good. Their goodness takes the form of tenderness towards their fellow-beings, and they cannot suffer the idea that men are going to hell. Therefore they say they must deny it. 'There is no hell at all.' What are we to do? We must face this question. Shall we deny it? It will be a very easy gospel. It will be a splendid Christianity for the future of our race not to have any hell at all. Don't preach hell-fire. Don't tell men that they are going to the devil because they refuse Jesus Christ. Don't talk about it. Deny hell torments. Let us all be comfortable. Let us all go on our way, making money honestly, if we can; but if we cannot, making money.

"Now I am not cruel. My brethren are not cruel. We are not monsters—Are we? I want to face the question honestly, and bring all my intellect to bear upon it, and therefore I will read my New Testament. I have been doing so, carefully, prayerfully, and I have brought to bear upon that question, in reading this Testament of mine, all the intellectual power God has given me. I tried hard to find that there is no hell. But it is here after all. It is burning after all. The smoke of it is ascending after all your denials. I tried my best to get it out of my New Testament. But I cannot. I am honestly bound to admit that Jesus Christ preached it. It is the tender Jesus who preaches hell-fire. It is the One who was willing to sacrifice Himself for the salvation of the world that preaches hell-fire to those who reject Him. Yes, brethren, there is such a thing as hell." Such are the words of Dr. Edwards.

And this place of punishment is eternal. Has my reader ever thought of the length of *Eternity*? An eminent writer says: "Suppose some little insect, so small as to be imperceptible to the human eye, were to carry this world by its tiny mouthfuls to the most distant star. Hundreds of millions of years are required for the performance of a single journey. The insect commences upon the leaf of a tree, and takes its little load, and sets out upon its almost endless journey. After millions and millions of years have rolled away, it arrives back again for its second load. Oh, what ages must pass before the one leaf be removed! In what period of coming time would the whole tree be borne away? When would the forest be gone? And when would that insect take the last particle of this globe, and bear it away in its long, long journey? Even then, Eternity would but have commenced."

Now, what is everlasting punishment? It is just the expression of God's hatred of sin. He cannot let the wicked go unpunished; and their punishment is just in proportion to their sins: and hell is God's own standard of the sinfulness of sin. " *Upon the wicked He shall rain snares, fire and brimstone, and an horrible tempest: this shall be the portion of their cup. For the righteous Lord loveth righteousness: His countenance doth behold the upright* " (Ps. xi. 6, 7).

4. *Look at sin in the light of Christ's death as an atonement for sin.* If anything less or anything else than the death of Christ could have atoned for sin, God would have spared His only-begotten Son. If all the angels in heaven had come down and died upon crosses on earth, they could not have atoned for one sin. It took God's own Son to become a babe, and a man of sorrows, and to be obedient unto death, even the death of the cross, in order to atone for our sins.

We think sin a trifle, and that God can pass it over without punishment. But if ever God could have let sin go unpunished, it was when the guilt of sinners was laid upon His Son, and when that Righteous One, who knew no sin in Himself, prayed " *with strong crying and tears unto Him that was able to save Him from death.*" Think of Him rending the air with His cries, and wetting the sod with His tears, as He cried three times over, " *O My Father, if it be possible, let this cup pass from Me: nevertheless not as I will, but as Thou wilt.*" What agony Jesus must have borne when He, made

strong by God to bear, cried out thus! Flesh and blood
seemed to be giving up. Christians, now, when about
to die, do not rend the air with their cries, and wet
their pillow with their tears, beseeching God to spare
them a little longer. Generally, they are "*willing to
depart and to be with Christ, which is far better.*" They
have looked death often in the face; and believing that
Jesus has borne the punishment of their sins, they are
not afraid. But what awful sufferings Christ must have
borne when He cried out thus, three times over, with
strong crying and tears!

If it had been possible that this cup could pass from
Him, and that we, poor sinners, could have been saved
without it, His cries would have been answered. But it
was not possible. God must show them His displeasure
at sin, even when borne by His own Son; and therefore
He hid His face from Him, and poured out upon Him
the punishment that we, otherwise, must have borne,
and Jesus cried, "*My God, My God, why hast Thou
forsaken Me?*" A godly minister once told me that for
about half an hour one day he thought he felt something
of what Jesus endured upon the cross. He felt as if
God had forsaken him, and as if he had no God to go
to; and he said that, if it had continued longer, he believed he would have asked God to send him to hell
rather than this. But, after all, he knew little about it.
God only, and Christ, and the damned soul know what
was in that cry, "*Why hast Thou forsaken Me?*"

"*It pleased the Lord to bruise Him; He hath put Him
to grief*" (Isa. liii. 10). What a wonderful text this is!
Rather than send us, wicked sinners, to hell, it pleased
the Lord to bruise His own Son! "*It pleased the Lord.*"
Who can see into the depths of this? Not all the
torments of hell show God's hatred of sin so much as
the agony of Jesus in Gethsemane and His cries on
Calvary. Think not, then, my reader, that the Lord can
let your sins go unpunished. He cannot. He must
show His abhorrence of sin. He never did let a sin go
unpunished. He never will let a sin go unpunished.
He never can let a sin go unpunished. He would not

be God if He did. This is how the matter stands: If you take Jesus as your Saviour, and His death as the atonement for your sins, then your sins are punished in Christ. His death stands for them. If you do not take Him as your Saviour, then you must bear the punishment of your own sins for ever; for God hates sin and must punish it.

5. *Look at sin in the light of God's goodness and love to you.* If you strike an enemy, it is a sin; if you strike your friend, it is a greater sin; but if you lift your unhallowed hand and strike your loving father, it is much greater still. How sinful, then, must it be to fight against so good a God as our God? Has He not showered down upon us loving-kindnesses and tender mercies since we were born? Has He not restrained us by His grace, and kept us from doing many wicked things that our hearts desired? Has He not sent His only-begotten Son to die, the just for the unjust, to bring us to Himself? Has He not striven with us by His Spirit in many ways to lead us to Christ?

How Jesus has knocked at the door of your hearts, wanting to come in, and carry away your guilt, and dwell in you by His Spirit, and make you holy! He knocked by your mother's prayers, and by your father's entreaties. He knocked by your teacher's instructions. He knocked that time when you were in earnest, and went away to your room alone to read your Bible and pray. He knocked by the reading of that tract or little book. He knocked again and again by the preaching of the gospel. How He knocked that time when some of your companions were converted, and you wished you were like them! How He knocked when your friend was taken away, and you saw him laid in the grave! How He knocked when you were sick, and you sat up in your bed, and wrapped the blankets round you, and asked Him to spare you, and promised Him that if He did, you would love Him and serve Him! He did spare you. Have you loved Him and served Him? Have you kept your vow? No; you have turned " *like the dog to his vomit again, and the sow that*

was washed to her wallowing in the mire." How sinful
your sin has been when you have had such a good and
kind God, and so many opportunities and advantages!

6. *Look especially at sin in the light of what is implied
in your rejection of Christ.* The greatest sin of all, the
damning sin, is that you will not come to Christ that
you may have life. God the Father has sent His only-
begotten Son to seek and save you. He is so satisfied
with the death of Christ in the room of sinners, that it
just delights Him to pardon you for Christ's sake. Yet
up till this moment you have refused His Son, and said,
"No, no; I will rather go to hell than be indebted to
Him," and you have flung Him back with contempt in
the face of His Father.

Jesus is beside you this moment,—He who died for
sinners on Calvary,—and He has made known to you
how delighted He would be to take all the guilt of your
sins off you, and to come into your heart and make you
holy. Yet up to the present you have rejected Him,
and said, "Get you gone, Lord Jesus. I don't want you
to rule over me." Just the old cry over again: "*Away
with Him, crucify Him!*"

The Holy Ghost has striven with you to lead you to
Christ; and you have heard His still, small voice, again
and again, saying, "You should accept Christ now, and
let Him be your Saviour." The Holy Ghost saith,
"*To-day, if ye will hear His voice, harden not your
hearts*" (Heb. iii. 7). But you have resisted the Holy
Spirit, and said, "Get you gone, Holy Spirit. I mean
to serve the devil while I have health, and when I
get sick and come to die, I hope the Lord will have
mercy on me." Yes, "*you have resisted the Holy Ghost.*"

Oh that you saw the sin of rejecting Christ, of
trampling under foot His blood, of rushing on to hell
over His dead body, of saying, "No, I will not have you
as my Saviour!" This is worse than theft, or lying, or
drunkenness, or adultery. It is "*crucifying the Son of
God afresh, and putting Him to an open shame.*" In the
Life of Walter Marshall, who wrote the great book called
The Gospel Mystery of Sanctification, we are told the

following incident :—When a young man he was anxious
to be saved. In his anxiety he went to Edmund Calamy,
a famous preacher of that time, and spoke to him about
his sins and his soul. To show Dr. Calamy that he was
in earnest, he had written down a list of his sins, arrang-
ing them under the Ten Commandments. The good
man looked over the black list from top to bottom, and
then said something like the following :—" Young man,
this is a sad catalogue, but there is one sin you are
committing not marked down at all, and which is worse
than any of these." " Please, sir, tell me what it is. I
made a clean breast of it, and marked down every one
that I remembered, even the worst." " It is," said Dr.
Calamy, " not taking all these sins and putting them
upon the head of the Lord Jesus. It is not doing what
He bids you: ' Come unto Me, all ye that labour and
are heavy laden, and I will give you rest.' "

   And oh that you saw not merely the *sin* but the
folly of rejecting Christ ! Suppose that there were a
famine in your neighbourhood, and that multitudes
were starving, and you were one of them. And suppose
that some kind rich man brought thousands of loaves,
and got them heaped up in the most public place. He
got placards printed and posted all round, saying that
any one who was in need was welcome to take as many
loaves as he needed. He employed messengers also to
go round the country for miles and tell the same. You
were starving, and you came to the place, and saw
the loaves, and heard the invitation, but you said, " I
cannot believe that any one would be so good as that—
to buy all these loaves, and give them for nothing to
anyone in need. It is too good news to be true.
Besides, I would not like just to be a poor beggar,
dependent on another. If I could pay half-price, or
even a penny, or a halfpenny, I would take them.
But I would not like to be altogether a beggar, like the
poorest creature on the street. I have a spirit above
that. But I am sure it cannot be true. It is too good.
No one would be so generous as that." And away you
went home, and were found dead the next morning

from hunger. Who would pity you? There were the loaves free to you, and you refused to take them.

Reader! you can make your own application of the story. You are perishing. Jesus has died for sinners, and is beside you this moment offering His death to you as a full atonement for your sins, without money or price. You have heard it; you have read it. But you say, "It is too good to be true. I cannot believe that He is so good as that. Besides, I would not like to be altogether a beggar, and to take salvation for nothing, and to depend entirely upon Jesus and His finished work. If I could do a little myself to atone for my sins or to prepare myself for being saved, I would be willing to be saved by Christ. But I would not like to come down so low as to be a beggar, and to take salvation for nothing, and to depend entirely upon Jesus and His finished work. If I could do a little myself to atone for my sins, or to prepare myself for being saved, I would be willing to be saved by Christ. But I would not like to come down so low as to be a beggar, depending entirely upon Christ, just as a thief or a harlot would. No; I have a spirit above that. But I am sure the Lord is not willing to save me just as I am. It is too easy. I cannot believe it!"

And so you reject Christ, and will perish if you do. Who, then, will pity you? No one. God the Father will not pity you, nor God the Son, nor God the Holy Ghost. The holy angels will not pity you, nor the wicked angels. Good men will not pity you, nor bad men. You were offered Christ again and again, and salvation along with Him, and you said, "No, no; it is too good to be true, and I cannot come down so low as that." And for what do you reject Christ? For a wicked companion? for a darling lust? for fear of a sneer? for a little money, perhaps less than Judas got for betraying his Master? Oh, the folly of it!

Seeing, then, that sin is such a terrible thing, how is it, dear reader, that you do not eagerly embrace Christ as your hope? Surely it must be because you

hate Him, and love sin. We showed in the last chapter
that you cannot get to heaven without pardon, founded
on a full atonement for your sins; we want now to
impress upon you that you cannot get to heaven without a new nature. God cannot let an unholy man into
heaven. " *Without holiness no man shall see the Lord.*"
" *Except a man be born again, he cannot see the kingdom
of God*" (John iii. 3). So Christ told Nicodemus three
times over one evening, with a double "Verily, verily."
But even if it were possible for you to slip into heaven
behind God's back,—which, however, is impossible,—
you would be miserable in heaven without a new
nature. Heaven would be a perfect hell to you.

A poor man was once left a large fortune by a
distant relative. Suddenly he found himself taken
from a cottage, and driven in a carriage, and mingling
in drawing-rooms with the rich and the great. They
just laughed at him, they called him an old fool, and
an uneducated clown; and he would have been far
happier in his humble abode. Why? Because he was
not fitted for his position: he was not educated for it.
And would you, unconverted reader, be happy in
heaven? What are they doing in heaven? Praising
and thanking the Lord. Sure you never thanked the
Lord heartily for anything—not even for coming from
heaven to save you? What more are they doing?
Talking about Jesus and His love, and about the way
in which the Lord led them upon earth. Now be
honest—would you not rather be in jail, but for the
shame of it, than be in a room alone with six people,
talking about Jesus and their religious experience?
You would be perfectly miserable there. If heaven
were a place such as the Mahometans believe it to be
—a place where they will get every wicked passion
gratified to the full, you would just be fitted for it.
But it is a holy place, and its inhabitants are all holy,
and its occupations are all holy, and you would be
miserable there without a new nature.

I have read somewhere that Whitfield once said
that if it were possible for a man to get to heaven

without a new nature, he would not be five minutes there till he would ask God to send him to hell for a change. If he ever said this, it was certainly an exaggeration. But I am sure this is no exaggeration, that he would ask God to send him down to the poorest, meanest, dirtiest hovel upon earth, rather than keep him there above. Heaven would be a perfect hell without a new nature. Surely you must see that "*Except a man be born again, he cannot see the kingdom of God.*"

Reader! I wish to ask you—Are you born again? Has any change that could be called a new birth ever passed upon you?—a change in your thoughts about Christ, in your thoughts about sin, in your objects in life. I do not ask, Are you perfect? I am sure you are not. John Newton once said, " I am not what I ought to be ; I am not what I wish to be ; I am not what I hope to be : but I can truly say, I am not what I was once, a slave to sin and Satan, and I can join heartily with the apostle, and say, '*By the grace of God I am what I am.*'" Can you say this? Are you born again? It may be you know as well as you are living that you are not. How, then, do you expect to get to heaven? Did the Lord tell lies when He said to Nicodemus three times over, "*Except a man be born again, he cannot see the kingdom of God*"?

But Jesus did not stop when He told Nicodemus that he must be born again. He went on to tell him how he was to be born again. "*As Moses lifted up the serpent in the wilderness, even so must the Son of Man be lifted up : that whosoever believeth in Him should not perish, but have eternal life*" (John iii. 14, 15). In the very act of looking to Christ, we are born again, just as the bitten Israelites were healed by looking to the serpent of brass. And there is no other way of being born again. "*As many as received Him, to them gave He the power to become the sons of God.*"

" There is life in a look at the Crucified One,
  There is life at this moment for thee ;
Then look, sinner, look unto Him and be saved,
  Unto Him who was nailed to the tree."

6

IV

The Wages of Sin

THE Apostle Paul says, "*The wages of sin is death,*" and Ezekiel says, "*The soul that sinneth, it shall die.*" Now the death thus threatened against sin is far more than the separation of the soul from the body. It includes all that God inflicts in consequence of sin. It is the curse that Paul speaks of: "*Cursed is every one that continueth not in all things which are written in the book of the law to do them.*" Mark, this curse is pronounced not only on open, unblushing sinners, but upon every sinner. "*The soul that sinneth, it shall die.*"

The Bible speaks of the *ungodly* and *sinners.* It asks, "*If the righteous scarcely be saved, where shall the ungodly and the sinner appear?*" (1 Pet. iv. 18). Now, what is the distinction between the *ungodly* and the *sinner* here? *Sinners* are open, unblushing sinners—thieves, liars, swearers, drunkards, unclean, and such like. The *ungodly* are not thieves, or liars, or swearers, or drunkards, or openly unclean persons. They are good neighbours, and outwardly moral. They may read their Bibles now and again, and say their prayers, and go to church, and to the Lord's Supper, and have family worship, and take an interest in religious things. But they are not godly. They do not love God; they do not trust Christ; they have never brought home Christ's death to themselves; they are not born again; they are not new creatures in Christ; they have not passed from death unto life. They forget God; and of them as well as of open, unblushing sinners it is written,

" The wicked shall be turned into hell, and all the nations that forget God" (Ps. ix. 17).

Let us look into the elements of this curse under which you lie if you have not got Christ as your Saviour, even though you may be amiable, and kind, and moral.

1. *You are condemned.* Jesus told Nicodemus, *"He that believeth on Him (Christ) is not condemned, but he that believeth not is condemned already, because he hath not believed in the name of the only-begotten Son of God"* (John iii. 18). Jesus does not say that you will be condemned hereafter. That is quite true. But He says you are *"condemned already"*! The sentence of death has been already pronounced upon you. You are just like that man condemned to die for murder, and lying in jail waiting for the moment of execution. *"Condemned already."* That is God's description of your state at this present moment. And His messenger, Death, may come soon to summon you. " Natural men," writes Jonathan Edwards, " hang over the pit of hell, as it were, by a thread that has a moth continually gnawing it. They know not when it will snap in twain and let them drop."

You say that you believe the Bible ; but if you really believed this, you could not sleep to-night, and be care-less as you are. You rise, and eat, and sleep, and laugh, and talk as if there were nothing wrong. And yet God says that you are *"condemned already."* Why is it you are so careless? Because you are blind. *" The god of this world (Satan) hath blinded the minds of them which believe not"* (2 Cor. iv. 4). Picture to yourself a blind man walking along the edge of a precipice, down which he is every moment in danger of falling. And yet he fears not. Why? Not because he is not in danger, but because he is blind. Blind sinner! God says you are "condemned already."

2. *The wrath of God abideth upon you, and you have no God to go to in your perplexities and sorrows.* God's people have a kind, loving Father to go to ; in their difficulties to guide them, in their dangers to deliver

them, in their sorrows to comfort them. What would they do if they had not? Oh, how good a thing it is to have such a God! But you have not. You have refused to accept Christ as your Saviour, and God says, "*He that believeth on the Son hath everlasting life: and he that believeth not the Son shall not see life, but the wrath of God abideth on him*" (John iii. 36). God's wrath was upon you when you lay down last night. God's wrath was upon you when you rose this morning. God's wrath is upon you now where you sit. "*God is angry with the wicked every day.*" "*Thou hatest all workers of iniquity.*" "*The Lord will abhor the bloody and deceitful man.*" Yes, He is dreadfully provoked by you. Jonathan Edwards says, "He is a great deal more angry with many of you that are now in this congregation, who, it may be, are at your ease, than He is with many of those that are now in hell." Many of them never had your advantages and opportunities.

3. *You are a child of the devil, and his slave.* The devil is the great enemy of God and man, going about to ruin people, body and soul. Jesus said to the Jews, "*Ye are of your father the devil, and the lusts of your father ye will do.*" God's people are the children of God, and they have His Spirit dwelling in them to enable them to love and serve Him. But you, who do not believe in Christ, are a child of the devil, and have the devil dwelling in you. Listen to what God says in Eph. ii. 1, 2: "*And you hath He quickened, who were dead in trespasses and sins; wherein in time past ye walked according to the course of this world, according to the prince of the power of the air, the spirit that now worketh in the children of disobedience.*" Just think of it, reader! The devil is *in* the children of disobedience, and *works* in them.

And he is not only your father, but your *master*. You are doing, day by day, what the devil wishes you. If your eyes were opened, like those of the prophet's servant at Dothan, you would see him leading you along with his chain round your neck, and making you do whatever he likes. And of all masters he is the most cruel. You remember what a tyrant he was to the poor Gadarene, who was possessed by demons, and over whom he had got complete control. "*Always, night and day, he was in the mountains, and in the tombs, crying and cutting himself with stones, and no man could bind him, no, not with chains.*" And look at the man yet, over whom the devil has got complete mastery. Driven on to drink, or to gamble, or to revel in debauchery—to ruin his character, to ruin his health, to ruin his circumstances, to ruin his wife, to ruin his children, to ruin his friends. And he knows it all. Yet on, on, on he goes, the devil driving him. What a cruel master you have got, my reader!

4. *God may give you up at any time, and cease to strive with you by His Spirit, and may let you alone.* God's Holy Spirit strives with men. There is not a man or woman in the world with whom He has not striven. He lights up the conscience even of the heathen. But specially He strives with those who have the Bible. There are ordinary operations of God's Spirit on the hearts of all who hear the gospel. There are far more people anxious about their souls than any one imagines. Sometimes people force a laugh on the face to hide the fear that is in the heart.

God's Spirit strives long, but He does not strive for ever. "*My Spirit shall not always strive with man*" (Gen. vi. 3). What a striking verse this is! He strives with men to lead them to Christ, and to induce them to give up their sins. If they resist, He strives on, and may strive often. But sometimes He ceases to strive. He gives one last trial, and if they continue to resist, and to say, "No, no, I will not take Christ as my Saviour; I will go on and live as I like," sometimes He ceases to strive, and lets them alone. And of all God's judgments that is the worst—to be let alone by God. People who are given up never think that they are given up, and usually become careless and unconcerned, laughing and mocking at religion. Reader! thank God if you are anxious yet to be saved by Christ, for this shows that you are not given up. What a solemn warning

is that given in Prov. i. 24-28: "*Because I have called,
and ye refused; I have stretched out my hand, and
no man regarded; but ye have set at naught all my
counsel, and would none of my reproof: I also will laugh
at your calamity; I will mock when your fear cometh;
when your fear cometh as desolation, and your destruction
cometh as a whirlwind; when distress and anguish
cometh upon you. Then shall they call upon me, but I
will not answer; they shall seek me diligently, but they
shall not find me.*" There are many in torment to-day
who have found these words true.

Christ-rejecting reader! God has striven with you
again and again; and up to this moment you have
rejected Him. He is striving with you now by means
of this book; and it may be that if you lay it down
rejecting Christ, He may give you up altogether. I say
—*it may be.* You cannot tell the day or hour when He
may take away His Holy Spirit, and cease to strive
with you. If you would come to Jesus even then, He
would receive you. But you will never come to Jesus
if God's Spirit give you up. You would be as sure of
hell as if you were in it. This is a solemn moment.

" There is a line by us unseen,
    That crosses every path;
The hidden boundary between
    God's patience and His wrath.

To pass that limit is to die—
    To die as if by stealth;
It does not quench the beaming eye,
    Or pale the glow of health.

The conscience may be still at ease,
    The spirits light and gay:
That which is pleasing still may please,
    And care be thrust away.

He thinks, he feels that all is well,
    And every fear is calm'd:
He lives, he dies, he wakes in hell,
    Not only doom'd but damn'd."

5. *You may die without Christ.* You shall die some day, and it may be very soon and very suddenly. How many diseases or accidents might take you off? God may be saying even now, " *Thou fool, this night thy soul shall be required of thee.*" You may die quietly ; for " *the wicked have no bands in their death, but their strength is firm.*" John Bunyan said that no persons die more quietly than bad people, for their eyes are blinded, that they do not see what is before them. Or you may die in fear and terror. The doctor will be sent for, and he will try some remedy, and it will fail. He will try another, and still another, and they too will fail. Then some friend will come to your bedside, and tell you that you cannot live more than an hour or two. Then you will turn your face to the wall, and all creatures will be withdrawn. You will know that you are not a Christian, that you have never accepted Christ. God only and you can tell what passes in your mind then. No wonder that sometimes the knees knock together, and the hair stands on end.

And what happens at death? Holy angels hover round the death-bed of the righteous, and sometimes the dying saint seems to see them, and his face is radiant ; and they carry him away into Abraham's bosom. Demons hover round the death-bed of the Christless, and as soon as he dies, they grasp him and carry him away to the bottomless pit. It may be that on the day of your funeral there will be a great display, and persons behind your coffin will be telling how much you died worth ; while in torment the demons will be laughing at you in mockery, saying, "You died worth so much, but we have you for ever." No wonder the poet speaks of "that loudest laugh of hell—the hope of dying rich." How shall you die without Christ ?

6. *You may stand at the judgment-seat without Christ.* The day will come when you will hear the voice of the archangel and the trump of God, and you will rise from your grave. If you have died without Christ, your damned soul will be forced to enter into

your damned body, and you will have to stand before
the Lord in judgment. You will call on the mountains,
"*Fall on us and hide us*"; but they will not hide you.

In that day the righteous shall stand upon the right
hand. When they were alive upon earth, they accepted
Christ's atonement as theirs, and "*their sins and iniquities
are remembered no more.*" Their good thoughts and
words and actions, which God's Spirit wrought in them
after conversion, will be read out from the Book of
Remembrance, and they will hear Jesus say, "*Come, ye
blessed of My Father, inherit the kingdom prepared for you
from the foundation of the world.*" "And these shall go
away into life eternal."

But the wicked shall stand upon the left hand, and
God's Book will be opened. Christless reader! every
wicked thought you ever had will be read out before
assembled worlds, and every wicked word you ever
spoke, and every wicked deed you ever did; and your
heart will be laid bare, and all your motives will be
discovered; and you will hear the voice of Jesus, who,
when you were upon earth, so often said to you, "*Come
unto Me,*" say to you then, "*Depart, ye cursed, into everlasting fire, prepared for the devil and his angels.*" And
the angels shall take hold of you, and drag you away,
and "cast you into outer darkness." "*These shall go
away into everlasting punishment.*" Yes, you shall "go
away"—away from your godly father and mother,
away from your godly brothers and sisters, away from
your homes, your Sabbaths, your meetings, your companions—away into everlasting punishment. How shall
you stand at the judgment-seat without Christ?

7. *You may suffer everlasting punishment.* I know
not what is meant by "*the lake which burneth with
fire and brimstone*" (Rev. xxi. 8); or by being "*cast
into outer darkness: there shall be weeping and gnashing of teeth*" (Matt. viii. 12); or by "*the bottomless
pit*" (Rev. xx. 3); or by "*the worm that dieth not, and
the fire that is not quenched*" (Mark ix. 48). These are
God's own pictures of the place of punishment. I
know not whether there will be material fire there or

not—probably not. But as God's pictures of heaven come far, far short of suggesting the greatness of the happiness there, so God's pictures of hell come far, far short of suggesting the greatness of the miseries there. Let us think, reader, of some of the worms that will be gnawing at you in the place of torment if you die without Christ.

One worm will be your wicked passions which you were able to get gratified on earth. These same wicked passions you will take with you into hell; for "*the wicked are driven away in their wickedness.*" But you will never get them gratified there. What a worm that will be!

Another worm will be your conscience. Even here conscience sometimes makes a man so miserable that he goes and gives himself up voluntarily to the officers of justice. Judas has the same conscience to-day in hell as made him go and hang himself. What a worm that will be!

Another worm will be your memory. "*Son, re-member*" (Luke xvi. 25). You will remember that place, that time, that man, that woman; and what misery this will bring with it! And specially you will remember times when God's Spirit strove with you, and Jesus knocked at the door of your heart, and you were not far from the kingdom of God. And now you are lost for ever. And for what did you sell heaven? For some wicked companion, or some darling lust. Wringing your hands in despair, you will cry out, "Oh, if I only had taken Christ's offer that day, I would have been happy for ever; and now I am lost—lost for ever. Oh, if I only had!"

Another worm will be the sight of others happy in heaven. "*There shall be weeping and gnashing of teeth when ye shall see Abraham, and Isaac, and Jacob, and all the prophets, in the kingdom of God, and you yourselves thrust out*" (Luke xiii. 28). The rich man in the parable (Luke xvi.) saw Abraham afar off and Lazarus in his bosom. You will see afar off in heaven persons who were once your bosom friends, and perhaps more wicked than yourself; but they closed with Christ's invitation, " *Come to Me*," and are now safe with Him, while you put it off, and off, and off, till one day death came and took you suddenly away ; and now you are lost for ever.

Another worm will be your companions in torment. How will you like to live for ever with the horribly wicked creatures whom you have met on earth, or whom you have read about ? But there is something more horrible still. You will meet there persons whom you were the means of leading into sin—into drinking, or gambling, or stealing, or adultery, and they will curse you for ever as being the cause of their ruin. How many children will curse their parents, and say, " Yes, father, mother, you worked hard for me, but you never prayed for me, nor taught me to pray ; you did not teach me the Bible, nor take me to the house of God ; you did not tell me of heaven, or hell, or Christ : and here I am for ever, and it was you brought me here " ?

Probably the wrath of God is denoted by the fire that shall never be quenched. And the fiercest fire is but a shadow of it. Who can tell what God's wrath is ? Jesus bore it on Calvary, and it made Him cry out, "*My God, My God, why hast Thou forsaken Me?*" Oh, my reader, if you refuse Christ, you will have to bear God's wrath yet, and you will know something of what Jesus endured when He uttered that cry. God grant that you may never know it ! " *It is a fearful thing to fall into the hands of the living God.*" Eye of man has never seen, ear of man has never heard, heart of man has never conceived, the agony of a lost soul.

And it will be for ever. This is the sting of the curse. " *The smoke of their torment ascendeth up for ever and ever.*" " *Who shall dwell with the devouring fire? Who shall dwell with the everlasting burnings?*" If there were any respite,—if after millions of years there were any prospect of getting free. But there will be none. No hope—for ever, and for ever, and again for ever ! Oh, eternity ! eternity ! Have you ever thought of being in hell throughout eternity ?

When Philip de Neri was living in a great university, a young man ran to him with a face full of delight, and told him that he had come to the law school of that place on account of its great fame, and that he meant to spare no pains to get through his studies as soon as possible. Philip waited with patience for his conclusion, and then said, "Well, and when you have got through your course of studies, what do you mean to do?" "Then I shall take my doctor's degree," said the young man. "And then?" asked Philip again. "And then," continued the youth, "I shall have a number of difficult questions to manage, and shall attract people's notice by my eloquence, my learning, my acuteness, and gain a great reputation." "And then?" repeated the good man. "And then," replied the youth, "why, there can't be a question. I shall be promoted to some high office or other, and make money, and grow rich." "And then?" repeated Philip. "And then," pursued the young lawyer, "then I shall live comfortably and honourably in wealth and dignity." "And then?" asked the aged man. "And then," said the youth, "and then, and then—then I shall die." Here Philip raised his voice—"*And what then?*" Whereupon the young man made no answer, but hung his head and went away. The last "And then?" had pierced his soul like lightning, and he could not get rid of it. Soon after he gave himself to the ministry of Christ, and lived a holy and useful life.

Again we must ask you to try to answer this question, "*What shall it profit a man if he shall gain the whole world, and lose his own soul?*" This was the question which led John Williams, the Apostle of the South Seas, to the foot of the Cross. This was the question which went to the heart of Francis Xavier, and sent him to India and Japan as a missionary. This was the question which Jesus asked eighteen hundred years ago, and no one since has been able to answer it. Can you, my reader? "*What shall it profit a man if he shall gain the whole world, and lose his own soul?*"

V

The Sinner Helpless, yet seeking to Work out his own Righteousness

I HAVE showed you that you cannot possibly get to heaven without the pardon of your sins, and without a new nature. A man was lying in jail condemned to die. On the day before that appointed for his execution, the governor of the jail opened the door of his cell, holding a letter in his hand, and said, "Cheer up! Here is a pardon for you from the Queen. You are free. Cheer up!" But he did not cheer up, but remained sad as before. "What do you mean?" asked the governor. Opening his prison clothes, and laying bare his breast, the prisoner said, "Look here, I have got the cancer. It will take me away in a few days, or weeks at the farthest. If the Queen could take away my cancer as well as give me pardon, then I would cheer up. I need both."

Sinners cannot get to heaven without pardon, and without a new power to overcome sin and to love God. How are these wants supplied in the gospel? In this way: When the poor sinner believes in Christ, and accepts Him as his Saviour, he gets at once two things. God pardons all his sins on account of Christ's death; and Christ comes into his heart and dwells in him by His Spirit, and puts good thoughts into him, and good words into him, and good deeds into him, and causes him to walk in His statutes. I have heard it illustrated thus: Suppose that you were owing ten thousand pounds, and had nothing whatever with which to pay the debt, and just suppose for the moment that I was rich as Rothschild,—a few thousand pounds would be nothing to me. I know you, and love you, and come to you and ask, "How much are you owing?" "Ten thousand pounds." "To how many persons?" "About twenty." "Call them all together, and I will pay them for you." They come. I pay one man fifty pounds, another five hundred, another a thousand, another two thousand, and so on till the whole ten thousand pounds are paid, and you are free from debt. Is not that an easy way of getting your debt paid? Another man comes and pays it for you, and you say "Thank you," and go on your way rejoicing. Well, that is just the way in which every believer in Christ has got his debt paid—as easily as that. And Christ offers, my reader, to take your debt on Him this moment, and pay it for you.

But even when your debts were paid, you might be as poor as Lazarus. You might not have a house to cover you to-night, nor breakfast for to-morrow morning. But I am as rich as Rothschild, and I go and invest fifty thousand pounds in your name, and come to you and say, "I have invested fifty thousand pounds in your name. Here are the legal documents. That will bring you in about two thousand per year. Go and live on that." Thus not only are your debts paid, but you have plenty to live on all your life.

This is a feeble illustration of what Jesus does for us when we believe on Him. He takes all our debt of sin on Him, and that moment it is gone from us. And besides, He comes into our hearts and dwells in them, and causes us to walk in His statutes. Think prayerfully over these texts: "*He that is joined unto the Lord is one spirit*" (1 Cor. vi. 17). The moment you are joined to the Lord, you get His Spirit to dwell in you. This is a fact, though you may not feel it or know it. But the Lord wishes you to believe it because He says it. "*Know ye not your own selves how that Jesus Christ is in you, except ye be reprobates?*" which means *counterfeits, hypocrites* (2 Cor. xiii. 15). If you are really believers in Christ, however weak, God wants you to know and believe that Jesus Christ is in you. "*I live*," said Paul, "*yet not I, but Christ liveth in me*" (Gal. ii. 20). Again he says: "*Know ye not that ye are the temple of God, and that the Spirit of God dwelleth in you?*" (1 Cor. iii. 16). And again: "*If any man have not the Spirit of Christ, he is none of His*" (Rom. viii. 9).

The moment you believe in Christ, you get both pardon of your sins and God's Spirit to dwell in you to make you holy. Both are *given to you* fully as gifts. "*Eternal life is the gift of God in Jesus Christ our Lord*" (Rom. vi. 23). Mark, it is a *gift*. Now we do not buy a gift, or work for a gift; we take a gift. God is so satisfied with Christ and His work on our behalf, that He is just delighted to give us pardon and His Spirit now for Christ's sake. We do not purchase or pay for these by any work of our own. They are gifts given to us. God will not sell them. He *gives* them freely along with Christ, and for His sake. We shall never get them unless we come down so low as to be willing to take them from Him for nothing, *as gifts*. "The king does not *sell* grapes; he *gives* them," said a king once to a little boy, who, not knowing who he was, had offered him a halfpenny for his grapes. And the Lord will not sell His pardon nor His Spirit. He gives them freely for Christ's sake, whenever a poor sinner is willing to take them *as gifts*. "*By grace are ye saved, through faith*." It is because you are not willing to come down so low as this that you are not saved. You do not think so, but it is really because of the wretched pride of your heart.

There are two things, my unconverted reader, of which you are ignorant—

First, How helpless you are. You have sinned against God hundreds of times, and what can you do now that would atone for your past sins? Even if you never got deeper into debt, that would not blot out the old debt. Surely you see that? But besides, you have a heart that hates God, and God knows it; and what does He care for works done by a heart that hates

Him? Perhaps there is some person who hates you, and you are well aware of it. Yet when he meets you, he bows and smiles, and says kind things. What do you care for his bows and smiles, when you know that in his heart he hates you? And God knows that your *"mind is enmity against God." "So then they that are in the flesh cannot please God."* Your *almsgiving!* What does the Lord care for it? It may do good to the poor, but it can merit nothing from God. *Your sitting down at the Lord's Table!* How would you like an enemy seated at your own table? Sitting there you tell the Lord, " Lord, I will take Thy bread and wine, but I will not take Thyself." *Your prayers!* They are like the prayers of Pharaoh when under the plagues. Can they merit anything from God?

If the Lord would make you this offer, that He would give you pardon and heaven for one good, pious, holy thought of your own manufacture, it would be a grand offer. But you could never give it. You are utterly helpless, and you do not know it. You are always thinking that you must do this and that and the other thing to help to save you, or to prepare yourself for being saved. Why, if you lived to the age of Methuselah, and prayed and fasted and wept, and did all the good you could, all put together could not blot out one sin. Oh that you knew how helpless you are! You would then not be far from the kingdom of heaven.

Second, You do not see that God is so satisfied with the obedience and death of Christ in the room of sinners, that He is delighted to pardon you this moment, wicked as you are, for His sake. You think that God is a kind of angry Esau who must be appeased by your gifts, as Jacob sought to propitiate Esau by sending one gift forward after another. *" For he said, I will appease him with the present that goeth before me, and afterwards I will see his face: peradventure he will accept of me."* You do not see that God is appeased by the death of Jesus Christ, and is delighted, for His sake, to give you at this moment pardon and His Holy Spirit. Oh that you saw this! Will the very greatness of His goodness be a barrier in your way? You cannot think that God is so good as that. But He is just as good as that. I know that you would not give your son to die for your enemy. But God says, "*My thoughts are not your thoughts, neither are your ways My ways, saith the Lord. For as the heavens are higher than the earth, so are My ways higher than your ways, and My thoughts than your thoughts.*" When God gives, it is like Himself, and nothing less than giving His Son and pardon for nothing could have saved you. Why then will you not come to Him this moment as a poor, helpless sinner, and be willing to let Christ's death stand for your sins, and His Spirit to come into your heart? The first thing that you will ever do that will please God will be to say, " Lord Jesus, here and now I do take Thee to be my Saviour, and Thy death to atone for my sins."

Having now got a glimpse of the real way to be saved, let us look, First, at some of the excuses of the careless sinner; and Second, at some of the efforts of the anxious sinner to work out a righteousness of his own.

Excuses of the Careless Sinner.

(1) "*God is merciful, and I am a poor, ignorant creature.*" Yes. God is merciful, but His mercy is the mercy of a holy God, who hates sin, and must punish it. He is delighted to pardon you if you consent to be saved by Christ; if you will not, you must perish.

Yes, you are a poor, ignorant creature. But have you acted up to the light you have? And could you not have got more light if you had wished it?

(2) "*I am a good neighbour, and a moral man. I am no thief, or liar, or drunkard, or swearer. I defy you to say anything against me.*" Tell me, reader, do you believe God's word that " *without shedding of blood there is no remission* " (Heb. ix. 22)? Is there any shedding

of blood in being a good neighbour? If you and I could have been saved by living outwardly moral lives, would Christ have come down from heaven and died upon the cross? God would have spared His only begotten Son. If you are a Christian, you will be a good neighbour, but it takes more than that to take you to heaven.

The Pharisee in the parable thanked God that he was not as other men, "*extortioners, unjust, adulterers, or even as this publican. I fast twice in the week, I give tithes of all that I possess.*" Probably this was all true. Christ does not deny it. Yet all these did not recommend him to God. Whereas the poor publican, who saw that he was a sinner, and cried out, "*God be merciful to me a sinner,*" went down to his house justified. The word that he used in his prayer, "*be merciful,*" has embedded in it the idea of propitiation through Christ, and he really asked God to pardon him for the sake of Christ.

When Christ was on His last journey to Jerusalem, a rich young man ran to meet Him. He was so moral, that he believed he had kept all the commandments from his youth up. He was so winsome, that when Jesus looked on him, He loved him for his amiability. Above all, he was anxiously seeking salvation, for he came running and fell down at Jesus' feet, and said, "Good Master, what good thing shall I do that I may have eternal life?" But Jesus looked at the young man, and saw that he did not know his own heart, and that his estate was his God; and therefore He said to him, "*Go and sell that thou hast, and give to the poor, and thou shalt have treasure in heaven: and come and follow Me.*" Alas! no; he loved the world more than he loved the Saviour, and slowly he turned him round, and went away sorrowful, for he had great possessions. Are you better than this young man was? Are you as good? Yet all his amiability and other excellent qualities could not save him. Nor will they save you. If you die trusting in them, you must perish. You are seeking to get to heaven without Christ, which is impossible,

7

(3) "*I hope I have had my sufferings in this life.*"
Satan tries to persuade people that sufferings here will
atone for their sins, and he refers to the parable of the
Rich Man and Lazarus. But Lazarus did not depend
on his sufferings to atone for his sins, but on Christ.
Your sufferings have perhaps been sent by God as a
punishment for your sins, or to lead you to Christ, who
has atoned for sinners. But nowhere in the Bible are
you taught that your sufferings here will atone for your
sins. Yet how prone are people, all over the world, to
believe this? The heathen cut themselves with knives,
and swing themselves on hooks, and torture themselves
in other ways, thinking in their ignorance that God
will be pleased with these tortures, and will put away
their sins. Roman Catholics crawl on their knees up
jagged rocks till the blood flows freely, and go on long
pilgrimages, which cost much money and much misery,
thinking that these will atone for their sins. Many
ignorant Protestants seem to think the same, and would
be glad to suffer some agony and pain before they die,
if it would help to blot out their sins. But it is all a
delusion of the devil. Nothing but the blood of Christ
blots out sin.

(4) "*I know the Bible, and I do believe in Christ.*"
Yes, you know the Bible with your head, and you
believe about Christ with your head. But have you
ever honestly brought home Christ's death to yourself?
Have you passed from death into life? Satan knows
the Bible probably better than you do. He quoted the
91st Psalm to Christ when he tempted Him. He knows
far more about God's holiness and justice, His power
and goodness, than you do. He knows more about
heaven and hell. He believes firmly that Christ died
for sinners, and is willing to save you. Nay more—he
not only believes, he trembles—trembles at the thought
of future punishment. "*The devils also believe and
tremble.*" Perhaps you have never got so far. But all
this does not save the demons, nor will it save you.

Christ never died to save demons. He never offered
His death as an atonement for their sins. If He did,

they think they would accept it at once. They try to persuade you that it is not offered to you, whereas they know well that it is. If they do persuade you to neglect Christ, they will taunt you for ever as being the author of your own damnation, and they will appeal to God to punish you, as being far worse than they are, as they never rejected Christ. Head-knowledge of the Bible is good as far as it goes. The more of it the better if you have got Christ. But without Christ it will save no one.

Let us look now at—

SOME OF THE EFFORTS OF ANXIOUS SINNERS TO WORK OUT THEIR OWN RIGHTEOUSNESS.

The Bible says: "*For they, being ignorant of God's righteousness, and going about to establish their own righteousness, have not submitted themselves unto the righteousness of God. For Christ is the end of the law for righteousness to every one that believeth*" (Rom. x. 3, 4).

A poor man was anxious, and asked a companion, whom he knew to be a real Christian, how he was to get peace. "Have you been long anxious?" asked his friend. "Yes." "What have you tried? Have you tried resolutions?" "Yes." "And have they not given you peace?" "No." "Have you tried struggling to live a better life?" "Yes." "And has it not given you peace?" "No." "Have you tried repentance, and sought to work yourself up to feel sorrow for sin?" "Yes." "And has it not given you peace?" "No." "Have you tried prayers—depending upon your earnest prayers?" "Yes." "And have they not given you peace?" "No." "Have you tried faith, and looked into your own heart to see if you believed?" "Yes." "And has it not given you peace?" "No." "Tell me, friend, have you ever tried Christ, and His blood that cleanseth from all sin?" "No."

(1) *They make vows and resolutions.* But they cannot

keep them. Have you not made vows, hundreds of times, and broken them? "Like snowflakes on a river —one moment white, then gone for ever." Hell is paved with good resolutions. Even a Christian cannot keep from his sins if he depends on his own strength; he must depend on Christ to keep him from falling. Much less can you, unconverted man! And even if you could keep your resolutions, this would not blot out past sins. "*Without shedding of blood there is no remission.*" You are not saved by keeping resolutions, but by depending on the death of Christ.

(2) *They attend meetings and observe religious ordinances.* Now it is right to attend the house of God. Those who do not do so, but "forsake the assembling of themselves together," are generally nearly as ignorant of the way of being saved as pagans. But meetings are for the purpose of leading you to Christ; and if you are not led to Christ, all your attendance at meetings will not save you. *It is right to read the Bible regularly.* But the Bible is to lead you to Christ; and if you are not led to Christ, reading the Bible will not save you. Christ's charge against the Jews was: "*Ye search the Scriptures, for in them ye think ye have eternal life, and they are they which testify of Me. And ye will not come to Me that ye might have life*" (John v. 39, 40). *It is right to pray.* By all means ask God to pardon you for the sake of Christ. But if you depend on your own prayers, and not on the merits of Christ, you will not be saved.

It is right to go to the Lord's Table, if you are a believer in Christ, and show forth the Lord's death. It reminds us of the Saviour, but it cannot be our Saviour. If you are depending on this to save you, and not on Christ, you are deceiving yourself. An old woman was asked on what she was depending to get to heaven. "Oh," she said, "I was a member of Dr. C.'s church in his time, and afterwards for forty years a regular joined member." She little thought that these privileges, if they did not lead her to Christ, would only deepen her damnation.

It is right for parents to dedicate their children to God in baptism. But Simon Magus was baptized; yet Peter told him that he was "in the gall of bitterness and in the bond of iniquity." Baptism did not save Simon, nor can it save you, nor any one. It is not baptism, but Christ, that saves. No one could possibly be more attentive to outward ordinances than the scribes and Pharisees; yet Jesus said, "*Except your righteousness shall exceed the righteousness of the scribes and Pharisees, ye shall in no case enter into the kingdom of heaven.*"

(3) *They depend on their prayers and good works.* A poor, but rather clever man, who had been lately converted, once said to me, "Oh, sir, give your congregation something to do that will make their peace with God, and you will please them mightily. It is just what people like. Why, the biggest miser in the parish would pull out his purse and give something to help to build a church ; and they would put a steeple on it that would reach up near the clouds, and put a weathercock on the top of it again, if you would just tell them that it would help to put away their sins. People don't like, sir, to think that they can do nothing that would help in some way to atone for their sins ; and when they hear ministers preaching, '*Believe on the Lord Jesus Christ, and thou shalt be saved,*' they step over it, and over it, and miss it, perhaps, like me, for seven-and-twenty years, and some, I am afraid, even till they die." This is quite true.

John Newton, often called *The African Blasphemer*, tells us of several earnest efforts he made to save himself. One of these lasted two years. Writing afterwards concerning this time, he said: "I spent the greatest part of every day in reading the Scriptures, meditation, and prayer ; I fasted often ; I even abstained from all animal food for three months ; I would hardly answer a question for fear of speaking an idle word. I seemed to bemoan my former miscarriages very earnestly, sometimes with tears. I continued in this serious mood for two years, without any considerable breaking off.

But it was a poor religion ; it left me in many respects under the power of sin, and, so far as it prevailed, only tended to make me gloomy, stupid, unsociable, and useless."

And how was he converted at last ?   He tells us in one of his hymns—

> "I saw One hanging on a tree
> In agony and blood,
> Who fixed His languid eyes on me,
> As near the Cross I stood."

He looked away to the Lord Jesus Christ, and he was saved.

Dr. Horatius Bonar says : " I knew an awakened soul, who in the bitterness of his spirit thus set himself to work and pray, in order to get peace.   He doubled the amount of his devotions, saying to himself, ' Surely God will give me peace.'   But the peace did not come.   He set up family worship, saying, ' Surely God will give me peace.'   But the peace came not.   At last he bethought himself of having a prayer meeting in his house, as a certain remedy.   He fixed the night, called his neighbours, and prepared himself for conducting the meeting by writing a prayer and learning it by heart. As he finished the operation of learning it, preparatory to the meeting, he threw it down on the table, saying, ' Surely *that* will do: God will give me peace now.'   In that moment a still, small voice seemed to speak in his ear, saying, ' No, that will *not* do ; but Christ will do.' Straightway the scales fell from his eyes, and the burden from his shoulders.   Peace poured in like a river. ' Christ will do,' was his motto ever after."

All such efforts to win heaven by prayers and good works are an insult to Jesus, whose finished work is rejected.   They are just the self-righteousness of men who are too proud to submit themselves to the righteousness of God.   Good works are very useful in their own place, and you will do them when you come to Christ, and get power from Him to do them.   But the first good work you will ever do will be to take Jesus.   Rev.

William Haslam tells that he once read the following
lines on an old tombstone near Bath:—

> " I would not work my soul to save:
> That work my Lord has done;
> But I will work like any slave
> For love of God's dear Son."

(4) *They strive to work themselves up to feel sorrow
for their sins, and to shed tears for them.*   Now we ought
to feel sorrow for our sins, and we will when we accept
Christ, and get a new heart from Him.   But if you
could shed as many tears as would fill the Atlantic, they
could not blot out one sin.   What is there in a tear to
blot out sin?   If you had committed a murder, or a
theft, and wept for it, would that atone for the crime?
Besides, no one ever did feel real godly sorrow for sin,
till he first came to Christ without it, and the Lord
gave him a new heart and His Holy Spirit, and put
repentance into him when he came.

I know well that there are many of my readers who
are trying earnestly to work themselves up to feel real
godly sorrow for sin, in order to make God willing to
save them.   Now, God is willing for Christ's sake to
save you this moment, as you are,—a poor, wicked,
hard-hearted, unfeeling sinner,—if you come to Him as
such.   And you will never make your hearts soft by all
your efforts.   Some have tried that for months with all
their might, but without avail.   The Bible does not say
how much or how little distress you must have before
coming to Christ.   You must know that you are a
sinner deserving punishment, otherwise you will never
come to Him; and you must honestly confess your sins
to Him.   But surely you have got that far; and if you
have, the Lord does not want you to wait one moment
before coming to Him.   Jesus does not say, " Him
that cometh to Me *under a deep sense of sin*, I will in no
wise cast out "; but " Him that cometh to Me, I will in
no wise cast out."   " *Whosoever will, let him take the
water of life freely.*"

The three thousand who received Christ on the day

of Pentecost no doubt varied greatly in their convictions, yet the Spirit of God taught none of them to
delay accepting Christ till he had become more anxious.
Lydia's heart seems to have opened gently, while the
Philippian jailor, in the same chapter, was almost in an
agony of despair ; and there has been the same variety
in all ages. Luther had great terror of conscience.
John Angell James said that he never had those great
terrors that others speak of. Cæsar Malan of Geneva,
after thirty years of a holy and useful life, said, "My
conversion to the Lord Jesus might, with propriety, be
compared to a mother rousing an infant with a kiss."
Jonathan Edwards wrote about the converts in his
days : "Some have had ten times less trouble of mind
than others, in whom yet the issue seems to be the
same." The Lord wants you to come to Him, not as
penitents, but as *sinners*, and to get penitence from Him.

(5) *They aim at feeling assurance and love, and think
that if they felt these first, they would be able to
depend on Christ.* "If I could only feel that
I was saved, then I could believe," says one. "If I
could only feel some love in my heart, then I would
have peace," says another. What is this but that
sinners do not see the value of Christ's "obedience unto
death," and are afraid to venture their souls upon Him
alone ? But if they could feel assurance or love in
themselves, they could trust in Christ and their feelings together. It is self-righteousness again, putting
assurance and love in the place of Christ.

How *foolish* is this, as well as *sinful !* A person
once spoke to a young woman who was trying thus to
work herself into these comfortable feelings before
believing, and told her that she must first believe, and
then she would feel comfort. He quoted 1 Peter i. 8:
" *Whom having not seen ye love; in whom, though now ye
see Him not, yet believing, ye rejoice* " ; but she could not
understand. The next day he paid her a visit, and
tried to teach her the same lesson. After talking for a
time, she offered him a cup of tea. He replied that he
could not take it just now, but that if he felt the taste

of it In his mouth first, he thought he could take it. She said he must first take it, and then he would feel the taste of it. "Yes," said he; "and you must first believe in Christ before you can feel assurance and love." Dear reader, you cannot possibly feel love to Christ till you first believe in His love to you. Love begets love. *"We love Him because He first loved us."*

(6) *They try to depend upon their own faith.* They have read that salvation is by faith; but they do not know what faith means—that it is simply believing what God says in His Word about Christ's Person and work, and looking to Him. Instead of looking to Him, they look within themselves. They think that faith is some feeling within them, or some great effort they have to make: they cannot tell what, but something more difficult than the best of good works. Anxious one! are you not looking to faith to save you, instead of to Christ; making a Saviour of your faith, instead of Jesus? If you want a good view, and go to the top of a mountain, you look out upon the landscape, you do not try to look in at the back of your own eye. So do not look at your own faith. Could faith speak, it would say, "Don't look at me; you cannot be believing when you are looking at me. Look away to Christ." If the bitten Israelites had looked at themselves, they would never have been healed; but they looked away from themselves to the serpent raised on the pole. So look you to Christ—that is faith.

Thank God, there is one thing that can put away sin; but there is only one—*"The blood of Jesus Christ, His Son, cleanseth us from all sin"* (1 John i. 7). This was the text that God blessed to give peace to Hedley Vicars, that dashing young officer who died at Sebastopol leading on his soldiers, and crying out, *"This way, men of the 97th!"* He had before this been a careless young man; but one day he went to a brother officer's room, and found him not within. There was a Bible lying on the table, and he took it up just to while away the time. The first verse that his eye lit on was this: *"The blood of Jesus Christ, His Son,*

cleanseth us from all sin."   *" Cleanseth us from all sin ? "*
said he.   "And is there really something that can
cleanse away all my sins?   If so, by the blessing of
God, I'll have them cleansed away."   And soon he was
rejoicing in Jesus, who died for his sins, and who was
then alive, and present with him continually.   Ever
afterwards till he died, this was his favourite verse:
*"The blood of Jesus Christ, His Son, cleanseth us from
all sin."*   Have you, dear reader, ever seen the beauty
of this verse?   Have your sins been blotted out in
Christ's precious blood ?

VI

God the Father's Love to Sinners

I WANT to tell you now of the love of God the Father to sinners. The devil tries to persuade people that God the Father is a hard taskmaster. You have the real opinion of every unconverted man about Him in the parable of the Talents in Matthew, 25th chapter. The man who had got the one talent said, "*Lord, I knew thee that thou art an hard man, reaping where thou hast not sown, and gathering where thou hast not strawed, and I was afraid.*" Or, as Luke gives it, "*I feared thee because thou art an austere man.*" Now, you could not love a hard taskmaster like that. Some children can scarcely love their parents, such hard taskmasters they are. You must get your ideas of God changed before you can love Him and trust Him.

It is true that God is a holy God, and hates your sin, and must punish it. He has a holy abhorrence of it. But there is something about you that He does not hate. He does not hate your souls. He does not hate your bodies. He does not hate your faculties. He hates your sins, but not your souls. Nay, He hates your sins because He loves your souls. The devil hates your souls, but loves your sins. And God, in His love, has opened up a way in which He can save you, and yet be holy. "*God is Love.*"

Let us look at some of the Bible texts about the love of God to wicked people.

Read Eph. ii. 4: "*But God, who is rich in mercy, for His great love wherewith He loved us, even when we*

were dead in sins." " *God, who is rich in mercy!"*
This is the Bible description of Him. It does not say,
God, who is rich in justice, but who is rich in mercy.
"*For His great love!"* How great it must be when
God Himself calls it great! And mark, "*His great
love wherewith He loved us, even when we were dead in
sins."* We think that God loves no one unless he be
good. Here Paul tells the Christians that God loved
them even when they were dead in sins, and that He
yearned for their salvation. God does not save *good*
people, but *bad* people. If they were good, they would
not need to be saved. Nor have they to wait to make
themselves good first. That they cannot do. God
takes them just as they are, and pardons them for
Christ's sake, and puts His Holy Spirit in them, and
makes them good afterwards.

Read John iii. 16: "*For God so loved the world, that
He gave His only-begotten Son, that whosoever believeth
in Him should not perish, but have everlasting life."*
Probably there is no verse in the Bible that God has
used more for the conversion of sinners than this. It
was with a sermon on this verse that John Williams
went from island to island in the South Seas, and
preached to savage cannibals; and as they heard the
wondrous story, that " *God so loved the world, that He
gave His only-begotten Son,"* they were melted and
subdued, cast their idols to the moles and to the bats,
and sat down at the feet of Jesus, clothed and in their
right mind.

Dear reader! I wish you understood and believed
this verse. "*Whosoever*" includes you. A little boy
was asked what was meant by "*whosoever.*" " It means
you, and me, and every other body," he replied; and
that is just what it means. There is no person in the
world has any *better* offer of Christ than you have, or
has any *other* offer of Christ than you have now. Be
you thief, or liar, or drunkard, or blasphemer, or harlot,
or murderer, "*whosoever believeth in Christ shall not
perish, but have everlasting life."* Here is the essence
of the Bible in a verse.

I knew a young man who was much indebted to this text. He was well acquainted with his Bible, so far as head knowledge was concerned ; he had been anxious by fits and starts for years; he had tried to get peace by resolutions, and by struggling, and by praying, and by making efforts to feel sorrow for sin and love to God, and by looking inside to see if he had got faith; and now, had he been asked, he would have said he was waiting for *the feelings.* " *What feelings ?* " " Why, the feelings that people have just before they are converted." He had been looking for something like an electric thrill from head to foot before he would find peace. There are no such feelings at all, dear readers ! It is a pure delusion of the devil to keep anxious ones from looking to Christ at once. All right feelings come after we have believed in Jesus. We must trust the word of Jesus without any feelings at all, and depend on Him. We shall never be saved if we do not take a step in advance of our feelings. The young man was *waiting for the feelings.*

One day he had been thinking over John iii. 16, and he lay down in bed at night, but not to sleep. The Spirit of God was working in his heart. He thought, " *God loved the world.*" That is wonderful—He loved the world—the wicked world that defied Him and dishonoured Him, and laughed His mercies to scorn. Yet He loved it. And "*He so loved the world, that He gave His only-begotten Son.*" Why, that was more wonderful still. He gave His one Son, His only-begotten Son, to die for His enemies, " *that whosoever believeth in Him should not perish, but have everlasting life.*" Why, he thought, that is the very thing I want—I want not to perish, but to have everlasting life. Let me look how this is to be got. " *God so loved the world.*" Wonderful ! " *God so loved the world, that He gave His only-begotten Son.*" More wonderful still ! And now Christ has died, and has finished the work. And "*whosoever*" —why, that means me as well as any other person !— "*whosoever believeth in Him*"—just dependeth on Christ —"*shall not perish, but have everlasting life.*"

And then and there he was enabled to believe it, and to rest on Christ. He leaped from his bed. Could this be conversion? So simple a thing as this! Was it just believing that God loved the world, and sent His Son; and just resting upon Christ? "Yes," whispered God's Spirit. "Why, I have been waiting for months for some feelings. How foolish I have been!" And down he got upon his knees, and thanked God for converting him, and asked Him to enable him to live like a Christian. And he looks back yet on that night as the night of his conversion. And why should not this day be the day of your conversion?

Read 1 John iv. 10: "*Herein is love, not that we loved God, but that He loved us, and sent His Son to be the propitiation for our sins.*" Some persons seem foolishly to imagine that it was Christ's coming and dying for us that made God the Father love us. No; but this made it possible for God to save us. It was God who loved us when we did not love Him, but when we hated Him, and sent His Son to be the "*propitiation for our sins.*"

The words "*propitiation for our sins*" show that God sent His Son to take our place, and die in our stead, and atone for our sins. Suppose that you had murdered a man, and that you were arrested, and tried, and condemned. And suppose that just after you were sentenced to be hung, the Queen's son stood up, and said to the judge: "My lord, this man is justly condemned, and deserves to die. But the Queen has deep compassion for him, and so have I. She has sent me to take his place, and die in his stead; and she wishes that afterwards he shall go to Windsor, and be her son for the rest of his life. If you will allow me, I will take his place and die for him, so that he may go free." Suppose the judge to consent. The handcuffs are taken off you, and the prison clothes, and put upon the young prince; and in a few days you see him hung up on the gallows for your crime. The murder you committed is atoned for, and your life is spared. Why? Because the Queen's son died in your stead.

If such had been the case, would you not love the

young prince? Would you not often think of him?
Whenever you heard his name mentioned, would you
not say, "Bless his name! he died for me"? And if
ever the policeman should come and attempt to arrest
you for this same murder, would you not plead that the
young prince died for you? This would be your only
plea.

Now, such a thing could not happen in any earthly
court of law, for no man has power over his own life—
not even the Queen's son. It belongs to God, and not
to him. And no earthly judge could agree to it. But
Jesus was God as well as man. "*He had power to lay
down His life, and power to take it again*" (John x. 18).
And some such thing has happened in heaven's court
of law, where Jehovah is judge of all. God's own Son
offered to become our Substitute, and was accepted.
He became man, and lived for us, and died for us, and
bore the punishment that our sins deserved. It was the
wrath of God due to us for sin, that wrung from Him
upon the cross the heart-rending cry, "*My God, My
God, why hast Thou forsaken Me?*" The agony that
Jesus endured for us would have swept the world out of
existence. But now justice is satisfied. The law demands no more. "*God can be just, and the justifier of
him which believeth in Jesus*" (Rom. iii. 26).

Is it any wonder that when Robert M'Cheyne and
Andrew Bonar were in the Holy Land, they went to
visit the Garden of Gethsemane? Dr. Bonar, who has
died lately, thus writes: "The sun had newly risen; few
people were upon the road, and the Valley of Jehoshaphat was lonely and still. We read over all the
passages of Scripture relating to Gethsemane, while
seated together there. It seemed nothing wonderful
to read of the wanderings of these three disciples, when
we remember that they were sinful men like disciples
now; but the compassion, the unwavering love of Jesus,
appeared by the contrast to be infinitely amazing. For
such souls as ours He rent this vale with His strong
crying and tears, wetted this ground with His bloody
sweat, and set His face like a flint to go forward and die.

While we were yet sinners, Christ died for us.' Each
of us occupied part of the time alone — in private
meditation — and then we joined together in prayer,
putting our sins into that cup which our Master drank
here, and pleading for our own souls, for our far distant
friends, and for the flocks committed to our care." Let
us also put our sins into that cup, now, just where we are.

Read 2 Cor. v. 20, 21 : "*Now then we are ambassadors
for Christ, as though God did beseech you by us : we pray
you in Christ's stead, be ye reconciled to God. For He
hath made Him to be sin for us, who knew no sin; that
we might be made the righteousness of God in Him.*"
Mark this expression, "*in Him.*" In union with Him.
This verse tells us that when we accept Christ, and thus
come into union with Him, our sins are made over to
Christ, and Christ's whole righteousness—His obedience
unto death—is made over to us, so that we are not only
made *righteous*, but "*made the righteousness of God in
Him.*" Just think of it. The holy and just God
punished Christ, though He was holy and lovely in
Himself, for our sins ; and the same holy and just God
can pardon you and me, and love you and me, though
we are unholy and unlovely in ourselves, for Christ's sake.

And here, in verse 20, God actually *beseeches* us to be
willing to let Christ take our place and die for us. "*As
though God did beseech you by us.*" I think I hear some
anxious reader say, " I am sure that God would not take
me as I am, so sinful and unholy. I must make myself
good first." Now, reader, look at this verse again. The
holy and just God punished Christ, though He was holy
and lovely in Himself, for our sins ; and the same holy
and just God can pardon and love you, sinful though
you are in yourself, for Christ's sake. Do ask God to
show you the meaning of these verses.

Learn the way of being saved from an Irish minister
of the gospel, who died a few years ago a glorious and
triumphant death. A short time before he died, he told
the minister under whom he had been brought up the
story of his conversion, in something like the following
words :—

" When I was seven years old, I began to be anxious
about my soul, and from that time till I was sixteen, I
tried to work out my own righteousness. When I used
to repeat my psalms and chapters and questions to my
mother, and she patted me on the head and praised me,
I thought God could never damn me after that. But
when I was nearly sixteen, I saw that all this could not
save me, and I became more anxious. I thought I
would go to your class for young communicants, and
to the Lord's Table, hoping this would do something
for me. One day in the class, you explained to
us very clearly that there were two different righteous-
nesses. One of these we might try and work out for
ourselves ; and if we did serve God with all our heart
and soul and mind and strength, from the day we were
born till the day we died, and never sinned once in
thought or word or deed, we might thus earn heaven ;
but nothing less than this would ever save any one. I
saw clearly that I could never get to heaven in this
way.

" You then showed us that there was another righteousness which Christ had wrought out ; that He had come
from heaven to earth, and for three-and-thirty years had
served God with all His heart and soul and strength and
mind, and never sinned once in thought or word or deed,
and that He had finished His obedience by dying on the
cross for sinners ; that this righteousness, which He had
wrought out in His life and death, was perfect—God saw
no flaw in it ; that Jesus did not work it out for Himself
but for sinners, and had it all to give away ; that He
offered it freely to each one of us without money or price,
and besought us in thorough earnestness to accept it
as our own ; and that the moment we believed this, and
accepted Him as our righteousness, all that He ever
did was reckoned as ours ; that we were not only
pardoned but made righteous—'*the righteousness of God
in Him.*'

" I did not see it clearly at the time ; but as I was
going home from the class I saw it. I saw that I did
not need to begin and work out a righteousness for **myself**

8

to recommend me to God, and that the years I had
spent in trying to do so were lost; but that I had simply
to accept one ready-made for me, and far better than my
own. And when I did see it, I leaped up from the road,
and clapped my hands, and went home 'walking and
leaping and praising God.'" Dear reader! have you
ever seen this?

Read Rom. iii. 20–26. This was the passage which God
used to give peace to Colonel Gardiner, and to Cowper
the poet, and to Brownlow North, and to many others:
"*Therefore by the deeds of the law there shall no flesh
be justified in His sight: for by the law is the knowledge
of sin. But now the righteousness of God without the law
is manifested, being witnessed by the law and the prophets;
even the righteousness of God which is by faith of Jesus
Christ unto all and upon all them that believe: for there
is no difference: for all have sinned and come short of the
glory of God; being justified freely by His grace, through
the redemption that is in Christ Jesus: whom God hath
set forth to be a propitiation, through faith in His blood,
to show His righteousness because of the passing over of
the sins done aforetime, in the forbearance of God; to show,
I say, at this time His righteousness: that He might be
just, and the justifier of him which believeth in Jesus.*"
Brownlow North was for more than forty years a very
wicked man. He tells how he was converted. After
many months of trouble about his soul, he rose from his
bed one night in sore agony, and went into his closet to
read the Bible. He says: "The portion I was reading
was the third of Romans, and as I read the twentieth
and following verses, a new light seemed to break in upon
my soul. '*But now the righteousness of God*,' etc. I can
see it as if it were this moment. Striking on the book
with my hand, and springing up from my chair, I cried,
' If that passage is true, I am a saved man; that is what
I want; that suits me; that is what I will have.' God
helping me, it was what I took—'*The righteousness of
God without the law*'—and it is what He has enabled me
to keep up to this moment."

Verse 25, as may be seen from the Revised Version,

refers to God's righteousness in paying the sins of those who lived before Christ died. It may be illustrated in this way. A farmer sells his farm for £2000. He gets no cash in hand for it, but agrees to accept a promissory note for the amount, to be paid at the end of three years. This promissory note is given, and the new owner enters on possession, and lives on his farm and works it years before he has paid anything. So God agreed to accept Christ's promise to come and die in the "fulness of time," in the room of sinners, and so "His righteousness is seen as passing over the sins done aforetime in the forbearance of God"! This seems to be the meaning of this verse.

Read also 1 Tim. ii. 4: "*This is good and acceptable in the sight of God our Saviour, who will have all men to be saved, and to come unto the knowledge of the truth.*" To the same purpose, 2 Pet. iii. 9: "*The Lord is long-suffering to us-ward, not willing that any should perish, but that all should come to repentance.*" I knew a lovely youth whom God used much to the conversion of sinners. Shortly before he died, he asked his sister to read to him 1 Timothy. She read it through, and then asked him why he had wished it to be read. "Chiefly," he said, "for the fourth verse of the second chapter, '*who will have all men to be saved, and to come to the knowledge of the truth.*'" This fact should never be kept in the back ground, but should ever be put in the front.

And now let us look at the parable of the Prodigal Son. What a lovely picture God gives here of Himself, and of His delight in saving the wicked! Please notice three points in it.

(1) The only thing that led the prodigal at first to return to his father was fear of starvation. And often the only motive that leads sinners at first to return to God is fear of hell. But God is very willing to receive sinners, when they come to Him through Christ, from any motive; and He puts better motives into them when they come. Reader! be not afraid that God will refuse to take you because you have no better motive than the fear of hell. "*Him that cometh to Me,*" from any motive,

"*I will in no wise cast out.*" Arise and go. Not merely resolve to go, but, like the prodigal, arise and go.

(2) The prodigal would have liked to come with better clothing than his rags, and with some money in his pocket. But the longer he remained away, he was getting the worse; and so he came just as he was, in rags and penniless. And you would like to come with a soft heart, and some works of righteousness to recommend you, but you cannot. The longer you remain away, you are getting the worse. Every day your sins are becoming more numerous, and your heart is getting harder, and you will never have as few sins as you have this moment till you come to Jesus, and get them all washed away in His blood. Why, then, talk such folly as that you are not good enough for Jesus? Ask, rather, are you not bad enough for Jesus? Have you not enough sins already?

(3) The father was delighted to receive the prodigal just as he was, in his rags and wretchedness. Look at God's photograph of Himself. Is there such another verse in all the Bible? "*But when he was yet a great way off, his father saw him*"—he had been out looking for him—"*and had compassion, and ran*"—actually *ran* —think of the father running to meet his prodigal son, hungry and in rags—"*and fell on his neck and kissed him*"—received him as he was, and pardoned him. Then immediately he got the wretched rags taken off him, and said to his servants: "*Bring forth the best robe and put it on him; and put a ring on his hand, and shoes on his feet: and bring hither the fatted calf and kill it, and let us eat and be merry: for this my son was dead and is alive again; he was lost, and is found. And they began to be merry.*" Mark, he did not receive him back as a servant, but as a son. That same hour he set him down at his own table as a son. This fifteenth chapter of Luke was written to show that it just delights the Lord—Father, Son, and Holy Ghost— to save sinners. "*There is joy in the presence of the angels of God over one sinner that repenteth*" (ver. 10). How the telegraph carries the news of the world to

every quarter of the earth! And when one sinner turns to God, it is telegraphed somehow throughout heaven. God the Father rejoices, and God the Son rejoices, and God the Holy Ghost rejoices, and the angels rejoice, and friends in heaven rejoice. Dear reader, if you were willing to-day to let Jesus take your sins, and come into your heart to make you holy, your friends in glory would rejoice, and you would send a thrill of joy through every inhabitant of heaven. Will you not?

Now let us look at two texts in the Old Testament, with the light of the New Testament cast on them, showing the delight of God the Father in saving the wicked.

Read Ezek. xxxiii. 11: "*Say unto them, As I live, saith the Lord God, I have no pleasure in the death of the wicked; but that the wicked turn from his way and live. Turn ye, turn ye from your evil ways; for why will ye die, O house of Israel?*" God says it. God swears it. God prints it. God commands preachers to preach it. God wishes sinners everywhere to know and believe it. Because He can swear by no greater, He swears by Himself: "*As I live,*" as sure as I live, "*saith the Lord God, I have no pleasure in the death of the wicked.*" And here is something better still: "*But I have pleasure that the wicked turn from his way and live.*" And He declares that this is as true as that He lives. Surely this puts an end to all doubt on the subject. Then He expostulates with the sinner, appeals to him, commands him: "*Turn ye, turn ye from your evil ways; for why will ye die?*" Here we have the heart of God the Father revealed. What an awful sin, after God the Father hath sworn this, to doubt the truth of it! And He commands His ministers to proclaim this, and let it be known: "*Say unto them, As I live.*" What a sin if ministers do not preach this as plainly as they ought!

Read another Old Testament text, Isa. i. 18: "*Come now, and let us reason together, saith the Lord: though your sins be as scarlet, they shall be as white as snow;*

though they be red like crimson, they shall be as wool."
This text has been more beautiful to me ever since I
read, many years ago, the outline of a lecture on paper-
making. The lecturer had before him rags and bits of
cloth of all colours. He had also a basin filled with
some liquid chemical compound. " Here is a black
rag," he said. He put it into the liquid, and it came
out white. "We make white paper out of this. Here
is a green piece of cloth." He put it into the liquid,
and it came out white also. And so with rags of other
colours. At last he took up a scarlet rag. " This is
a piece of a soldier's old coat. Now scarlet is the
fastest of all colours. I could make this white, but in
order to do so I would require to keep it so long in the
liquid that the very fibre of the cloth would be destroyed.
So we keep it in for a certain length of time, and it
comes out pink, and we make pink blotting-paper out
of scarlet rags. Scarlet is the fastest of all colours.
This is the reason why so much flannel is scarlet."
After reading this, I saw a fresh beauty in this verse.
God does not say, Though your sins be as black as
midnight, or as green as the laurel-leaf; but, Though
your sins be as scarlet, they shall be as white as snow.
And He invites the sinner to talk freely with Him:
" *Come now, and let us reason together, saith the Lord."*
O sinner, can you any longer doubt the delight of God
the Father to save you after reading these passages?
It is awfully sinful to make God a liar, and not to
believe His word and His oath. *God is love.* Yes, God
is love,—not *was* love, or *has* love, or *will be* love—but
God *is Love.*

I will end this chapter by telling you about an
American colonel. The story has been written by a
minister of the gospel about his own son, and he
vouches for its truth. It is some time since I read
the account, and I give the substance of it from
memory.

This son was a colonel in the Northern army during
the American war, and was dangerously wounded in
the battle of Bull's Run. Word was at once sent to

his father, but he lived so far away that it was eleven days before he arrived at the hospital where his son lay.   When he did arrive, the colonel was half-sleeping ; but when he heard his father's voice, he rose up, and said in an excited way, " How are you, father? And how is my mother, and my sister?" The father saw that the doctor and the nurses looked rather alarmed. He took the doctor aside into a room, and asked, " What about my son?   Will he live?"   " No."   " Is he surely going to die?"   " Yes."   " How long is he likely to live?"   " He may possibly live three or four days, but he may die any hour."   The father saw that it was no time for tears, so he went back with as calm a face as possible to his son.   " Father, you have been speaking to the doctor.   Tell me—am I going to live or die?"   The father tried to evade the question, but could not.   " Father, you must tell me.   Better for me to know the worst."   " The doctor says you are going to die."   " Is it certain that I am going to die?" " Yes."   " How long may I live?"   " He says that you may possibly live for three or four days, but that you may die any hour."

The poor sufferer leaned back on the pillow, and began to sob and weep.   " Father, I cannot die.   I must not die.   I have been a thoughtless young officer like many others.   I am not prepared to die.   Tell me, father—I know that you often speak to anxious people —tell me, can I get pardon yet before I die?"   " Yes, certainly, my son."   " Tell me, can I know that I have got pardon before I die?"   " Yes, certainly, my son." " Well, now, father, tell me in as few words as possible, and as plainly as you can, so that a poor sinner can pick it up, how I am to get pardon before I die."   The father says that just at that moment God brought up to his mind a circumstance that he had forgotten for years.

" Do you remember, my son, that when you were a boy, you did a thing that was very wrong, and I chastised you ; and you were very angry, and spoke to me in a way that you should not?"   " Oh, father, I remember it very well, and I have been wishing since I lay down here that I might see you again to ask your forgiveness for it again before I died." "Do you remember that some days after you came and confessed that you had spoken very wrongly, and asked me to forgive you?" "Yes, I do; and I remember the very words you spoke to me—you kissed me, and said, 'I forgive you with all my heart.' I have gone over it all again and again since I lay down here." "Did you believe that I forgave you?" "Of course I did." "Why?" "Because you said you did. And I knew that you did not tell lies." "And you believed me when I said I forgave you, just because I said it?" "Yes," said the colonel.

"Now, my son, listen attentively. You have often heard of Jesus Christ. God so loved this wicked world that He gave His only-begotten Son to die for sinners, even the chief. And God the Father is so satisfied with the death of Jesus Christ in the room of sinners, that He is delighted, for His sake, to pardon you. He is a thousand times more willing to pardon you, if you depend upon Jesus, than I was to pardon you. Now do this. The Lord is here beside you; and just now go to Him and tell Him out your sins—bad thoughts, and words, and deeds—as openly and frankly as you confessed to me. Make a clean breast of them. Tell Him how wicked you are, and make no excuses. Then ask Him for the sake of Jesus Christ, who died for you upon the cross, to pardon you, and depend for pardon, not upon your prayers, but entirely upon the death of the Lord Jesus upon Calvary. And here is what He promises: '*If we confess our sins, He is faithful and just to forgive us our sins.*' Believe that He forgives you, just because He says He does, in the same way that you believed me when I said I did. He promises that if you confess your sins, depending entirely upon Christ, He will forgive you. Believe Him." "And is that the way to get pardon?" said the son. "Yes." "Well, father, let me alone for a little time till I talk to God." The father went aside, and began to weep, as quietly as possible, still keeping within view of his son. After a considerable time he heard a voice, "Father." "Here I am, my son." "Father, I have gone to God, and have told Him all my sins, just as I told you; and I have asked Him for the sake of Jesus Christ, who died for me upon the cross, to pardon all my sins; and I have heard Him say to me, 'I, even I, am He that blotteth out thy transgressions for Mine own sake, and will not remember thy sins'; and, father, I do believe that when I die He will take me to heaven."

"Strange to say," writes the father, "from that hour he began to amend, and he lives yet, a real, earnest Christian, and an office-bearer in the Christian Church." Dear reader, just at this moment take a little time to be alone with God, and tell Him your sins, and ask Him, depending entirely on the death of Jesus, to pardon you; and He will pardon you. It just delights Him to save sinners.

VII

Christ's Love to Sinners

I WISH to tell you now about the love of Christ to sinners. He describes Himself in Luke xv. as the Good Shepherd, who went after the one lost sheep over hedges and ditches till he found it, and then laid it on his shoulders rejoicing, and called his friends and neighbours to rejoice with him. Oh that you would allow Him to carry you upon His shoulders to-day! He would rejoice; and He would call upon the angels and redeemed spirits to rejoice with Him: "*Likewise, I say unto you, there is joy in the presence of the angels of God over one sinner that repenteth*" (Luke xv. 10). What a verse this is to show the heart of Jesus! Did He not say when on earth that the one grand object of His coming from heaven was "*to seek and to save that which was lost*" (Luke xix. 10)? and Paul says, "*This is a faithful saying, and worthy of all acceptation, that Christ Jesus came into the world to save sinners, of whom I am chief*" (1 Tim. i. 15). Surely we should expect Christ to save sinners when it delights Him to save them, and when the grand object of His coming into the world was just to save them.

1. *Christ's love to sinners was seen in His life upon earth.* "Ye know the grace of our Lord Jesus Christ, that, though He was rich, yet for your sakes He became poor, that ye through His poverty might be rich" (2 Cor. viii. 9). Think of Him who made the sun and moon and stars, and keeps them in their orbits; who was rich in the communion of the Godhead, and rich

In the worship of the angels, stooping from heaven to be a little babe, born in a beggar's bed for us! If Queen Victoria had left her palace in Windsor and lived all her life in the poorest house in Ireland, from love to us, it would have been no such condescension. If the angel Gabriel had become a worm and crawled along the ground for us, it would have been only one creature becoming a lower creature. But here is God becoming a babe for us! Oh, what a stoop the great God made when He stooped from heaven into a frail tabernacle of clay! Think of Him who was in the form of God, and thought it not robbery to be equal with God, for our sakes making Himself of no reputation, and taking on Him the form of a servant, and being made in the likeness of men!

We will look over His public ministry, and see how full of love He was ; and as we proceed, let us remember two things—First, that the Lord Jesus is just beside us now; and, second, that He is just the same Jesus—"the same yesterday, and to-day, and for ever."

How He talked to that poor woman of Samaria ! He knew very well who she was—that she had had five husbands, and was now living with one who was not her husband. Yet He did not draw Himself up in His dignity, and say, "You are a wicked woman, I will not speak a word to you." You or I might probably have done that, and have thought ourselves very good because we did so. But Jesus did nothing of the kind. He first put Himself under a compliment to her, and asked her for a drink of water. Please remember that water in the East is always valuable, and that there were fewer dealings between Jews and Samaritans then, than there are between Protestants and Roman Catholics in Ireland now. He thus put Himself under a compliment to her ; and we do not put ourselves under a compliment to people whom we dislike. Then he told her of *living water* which He could give her; and when she asked Him for it, He said so gently, yet so faithfully, "*Go, call thy husband, and come hither*," and thus turned her thoughts into the channel of her past life, and showed her all her history. Then, having shown her her sins, He made known to her that He was the promised Messiah—"I that speak unto thee am He." And in about an hour—for it took about that time for the disciples to go to the town and back—He led her to trust in Himself. At twelve o'clock, a sinner; at one o'clock, a believer; at two o'clock, a female missionary, and one of the best missionaries ever known, for that very evening she was the means of leading a great many of her townspeople to the Lord Jesus. And He is just the same Jesus *now* and *here*—as willing to save any poor woman of Samaria who may be among my readers. Oh that you knew His love to bad people!

Look now at the woman who was a sinner, in the seventh chapter of Luke. She quietly went into the Pharisee's house when Jesus was sitting at meat. She got behind Him, and washed His feet with her tears, and wiped them with the hairs of her head, and kissed His feet, and anointed them with ointment. Jesus did not rebuke her, did not cast her off, but said: *"Her sins, which are many, are forgiven; for she loved much."* Look here, reader—a wicked woman welcome to Jesus! Just look at her—a wicked woman of the town welcome to Jesus! And He is the same Jesus to-day, and just beside you.

Look again at Zacchæus, the tax-gatherer and extortioner. He wanted to see Jesus as He passed through Jericho, and as he was small in stature, he went before and climbed up a sycamore-tree. Jesus came along, and looked up, and said, " Zacchæus, come down, for to-day I must abide at thy house "; and Zacchæus came down, and received Him joyfully. When he got down, he said, " Lord, whatever I have taken unjustly from any man, I will restore unto him fourfold, and the half of all the rest that is left I will give to the poor."

Here was evidence that his heart had been changed, and his besetting sin taken away—somewhere between the branch and the ground. And Jesus is just the same Jesus, as able and willing to save any sinner, small or great, who may be among my readers.

I love to think of Jesus riding into Jerusalem upon the ass's colt. There was a multitude before Him, and a multitude behind Him, crying, " Hosanna to the Son of David !" At length He came to the brow of the hill, from which He could look over the Valley of Jehoshaphat, and see the city. He knew that on the following Friday the people walking its streets would cry, "*Away with Him—crucify Him—crucify Him !*" Yet He pulled the reins, and stopped the colt, and looked over the valley at the guilty city, and the tears streamed down His cheeks as He said, "*If thou hadst known, even thou, at least in this thy day, the things which belong unto thy peace ! but now they are hid from thine eyes*" (Luke xix. 42).

See Him again on the following Tuesday, when He left the Temple for the last time, and as He left it, said, "*O Jerusalem, Jerusalem, that killest the prophets, and stonest them that are sent unto thee, how often would I have gathered thy children together, even as a hen gathereth her chickens under her wings, and ye would not*" (Matt. xxiii. 37). "*I would—but ye would not.*" Oh that thou wouldst fly to Me and take refuge under My wings, as the chickens fly and take refuge under the wings of their mother bird ! "*But ye would not.*" Were these words the words of a hypocrite ? Were these tears the tears of a hypocrite ? Oh, the love of compassion that Jesus has for the wicked and sinful !

Look at Jesus on the day of His death. As the soldiers were nailing Him to the cross, He prayed, "*Father, forgive them, for they know not what they do.*" And surely one of the most wondrous events of that wondrous Friday was this: a thief—one of the gang of which Barabbas was the leader—going into heaven arm-in-arm with Jesus. "*Verily I say unto thee, To-day shalt thou be with Me in paradise.*" In the morning, this thief was in a state of nature ; in the middle of the day, in a state of grace ; in the evening, in glory—justified, sanctified, made meet for heaven in a few hours. Oh, the grace of the Lord Jesus to bad people !

But if you want to see the love of the Lord Jesus

to the wicked, *look at that cross on Calvary*. For whom did He die? "*Christ died for the ungodly*" (Rom. v. 6). Yes, thank God, Christ died, not for the godly, but for the ungodly. What good would it have done you and me if Christ had died for the godly? None. Indeed, there would have been no need of Him dying *for the godly*. It was because we were ungodly that He needed to die. And now, if we are willing to let Christ take our place and die for us, and if we depend on Him, we don't need to die for our sins, or to atone for them at all. "*When we were yet sinners, Christ died for us*" (Rom. v. 8).

How is it that we can read about the sufferings of the Lord Jesus so coldly, and write about them so coldly? Oh for some of the feeling of Kajarnak, the Greenlander, when he heard Beck, the Moravian missionary, read for the first time the account of the sufferings and death of Jesus! He went forward to the missionary, and said in a tone of voice which bespoke deep emotion, "What do you tell us there? Repeat that to us! I also wish to be saved!" And before long Kajarnak was saved—the first fruits of an abundant harvest.

Think of Jesus being scourged, as now they scourge garrotters in our jails,—of Him, the blessed Son of God, being stripped and tied to a post, while the Roman soldiers laid on His back that horrid scourge, tipped with steel or lead, till the skin peeled off and the blood streamed down His back! Then think of them throwing over His bleeding back an old scarlet cloak, and putting on His head a crown of thorns, and a stick in His hand, and, in mockery, coming forward and bowing their knees before Him, and saying, "Hail, King of the Jews": then snatching the stick out of His hand, and beating Him with it on the head! Oh, the grace of the Lord Jesus to bad people!

See Him entering Gethsemane on that dark night, and bearing God's wrath and curse for sinners, till three times over He cried, "*Abba, Father, if it be possible, let this cup pass from Me; nevertheless, not My will, but*

Thine, be done." As old Traill says, "He filled the silent night with His crying, and watered the cold earth with His tears, more precious than the dew of Hermon, or any moisture, next unto His own blood, that ever fell on God's earth since the creation." And all for the ungodly!

And then see Him on Calvary, where He "*bare our sins in His own body on the tree.*" The sufferings of His body during those hours were excruciating; but His chief sufferings were those of His soul. His own Father hid His face from Him because of the sin which He bare, and Jesus felt as if He had no God, and He cried, "*My God, My God, why hast Thou forsaken Me?*" Oh, sinner! you will know something yet of what Jesus endured that day, if you do not take Him as your Saviour. You will have to bear the punishment of your own sins in hell for ever. But if you take Jesus as your Saviour, then His death stands for your sins, and you have not to bear the punishment of them at all. Oh, the grace of the Lord Jesus to bad people!—that you knew it, and believed it, and reaped the benefit of it!

I happen to know somewhat of the early history of a clergyman now labouring in England, who was led to Christ by seeing the grace of the Lord Jesus to bad people. He had a pious mother and grandfather who prayed for him; but he grew up very careless and godless. He was a boarder in one of the endowed schools in Ulster, where there were about thirty other boys. We shall call him John Thompson, though that is not his real name. He was the biggest boy in the school, and the cleverest boy in the school. He was also the bully of the school. So godless was he, that he would not allow any of the thirty boys sleeping in the same dormitory with him to kneel down and pray. If any one dared to do so, John Thompson bullied and battered him till he had to rise. Not a boy dared to kneel, for fear of this big bully.

At length, one Sabbath, the late Rev. Achilles Daunt, from Dublin, came to preach a charity sermon in the church there. The other boys went to the service on

Sabbath morning, but John Thompson was studying for prizes, and had risen at four o'clock that morning, and studied classics and mathematics till they came home. They spoke well of the preacher, and John Thompson thought that he would go in the evening. When he got the first glimpse of Mr. Daunt in the pulpit, he elbowed his companion, and whispered, "There's not much good in that fellow." After a little, he fell asleep. When the text was given out, he began to listen. It was Heb. xiii. 8: "*Jesus Christ the same yesterday, and to-day, and for ever.*" The preacher said that he would show three things,—*First*, That when Jesus Christ was on earth, He loved bad people in spite of their badness, and did them good; and that He is the same now. *Second*, That when Jesus Christ was on earth, He spake the truth, and never told a lie, and always did what He promised; and that He was the same now. *Third*, That when Jesus Christ was on earth, He never cast away any one, however bad, who came to Him; and that He is the same now. As he proceeded to show these things, John Thompson said to himself, "If Jesus Christ is like that, He is very different from what I ever thought." As he left the church, he touched his companion, and said, "There is something in that fellow after all." That evening, for about two hours, he walked round the playground. God was answering the prayers of his mother and grandfather. That night, before they went to bed, he kneeled down before his thirty companions to pray. When they saw it they were amazed. One shouted, "John Thompson's converted — John Thompson's converted!" Another shouted, "And a hard job the Lord had of it." John Thompson tells that he had forgotten even the words of the Lord's Prayer, and did not know well what to pray. But he rose from his knees, and said to the next biggest boy, "Kneel down." The boy said, "If John Thompson kneels down, so may I." And in a moment the thirty boys were on their knees. John Thompson looks back on that night as the night on which he was converted. And how was he converted? By seeing the great grace of the Lord Jesus to bad people; by seeing that Jesus, when on earth, loved bad people, and did them good; that He always spoke the truth, and never told a lie; and that He never cast away any one, however bad, who came to Him; and that He is just the same now.

And oh, unpardoned sinner! if you saw this, you could not help trusting Christ, and loving Him. He wishes this moment to take all your sins off you, and to carry them for you. If you are willing for this, and tell Him so, He takes them, and your iniquities are forgiven, and your sins are covered. "*Come unto Me, all ye that labour and are heavy laden, and I will give you rest.*"

2. *Christ's sufferings and death were in the room of the ungodly, to atone for their sins.* Did you ever ask yourself this question: Why did Christ die? He had no sin of His own. Then why did He die? The Bible answer is very clear: "He was wounded for our transgressions; He was bruised for our iniquities: the chastisement of our peace was upon Him; and with His stripes we are healed. All we like sheep have gone astray; we have turned every one to his own way; and the Lord hath laid upon Him the iniquity of us all" (Isa. liii. 5, 6). I know several persons who were brought to Christ through this text.

I never read it or hear it without thinking of a young boy in Dublin, about sixteen years of age, whom I was asked to visit. He had been ill for about two years, and the doctors did not seem to understand the nature of his disease. He told me that they all said there was something wrong with the circulation of his blood, and that, according to all the laws of doctors, he should have been dead long ago. "But," he said, " I am alive yet." "Yes, and you seem quite happy and cheerful; you must expect to get to heaven when you die?" "Certainly I do." "Have you not sinned often?" "Yes." "Have you not thought wicked thoughts?" "Yes." "Have you not spoken wicked and idle words?" "Yes." "Have you not done many things that you should not?" "Yes." "Have you loved God as much as you ought?" "No." "Have you prayed as much as you ought?" "No." "Have you served God as well as you ought?" "No." Does not God hate sin?" "Yes." "Does not He punish it?" "Yes." "Please, then, tell me how you expect to get to heaven?"

He looked up quietly from his chair, and said, "'*He was wounded for our transgressions; He was bruised for our iniquities.*' I cannot understand," he continued, "some boys who come in to see me. They say they cannot see the way of being saved. Why, it seems to me as clear as that two and two make four. It is just this: I sinned, and must have died. Jesus came and took my place, and bore my punishment, and died in my stead; and now I get free, because He died for me. That is all." I asked, "Do you never remember a time when you did not see that?" "No." "You must have a pious mother, I think, who prayed for you before you were born, and many a time since?" "Yes; my mother is a very good woman." And again, before I left, he expressed his astonishment that any one could hear about the Lord Jesus dying for sinners, and being willing to save him, without seeing the way to be saved. I told him he had great reason to be thankful, for "Flesh and blood had not revealed it unto him, but his Father who is in heaven"; and that I would tell boys and girls in other places what a Dublin boy had said to me. So now I have kept my promise. Boys and girls, let me ask, do *you* see this? Are you relying with your heart on the Lord Jesus having died for your sins?

Read also 1 Pet. ii. 24: "*Who, His own self, bare our sins in His own body on the tree.*" What was it that Jesus bore upon the cross? He "*bare our sins,*"—not the *pollution* of them certainly, that was impossible,— but the *guilt* of our sins, or our liability to punishment, and also the *punishment* of our sins. His sufferings and death were the full equivalent of the woe which our sins deserved. If we saw who Jesus was,—God and Man,— and if we saw the greatness of His sufferings in His life and death, we could not doubt that the sufferings of this God-Man were enough to blot out all our sins.

To the same purpose is another verse in 1 Pet. iii. 18:

"*For Christ also hath once suffered for sins, the just for the unjust, to bring us to God.*" What has given peace to thousands is this: They have come to see that Christ's death has satisfied God for their sins, so that God can now be just in pardoning them; and this has satisfied their consciences;

> "For when they saw the blood,
> And looked to Him who shed it,
> Their right to peace was seen at once,
> And they with transport read it."

Reader! have you seen this?

To the same effect is that wonderful verse, Gal. iii. 13: "*Christ redeemed us from the curse of the law, having become a curse for us.*" What strange language! No one, unless he had been inspired by God, would have dared to say that Christ "*became a curse* for us." Indeed, it is so strange that even Christians are afraid to use the language, and they speak of "*the cursed death of the cross*"! But that is not what this verse says. It does not say that the cross was cursed, but that Christ Himself "*became a curse for us.*" What can this mean, but that He bare the guilt and punishment of our sins in our stead?

Read again Phil. iii. 8, 9: "I count all things *but dung, that I may win Christ, and be found in Him, not having mine own righteousness, which is of the law, but that which is through the faith of Christ, the righteousness which is of God by faith.*" Read also 1 Cor. i. 30: "*Of Him are ye in Christ Jesus, who of God is made unto us . . . righteousness.*" My reader must have observed how often the Bible speaks, not only of the death of Christ, but of His righteousness, and tells that, when we believe in Christ, we get His righteousness made over to us, and are not only pardoned, but are made the righteousness of God in Him. Christ did more for us than die; He lived. And His righteous life and atoning death together make up His *righteousness*, or His "*obedience unto death.*"

To be pardoned is one thing; to be pronounced

righteous is another and still better. To be free from
debt is one thing; to be rich is another. Reader! the
moment that you accept Christ as your Substitute, all
your sins are made over to Him, and His death atones
for them ; and all His righteousness is made over to you,
and you are "*made the righteousness of God in Him.*"
" *Christ is made of God unto you righteousness.*" *You
are found in Him, not having your own righteousness,
" but that which is through the faith of Christ, the righteousness which is of God by faith.*" Christ's righteousness is
" *upon all them that believe* " (Rom. iii. 22).

And we need this righteousness. Look at the curse
pronounced upon us : "*Cursed is every one that continueth
not in all things which are written in the book of the law
to do them.*" Now, how can we get from under this
curse?   How can we present God with a perfect
"*continuance in all things*"?   Not in ourselves. But
Christ, throughout His life, "*continued in all things which
are written in the book of the law,*" and He died upon the
cross ; and when we believe, all this "obedience unto
death" is made over to us. We can thus present God
with a perfect continuance in all things which are
written in the book of the law to do them, as well as
with a perfect atonement for our sins. Could God
pronounce us *righteous* if nothing but Christ's death
were made over to us ?

Luther could not understand the Bible at all until
he saw the meaning of this phrase, " *The righteousness of
God,*" in Rom. i. 17. At first he thought it referred to
God's attribute of righteousness, but he saw that this
did not open up the meaning of the passages in which
it occurred.   But when he saw that it meant the
righteousness which God *provided,* the righteousness
which Christ the God-Man *wrought out* in His righteous
life and atoning death, the righteousness which God *is
pleased to accept* for us, his heart exulted with joy.
Writing to a friend, he said: " Learn to sing unto Him
a new song, to despair of yourself, and say to Him—
Thou, Lord Jesus Christ, art my righteousness, and I
am Thy sin. Thou hast taken what was mine, and

hast given me what was Thine. What Thou wast not,
Thou didst become, in order that I might become what
I was not. Learn with what love He opens His arms
to thee, taking all your sins upon Himself, and giving
thee all His righteousness."

No doubt it is His *death* that is most prominent in
the Bible, or His *blood*. The *death* and the *blood* mean
just the same. This is the most striking part of His
righteousness. But His *blood* and His *death* seem to
be just short names for His whole "*obedience unto death,
even the death of the cross.*"

Read one other text, Rom. v. 19: "*For as by one
man's disobedience many were made sinners, so by the
obedience of one shall many be made righteous.*" Mark
the expression: "*By the obedience of one*" — "*the
obedience*"—shall many be made righteous; not merely
be pardoned, but "*be made righteous.*"

"*As by one man's disobedience many were made sinners.*"
I remember well, when a boy, wishing that Adam had
not stood for me, and that each of us had stood for
himself, unconnected with Adam. But when Adam,
who was made in God's own image, sinned in Paradise,
is it likely that you and I should have done better?
And now there is a far safer way of being saved than
if Adam had not stood as our head. For then each one
of us must have been saved by working out a righteousness for himself that would entitle him to heaven.
Whereas now Christ offers His perfect righteousness to
each one of us, and when we accept Him, we get
His righteousness as ours to entitle us to heaven.
And the heaven we will get will be a far better
heaven than if Adam had not stood for us. For then
the heaven we would have got would have been the
full value of our own righteousness. But now the
heaven we will get will be the full value of Christ's
righteousness.

When Duncan Matheson was dying, he said, "*If I
had my life to live over again, I would preach substitution
more than ever*"; and he was right. It is the essence of
the Bible, and of the way to be saved. And now, my

reader, Jesus Christ is just beside you this moment, wherever you are. And He offers you now, just as you are, His obedience unto death, as the atonement for your sins, and as your robe of righteousness.

You remember the king who made the marriage supper for his son, in Matthew, 22nd chapter. He sent his servants to bid those in the highways to come to the feast. And " *they gathered together all, as many as they found, both good and bad.*" Yes, " *both good and bad,*" and the wedding was furnished with guests. In the East, then as now, a large part of rich men's riches consisted in costly garments stored past them. Horace tells of 5000 mantles, which Lucullus, on examining his wardrobe, found that he possessed. When a great king made a feast, he had a robe provided for each guest, and it was reckoned then, as it is reckoned yet, a great insult to refuse to put it on, or to appear in one's own dress at the king's feast. " When the king came in, he saw a man which had not on a wedding garment. And he saith unto him, Friend, how camest thou in hither, not having a wedding garment ? And he was speechless."

And oh, sinner, you will be speechless in the day of judgment if you do not put on the robe of righteousness provided for you, and freely offered to you. " *Put ye on the Lord Jesus Christ.*" Have you accepted Christ ? I must ask you this question, and must press it on you : " *Have you accepted Christ ?* " Yes or no ? I know more than one instance in which this question has been the means of leading persons to decision. Do not evade it, I beseech you ; for on your acceptance of Him depends your everlasting salvation. Five years ago, say, two men lived in your neighbourhood. They are now both dead. One of them is in heaven ; the other is in hell. What was the difference between them ? It was not that at that time the man now in heaven was a better man than the man now in hell. Perhaps he was the worse of the two. But the difference was that the one man was led to see that he was a sinner ; and that Jesus was offered to him as his Saviour. He accepted Him as such, and was enabled afterwards to live a holy life; and, when he died, went to heaven. The other man resolved that some day, before he died, he would accept Christ, but he put it off. In the meanwhile he rejected the only Saviour. God cut him down in his sins, and now he is in hell, bewailing his madness in neglecting so great salvation. Oh, the folly of this putting off—this waiting for a more convenient season, which is always coming, but which never comes! Of all Satan's baits, this is the most taking one: "You are not going to die to-night, are you? Time enough yet."

VIII

Christ's Work Finished and Free to All

THE Rev. Hay Aitken, the English evangelist,
tells the following incident. He had been
preaching for a week or two in a town in England,
and had finished his work, and was to leave on
Monday. About an hour before his departure, a
knock was heard at the door of the clergyman's house
where he stayed. The door was opened, and a young
man asked, "Is Mr. Aitken here?" "Yes; please
walk in." Mr. Aitken did not know at the time who
his visitor was, but he found out afterwards. His
father was a clergyman, and had got his son into a
good situation; but he had lost it, and had run away
to Paris. His father had followed him, found him in
the slums of that city, and brought him back; and
the young man was now in an inferior situation.

Something like the following conversation occurred :—
"Mr. Aitken, I have walked eight miles this morning
to see you." "I am very glad to see you," Mr. Aitken
replied. "I heard you preach last night, and I think
you said that the more God's Spirit strove with us,
when we resisted Him, the less likelihood there was of
our being saved." "Yes, I did." "I believe it is true.
God's Spirit has been striving with me again and again,
and He is striving with me now; and I believe that if
I am not saved now, I never will be saved at all, and I
am resolved to be saved now, if God is willing to save
me." "I am sure He is willing to save you now
through Jesus Christ; but before we talk further, my

young friend, let us kneel down and ask God to teach us."

Having risen from their knees, Mr. Aitken said " Please be seated. I wish just to ask you two questions: First, Do you see that when Christ died upon the cross He suffered all, paid all that was needed to atone for your sins ; that His work is finished, and not half-finished; that when you get His death, you get a full atonement for your sins, and don't need to eke it out by doing anything else *as an atonement* for your sins ? Do you see that Christ's work is finished ? " " Oh yes, Mr. Aitken, I see that quite well; my father used to preach often about Christ's finished work." " Well, I hope you do. Now for the second question : Young man, here you are, a poor, wicked, hell-deserving, unfeeling, helpless sinner." " Yes, that is just what I am." " Now, are you willing, just as a poor sinner, to take Christ's finished work offered to you as yours ? Remember, He is just here beside you, offering Himself and His death to you. Are you willing to go to heaven just as a poor sinner, relying entirely on Christ and His work — to be a beggar, dependent entirely on Him ? " After a pause, the reply came : " Well, I think I am ; but I don't feel a bit different, Mr. Aitken." " I was not asking you," said Mr. Aitken, " what you *feel*, but what you *mean*. I wish you would let your feelings alone. Do you mean this—are you willing for this—to take Christ's death as the full, finished atonement for your sins, and to rely entirely for pardon and heaven on Christ's finished work ? Are you willing for this ? " After another pause : " Well, I think I am ; but I don't feel a bit different yet."

" Now, my young friend, I wish that you would let your feelings alone for a little. I will ask you the same two questions over again." Again he answered yes to the first one ; and at the end of the second said, " Yes, by the grace of God, I am willing to be a poor sinner depending entirely upon Christ." " Well, I hope so," said Mr. Aitken. " And now, young friend, about those feelings of yours. You are a poor, wicked, hell-deserving sinner, depending entirely for salvation upon Christ and His cross. Where is your condemnation to come from? Can the devils condemn a poor sinner depending on Christ?" "No," said the young man. "Now, young friend, look up: can God, will God, condemn a poor sinner depending entirely for salvation on Christ and His cross? Can He? Will He?" There was a pause—a few moments of silence; then the tears burst from his eyes. He rushed forward and clasped Mr. Aitken round the neck, and said, "I see it, I see it! There is no condemnation to them that are in Christ Jesus." Dear reader! have you ever seen this?

1. *Christ's work is a finished work.* This is what is taught so clearly and so frequently in the Epistle to the Hebrews. Have you observed that between the last verse of the seventh chapter and the fourteenth verse of the tenth chapter the writer tells us no fewer than seven times that Christ died "*once for all*,"— "Once for all,"—and that "*by one offering He hath perfected for ever them that are sanctified*"? (Heb. vii. 28; also ix. 12, 26, 28; also x. 10, 12, 14). If we saw who He was who suffered, and how much He suffered, we could not doubt that the sufferings and death of this God-Man were enough to atone for the sins of the whole world. If only one person had been saved, Christ must have died; but now His sufferings and death are enough for all, and free to all.

On the cross He cried, "It is finished." On the night before He died, He prayed, "*Father, I have finished the work which Thou gavest Me to do*" (John xvii. 4). He finished the working out of a perfect obedience, and made a complete atonement for sinners. Daniel predicted that when He came, He would "*finish the transgression, and make an end of sins, and bring in everlasting righteousness*" (Dan. ix. 24); and He did all this. If God had not been satisfied with Christ's death, as a full and complete atonement for sinners, He would not have raised Him from the dead. Christ

would have been lying in the grave yet. Nor would
He have taken Him to sit at His right hand in heaven.
These are God's evidences that Iie is satisfied with
Christ's work on our behalf, and has taken it off His
hands as a finished work. Christ's death was the payment of our debt; Christ's resurrection and sitting down
in heaven are God's stamped receipt that the payment
is made and is sufficient.

And now, when we get Christ's finished atonement
as ours, we do not need to atone for our own sins more
or less. "*It is finished.*" We do not need to eke it
out as an atonement by our tears, or prayers, or sufferings. "*It is finished.*" We need just to thank the
Lord that He died for us, and to love the Lord
because He died for us, and to seek to please the Lord
because He died for us, and to go on our way rejoicing,
trusting in Christ's finished work.

> "Nothing, either great or small,
> Nothing, sinner, no;
> Jesus did it, did it *all*,
> Long, long ago.
> '*It is finished!*' Yes, indeed,
> Finished every jot;
> Sinner, this is all you need,
> Tell me, is it not?"

In the *Life of Robert Haldane*, we are told of
a Rationalist or Unitarian minister who had argued
with him against the Atonement again and again at
Montauban in France. Mr. Haldane had been trying
to show him that Christ's death was sufficient as an
atonement for his sins, and was offered to him freely
as a gift, and that the moment he took it he got a full,
finished atonement for his sins; that he got not a
quarter-payment, nor a *half*-payment, nor a *part*-pay-
ment, but a finished payment of his debts—not £999
paid out of £1000, but the whole £1000 paid. The
minister argued stoutly against this. At length, one
Friday, they went out to walk together, and Mr.
Haldane began to speak about the words, "*It is
finished*," and dwelt on the value of Christ's death, and

His love in offering His death to sinners, and in beseeching them to accept it. As he proceeded, the minister
stopped on the road, and stood still for a little ; then,
looking Mr. Haldane earnestly in the face, he said in
French, " *It is too good—it is too good.*" God's Spirit
had shown him somewhat of the meaning of those three
words, " *It is finished,*" and he went home to preach
the glad tidings of pardon for nothing through the
finished work of Christ. Dear reader, again we ask,
Have you ever seen this?

Need we say what an insult to the atonement of
Christ is the Roman Catholic doctrine of the Mass,—
that in every mass there is offered to God an atonement
for the sins of the living and of the dead? As if
Christ's one offering were not sufficient ! as if all those
seven texts in Hebrews about Christ being offered
" once for all " were a lie ! as if Christ's work were not
finished, and needed to be eked out !

2. *Christ's finished work is free to every sinner.* Unpardoned sinner ! God's justice does not now stand
in the way of your salvation. There is nothing hindering you to be saved *outside yourself.* There are
three truths about Christ's death that are held by
all Evangelical Christians : *First,* Christ's death was
sufficient for all men. *Second,* Christ's death was suited
to all men—adapted to all men—just what all men
need. *Third,* Christ's death is, by God's command, to
be offered to all men. No one disputes these three
facts. But you must take His death home to yourself.

The ark was finished, and all the provisions in it
were complete ; but Noah and his family had to step
into the ark, and if they had not done so, they must
have perished. What a change when they stepped in,
and the Lord shut them in ! It was just a step, but it
must be taken.

On that night in Egypt the lamb was slain, and the
promise given that wherever God saw the blood He
would pass over that house, and spare its inhabitants.
But the blood must be sprinkled upon each door-post,
otherwise the destroying angel would have come in.

So the blood of Christ must be sprinkled on each conscience. God must see the blood upon your heart, and that you are resting upon Christ. The difference between the houses passed over that night and the houses where the destroying angel entered, was, that God saw blood upon the one and not upon the other. Thank the Lord for this, that it is God who must see the blood, and not ourselves or our neighbours. Not seldom God sees the blood on us when we cannot see it on ourselves, or when our neighbours cannot see it.

When the burnt-offering was sacrificed in Old Testament times, of the person who offered it, it was said, "*He shall put his hand upon the head of the burnt-offering, and it shall be accepted for him to make atonement for his sin*" (Lev. i. 4). So we must honestly confess our sins to God, telling them out to Him, and put them upon the head of Jesus, otherwise we cannot be saved.

But who enables us to accept Jesus as our Substitute? It is God's Spirit, and it just delights God's Spirit to lead us to Christ. You have not to wait on Him a moment to make Him willing. His great work with the unconverted is to show them the sin of not believing in Jesus. "*And when He is come, He will convince the world of sin . . . because they believe not on Me*" (John xvi. 8, 9). He points to Jesus, and says, "*Behold the Lamb of God, who taketh away the sin of the world.*" He is a hundred times more willing to lead you to Christ than you are to be led. Whenever you take one step towards Christ, it is because the Spirit of God has taken a hundred steps towards you. "*The Spirit and the Bride say, Come*" to Jesus. "*The Holy Ghost saith, To-day, if ye will hear His voice, harden not your heart.*"

Now, how do you get the death of Christ as an atonement for your sins? Just by *taking* it; and you will never get it till you do take it. And what do you mean by *taking* it? Why, the Lord Jesus Christ is just beside you, though you do not see Him, and He honestly offers His death to you this moment as an atonement for all your sins ; and taking it means believing this honestly, and saying to Him just this moment, where you are, " *Lord Jesus, Thou dost offer Thy death to me to atone for my sins. Here and now I do accept Thine offer, I do take Thy death as an atonement for my sins, and I do take Thee as my Saviour.*" If you honestly tell the Lord this, meaning it,—that is, taking His offer, and taking Himself,—when He gives, and you take, the thing is done : no one else has any business in the matter. You may not do it *perfectly*, but do it *honestly*. Oh, dear readers! how supremely foolish it is not to say yes at once. A little boy in Edinburgh was dying. "*Father, say yes to Jesus,*" were among his last words. Dr. Charles Brown of Edinburgh said he had never heard a better account of what faith is than that "*Say yes to Jesus.*" An honest *yes* to His offer is salvation begun! Now, kneel down this moment, and say yes, and the Lord will enable you.

Remember that Christ's atonement is for sinners. Whatever else may not be for sinners, Christ's death is for none but sinners, and it is offered to you as freely as to any other person in the world. No person in the world ever had any better offer of Christ than you have, or any other offer of Christ than you have. There is nothing freer to you upon the earth than the death of Christ. It is as free to you as the rain from heaven. You have no right in yourself to Christ's death, but He offers it to you, beseeching you to accept it, and to give Him the credit and the pleasure of saving you. If He did not offer it to you, you would have no right to take it ; but when He offers it, it is no presumption to take it. Nay, it is the height of presumption not to take it —a great sin, and a great folly as well.

There are four things I wish to tell you about Christ's death. *First*, God *permits* you, a poor sinner, just as you are, to take Christ's death as a full atonement for your sins. *Second*, God *invites* you to do so. *Third*, God *commands* you to do so. *Fourth*, God *entreats* you to do so. We will quote a text or two on each point.

(1) *God* PERMITS *you, a poor sinner, just as you are, to take Christ's death as a full atonement for your sins.* Read John vi. 37: "*Him that cometh to Me, I will in no wise cast out.*" *Any him or her!* Surely this includes you, be you rich or poor, young or old, learned or ignorant, moral or immoral, feeling or unfeeling, hard heart or soft heart. Any one who comes to *Me*, Jesus says, "*I will in no wise cast out.*" There are very few verses in the Bible that have been so much blessed by God to give light and peace to sinners as this one. Did any one ever come to Jesus, and say to Him honestly, "Lord Jesus, I want Thee to carry my sins for me," and Jesus said, "No, I will not"? I tell you that if the devil knew even one instance of this in the wide world, he would have it telegraphed over the earth, and to-morrow morning it would be read in the Belfast *Whig* and *News Letter* and *Irish News*; in the *Derry Standard* and *Sentinel*; in the *Irish Times* and *Freeman's Journal*; in the London *Times* and *Standard* and *Daily Telegraph* and *Daily News*; in the *New York Herald* and *Times*; in the *Melbourne Argus*; and in hosts of other papers,—that in such a place, such an one, boy or girl, man or woman,—giving the name, —came honestly to the Lord Jesus and asked Him to carry his sins for him, and to let His death stand for him, and that Jesus said, *No*. Such a thing never did happen, and never will happen. Why, then, do you not this moment go to the Lord, who is just beside you, and ask Him to take your sins, *and believe that He does,* —yes, *believe that He does?*

But how are you to know that if you come to Jesus, and are ready to make over your sins to Him, He will receive you? Just because He says He will, and He does not tell lies. You do not feel it, you believe it.

(2) God not only *permits* you, He INVITES you to take Christ. Read Rev. xxii. 17: "*Whosoever will, let him take the water of life freely.*" What you have to do is to *take, take*; and it is for *whosoever will.* Surely that means you?

If some rich man offered you a hundred-pound note,

you perhaps could scarce believe he was in earnest. But if he assured you that he was in earnest, and that he wanted you to take it as a gift, would you not take it, and would it not be yours in God's sight, and in man's sight, as much as if you had laboured hard for years to get it? Why will you not believe that God is in earnest, and take His Son, and pardon along with Him? How long does it require to take a gift? Does it require months or days? No, just a moment. And the moment you accept Christ and His death, that moment you get Christ's death as an atonement for your sins, and God pardons you for Christ's sake. But you must take.

"I must say," wrote Dr. Chalmers in a letter to a friend, "that I never have had so close and satisfactory a view of the gospel salvation, as when I have been led to contemplate it in the light of a simple offer on the one side, and a simple acceptance on the other. It is just saying to one and all of us, 'There is forgiveness through the blood of My Son: take it'; and whoever believes the reality of the offer takes it. It is not, in any shape, the reward of our own services; it is the gift of God through Jesus Christ our Lord. Make a clear outset in the business, and understand that your first step is simply a confiding acceptance of an offer that is most free, most frank, most generous, and most unconditional."

I remember once going to see a dying man in County Tyrone. He was sitting in his bed, propped up by pillows, and scarcely able to speak; he died the next morning. He told me that he had been careless till a few months before. He had thought that, in order to get pardon, he must do more good works than he had ever done bad ones, and thus have the weight on his side of the balance, as he expressed it; but as this would take a long time, and as it was doubtful whether he could ever do it at all, he never commenced to try. Consumption set in, and he was sent to a Belfast Hospital, where a lady came and talked to him, and gave him little books to read. He was sent home as incurable, and the lady continued to write letters to him. "Two things did me real good," he said: "I heard a person tell about a poor weak man walking along a road, carrying on his back a heavy burden. By and by a large strong man came along, and said, 'That burden is too heavy for you; give it to me and I will carry it for you, and give you rest from it.' And the poor man just handed over the burden to the strong one, and walked alongside him. And so," he continued, "I was carrying the load of my sins, and Jesus came along and said, '*Cast thy burden upon the Lord, and He will sustain thee*,' and I just gave my load of sin to Him, and He has taken it, and it is off me.

"A second thing did me good. I read in a little book about a poor labouring man working hard in the fields. His wife knew that he would be weary, and so she had got tea ready, and when she saw him coming near home, she poured it out and had it waiting for him on the table. When he entered, he said, 'Jane, I am weary; please get me a cup of tea.' She replied, 'I knew that you would be weary, so I made it, and there it is poured out, and all ready; sit down and take it.' But he did not sit down and take it, but kept walking about, and saying with great earnestness, 'Jane, give me a cup of tea.' 'My dear, there it is; do sit down and take it.' And again and again, 'Do give me a cup of tea'; and again and again, 'Do sit down and take it.'

"That is just a picture of me," said the dying man. "God sent His Son to die for me, and Jesus finished the work, and offered His death to me without money and without price. But I did not take Him, but kept saying, Lord, save me! Lord, save me! And still again, Lord, pardon my sins, and save me! And the Lord said, 'There is My Son, take His death as the atonement for your sins, and you will get pardon and peace along with Him.' But I did not take Him, but kept crying earnestly, Lord, save me! Lord, pardon me! And I thought it was a great pity of me. At last I saw my mistake, and saw how willing Christ was

10

to make over His death to me, and I took Him as my Saviour, and His death to atone for me; and now, I do believe that when I die I will get to heaven."

What a startling picture this is of many of my readers—crying earnestly to the Lord to pardon them and save them, and yet rejecting Christ! You must not only *ask*, you must *take* Christ and His death home to yourselves.

You might pray to the Lord for a lifetime without getting pardon, if you did not depend upon Christ. And the moment you do ask Him to pardon you, depending upon Christ, that moment He does pardon you. What a difference there is between unbelieving prayer and believing prayer in the name of Jesus!

(3) God not only *permits* and *invites* you, but COM-MANDS you to take Christ as your Saviour. Read John vi. 28, 29. The Jews said unto Jesus: "*What must we do, that we may work the works of God? Jesus answered and said unto them, This is the work of God, that ye believe on Him whom He hath sent.*" And again: "*This is His commandment, That we should believe in the name of His Son Jesus Christ*" (1 John iii. 23). When we obey this commandment, it is the first work we do that pleases God. Oh, my reader! you have no right to disobey this commandment, even for a moment. You will be lost for ever if you disobey it; for "*he that believeth not shall be damned.*" This is the greatest sin —the greatest sin of all. Christ commands you to go to Him with your sins, and this is the best warrant you can have why you should go.

Mr. Spurgeon tells about the foreman of certain works in England, who had often heard the gospel, but was afraid that he had no *right* or *warrant* to come to Christ, seeing he was a poor sinner. His master, who was a Christian, sent a card one day round to the works: "Come to my house immediately after work." The foreman appeared at his master's door, and the master came out, and said somewhat roughly, "What do you want, John, troubling me at this time? Work is done: what right have you here?" "Sir," said he,

"I had a card from you saying that I was to come after work." "Do you mean to say that merely because you had a card from me, you are to come to my house and call me out after business hours?" "Well, sir," replied the foreman, "I do not understand you, but it seems to me that, as you sent for me, I had a right to come." "Come in, John," said his master. "I have another message that I want to read to you: '*Come unto Me, all ye that labour and are heavy laden, and I will give you rest.*'" The foreman saw that he had the best authority for coming to Christ with his sins, when Christ *commanded* him to do so.

Yes, read this command: "*Come unto Me, all ye that labour and are heavy laden, and I will give you rest*" (Matt. xi. 28). How many weary hearts have been relieved by this verse! Reader! are you not heavy laden with sin, whether you feel it or not? And have you not been labouring in various ways to get rid of your load? Then this verse is for you. Jesus says: "Quit your labouring, and try a new plan altogether. I am here. Let Me take your load, and carry it for you, and *I—will—give—you—rest.*" So Jesus promises. Did He ever make a promise, and not fulfil it? Never. And mark—this is a *command*. You have no right to refuse Christ and His death. You may refuse to walk in the fresh air. You may refuse to drink the rain that falls from heaven. But you have no liberty to refuse Christ, and being saved by Him.

How foolish, then, for people to say they would accept Christ if they had liberty to do so! God gives you no liberty to refuse Him.

Mr. Spurgeon tells of a young woman who was in great concern about her soul. "I placed Christ before her very plainly, but she did not seem to understand the way. One morning she came to me after service. 'Dear sir, will you pray for me?' She was thunderstruck when I said 'No.' 'But, sir, I am anxious to be saved: won't you pray for me?' 'No.' 'Oh, sir, you don't mean it?' 'I do. I have set Jesus Christ before you; if you will not have Him, there is no use praying;

you will be lost. There is no other way, and I don't wish that there should be any other way. Will you have Christ, or will you not?' There was a pause, then she said, 'Yes, I will, if I may.' 'May? He has put it, "He that believeth shall be saved, and he that believeth not shall be damned." Surely you may have Him, when there is such a dreadful threatening against unbelief?' 'Well, I will.' 'Then let us get down directly and pray now. If you are willing to obey God's command, then we may pray.' We did pray," said Mr. Spurgeon, "and I am sure that young woman has never doubted that she was saved from that hour. If you won't believe in Jesus, all the praying between heaven and earth won't save you. But if you seek Him in simple faith, soon shall you say with rejoicing, ' I have found Him whom my soul loveth, and I will never let Him go.'"

Read another command : "*Look unto Me, and be ye saved, all the ends of the earth*" (Isa. xlv. 22). This refers to the bitten Israelites in the desert. They had sinned, and God sent fiery serpents that bit them, and they were dying. Here was a man bitten in the leg ; there was a woman with a serpent coiled round her arm—both dying. What were they to do? God told Moses to make a serpent of brass, and to put it upon a pole, and promised that whosoever looked at the serpent of brass would live.

No doubt many of the Israelites scoffed at this strange mode of cure, and refused it. One tried poultices ; but all the poultices in the world could not cure the bite. Another tried a drawing salve ; but all the salves in the world could not cure the bite. But one man said, "I will try God's plan," and he looked away towards the pole, and saw it, and raised his eyes up to the serpent at the top ; and lo ! in a moment he was cured. God had promised He would cure him, and He did. The woman near him was very weak, and not able to raise her head ; but her neighbours put their hands round her head, and turned it towards the pole. " Now look. Do you see the pole?" "Yes." "Look up higher to the top." And she saw the serpent of brass, and in a moment she was cured.

Mark, this man had not to rise and walk to the pole. He might not have been able to do so. He had just to look where he was. And whosoever looked lived. And this is Christ's own illustration of the way to be saved. "*As Moses lifted up the serpent in the wilderness, even so must the Son of man be lifted up, that whosoever believeth in Him should not perish, but have eternal life*" (John iii. 14, 15). There is no other way to be saved. This is the short and easy method. You may be saved this way to-day, and should you live for fifty years and be saved then, you must just be saved in this way. Jesus says: "*Look unto Me, and be ye saved.*" It is not, Look at your sins, but at Me. If the Israelites had kept looking at their bites, they would never have been cured. They must look to the serpent of brass. Look then to Jesus. *It is a command.*

(4) God not only *commands*, but ENTREATS AND BESEECHES you to take Christ's death as a full atonement for all your sins. Read 2 Cor. v. 20: "*Now then we are ambassadors for Christ, as though God did beseech you by us : we pray you in Christ's stead, be ye reconciled to God.*" You may think you are willing to be saved, and that you have to make God willing to save you. But that is a delusion of the devil to keep you away from Christ. God the Father is here *beseeching* you this moment that you will accept His Son, and not rush on to hell over Christ's dead body. And Jesus is here *praying you.* Just think of Jesus at this moment *praying* you that you would let Him carry your guilt, and have the credit of saving you! And will you refuse? All that is wanted is your own consent. Will you not consent to this? and say, "Yes, Lord Jesus, here are my sins. Take them off me, and carry them for me, and come into my heart and make me holy. I consent to be saved by Thy righteousness and death!" If you honestly mean this, He takes them off you, and your salvation is begun.

This verse has been the means of giving peace to

multitudes. When John Howard heard Joseph Milner preach from it, and explain from it God's delight in saving the worst of sinners, he thought it so good that he feared it was not in his own Bible at home. And when he found the same words *beseech* and *pray* in his own Bible, he was delighted and overcome, and from that moment all his passions were put under the feet of Jesus. We have often thought that there are four words in these two verses (20, 21) that no one would have dared to write unless he had been inspired by God—Christ was made *sin for us*. We are *made the righteousness of God in Him*. God *beseeches us* to be reconciled to Him. Jesus *prays us*. What a verse this is! We ourselves know at least two excellent ministers who have told us they were brought to Christ through this verse. They had thought that they were willing to be saved, and that God was not willing to save them. And here they learned that God was *beseeching* them, and Jesus *praying* them to let Christ save them.

Oh, my reader! have you ever had a real trans-action with Jesus—as real a transaction as you ever had behind a counter, or in a fair? Have you ever said to Him, "Lord Jesus, Thou dost offer Thy death to me, as a full atonement for my sins. Here and now I take Thine offer"? Remember, if you are lost, it will be for want of an honest "yes" to Christ's offer. Oh, settle the matter now upon your knees.

> " 'Tis done! the great transaction's done!—
> I am my Lord's, and He is mine."

IX

Groundless Fears

A N old writer says: "The gospel is much clouded by legal terms, conditions, and qualifications. If my doctrine were, *Upon condition* that you do so and so,—that you believe, and repent, and mourn, and pray, and obey, and the like,—*then* you shall have the favour of God,—I dare not for my life say that is the gospel. But the gospel I desire to preach to you is—Will you have a Christ *to work* faith, repentance, love, and all good in you, and to stand between you and the sword of divine wrath? Here there is no room for you to object that you are not qualified because you are such a hardened, unhumbled, blind, and stupid wretch. For the question is not, Will you remove these evils, and then come to Christ? but, *Will you have a Christ to remove them from you?* It is because you are plagued with these diseases that I call you to come to the Physician that He may heal you."

I wish in this chapter to notice some groundless fears which often make sinners think that they cannot accept Christ and be saved now.

1. I HAVE NO RIGHT SENSE OF SIN, AND I FEAR I SHALL NEVER BE CONVERTED WITHOUT STRONGER CONVICTIONS OF SIN AND GREATER TERRORS OF CONSCIENCE.

You have read, probably, of some persons who had great terrors before they believed, and you think you must have the same. Now, it is quite true that you have no right sense of sin. But you know that you are a sinner deserving hell. Thousands have been saved

without the deep sense of sin that you are looking for.
That will come after conversion. In fact, no one ever
got farther before conversion than this—to sorrow that
he did not feel more sorrow for sin, to grieve that he did
not feel more grief for sin, and to cry, I wish I was
converted. This is conviction, and is just the state to
which God brings persons the moment before conversion. Jesus does not wish you to wait one moment for
more conviction, but just to come to Him as the poor,
hard-hearted, unfeeling sinner that you are, and He will
take your sins, and put a new heart into you, and give
you the sorrow for sin that you are now trying to work
up in yourself. "*A new heart also will I give you, and
a new spirit will I put within you ; and I will take away
the stony heart out of your flesh, and I will give you an
heart of flesh. And I will put My spirit within you, and
cause you to walk in My statutes, and ye shall keep My
judgments and do them*" (Ezek. xxxvi. 26, 27). You are
putting your convictions in the place of Christ. Look
not at your convictions, but look at Christ, and the convictions will follow.

I have often thought that the answer to the question, *What is Repentance unto Life?* in the Shorter
Catechism of the Westminster Assembly, is remarkably
good. " Repentance unto life is a saving grace, whereby
a sinner, out of a true sense of his sin, and apprehension
of the mercy of God in Christ, doth, with grief and
hatred of his sin, turn from it unto God, with full
purpose of, and endeavour after, new obedience." The
first thing the sinner gets is a true sense of sin—that is,
he comes to see that he is a sinner deserving punishment.
He will never go to Jesus till he sees this. He must
have a *true* sense of sin. It does not say a *deep* sense
of sin, or a *clear* sense of sin. It may be deep or not so
deep, clear or not so clear. But it must be true so far
as it goes—a *true* sense of sin. Then comes an
apprehension of the mercy of God in Christ. He learns
that God is satisfied with the death of Christ in his
room, and is willing to save him, and he is enabled to
rest on Christ. Then, *after that*, comes grief for sin,

and hatred of sin, and turning from it unto God—not before it, but after it. Jesus gives it to him when he comes. With the one hand He gives him repentance, and with the other remission of sins. " *Him hath God exalted with His right hand to be a Prince and a Saviour, for to give repentance to Israel and forgiveness of sins*"(Acts v. 31).

Dr. Horatius Bonar writes : " That *terror of conscience* may go before faith, I do not doubt. But such terror is very unlike Bible repentance ; and its tendency is to draw men *away from*, and not *to* the Cross. But this is not godly sorrow, and is not uncommon among unbelieving men, as Ahab and Judas. The broken and contrite heart is the result of our believing the glad tidings of God's free love.

" Few things are more dangerous to the anxious soul than the endeavours to get convictions, and terrors, and humiliations, as preliminaries to believing the gospel. They who would tell a sinner that the reason of his not finding peace is that he is not anxious enough, are enemies to the Cross of Christ. Christ asks no preparation of any kind whatsoever, legal or evangelical, outward or inward, in the coming sinner. And he that will not come *as he is* shall never be received at all. It is not 'exercised souls,' nor 'penitent believers,' nor ' well-humbled seekers,' nor ' earnest users of the means,' nor any of the better class of Adam's sons and daughters, but SINNERS that Christ welcomes. He came not to call the righteous, but *sinners* to repentance."

2. I FEAR THAT THE LORD WOULD NOT TAKE ME TILL I WOULD SPEND SOME TIME FIRST IN DOING GOOD WORKS, AND IN MAKING MYSELF BETTER PREPARED FOR RECEIVING CHRIST.

What good works could you do, with your heart hating God, that would please Him ? And it is a blessed fact that He is willing to take you as you are. You sing, " Just as I am " ; but you don't believe a word of it. Or you sing, " O take me as I am " ; and you really think you have to coax God to make Him willing to save you. Why, He just delights for Christ's sake to take you as you are.

One of the most successful of modern evangelists tells that he was once in a room with sixteen intelligent men, and he took the liberty of asking them two questions: *First*, what kind of people do you think God saves? They all said that He saves good people, praying people, righteous people. *Second*, on what ground does the Lord save people? They all said He saves good people because they were in earnest, or prayed, or were good. He told them that there was a verse (Rom. iv. 5) which answered both questions: " *To him that worketh not*,"—does not depend on his own work,—" *but believeth on Him that justifieth the ungodly, his faith is reckoned for righteousness.*" Mark, it is the ungodly that He saves—not the godly. And He saves not on the ground of their works, but because they believe on Jesus.

Perhaps, reader, you have been thinking very much the same as these men, and have been trying for days or weeks to make yourself good. Have you succeeded? No, you have not. You have been putting your works in the place of Christ, and trying to make a saviour of your works. Be not afraid. Good works will follow when you accept Christ, but it is not by works you get pardon and peace.

Can you swim? You remember that when first you tried to swim, you were afraid to trust yourself to the water. When the water came over your face, you feared you would be drowned, and you put your foot down to the bottom again and again to help to save yourself. And the next day it was the same; down went your foot when the water went over you. You could never swim as long as you put your foot to the ground. But you were told that if you trusted yourself to the water, and lay quietly on your back, it would float you and keep you up; that it floated great vessels of iron, and much more it would you. You ceased to struggle, and to put your foot to the ground, and you lay quietly on your back, and you found that the water did float you. So now you think you must do this thing and that thing to help to save yourself. If you would learn that Jesus is enough, and lean on Him, He would save you   These efforts to save yourself are really hindering you from being saved.

You have read about the Philippian jailor. Remember that he was a heathen, and, perhaps, had never heard about Christ before ; moreover, that he was a jailor, and a hard-hearted one, who had made the feet of the apostles fast in the stocks. But God suddenly awakened him, and he came to Paul, asking, " *What must I do to be saved?* "   Mark what Paul said to this ignorant heathen : " *Believe on the Lord Jesus Christ, and thou shalt be saved, and thy house* " (Acts xvi. 31) ; and he was saved that very night. Paul did not say to him, " I am very glad to see you anxious. It is God who has made you so. Now, give up your wicked companions and your wicked ways, and lead a new life. Come regularly to our meetings. *There* is a Bible for you—read it carefully. Pray to the Lord to give you pardon and to give you grace. Begin family worship also. And in God's own time He will lead you on to pardon and to Christ." Are there not hundreds of professing Christians over the world who would just have said something like this to the jailor ? Remember, the Lord saved this ignorant heathen on the spot, that very night. There is not one of us who believes that the Lord is as willing to pardon poor sinners as He really is.

3. I FEAR THAT MY SINS ARE TOO GREAT TO BE FORGIVEN.

Indeed they are very great—far greater than you imagine. But think of the sufferings of Christ, the God-Man, and believe what God says : " *The blood of Jesus Christ, His Son, cleanseth us from all sin.* " Think of the persons who have been saved : Rahab, the harlot of Jericho ; and Manasseh, the son of godly Hezekiah, who offered his children in sacrifice to Moloch, and made the streets of Jerusalem flow with the blood of God's people ; and the thief on the cross ; and Saul of Tarsus, the chief of sinners ; and John Newton, the African blasphemer ; and Brownlow North, once one of the most wicked men in Scotland, and afterwards for

twenty years one of the most useful men in Scotland ;
and Africaner, the African chief, whose hands were
dripping with the blood of his slaughtered enemies.

Have you ever considered 1 Cor. vi. 9, 10: "*Know
ye not that the unrighteous shall not inherit the kingdom
of God? Be not deceived: neither fornicators, nor
idolaters, nor adulterers, nor effeminate, nor abusers of
themselves with men; nor thieves, nor covetous, nor
drunkards, nor revilers, nor extortioners, shall inherit the
kingdom of God.*" What a black catalogue! But do
not stop there. Read the next verse: "*And such were
some of you; but ye are washed, but ye are sanctified, but
ye are justified in the name of the Lord Jesus, and by the
Spirit of our God.*" While that verse remains in the
Bible, never despair of your own salvation, or of the
salvation of any man alive. Think no longer of what
you are, but think of what Jesus is.

4. I FEAR THAT I HAVE COMMITTED THE UN-
PARDONABLE SIN.

Now the Bible does speak of "*the blasphemy against
the Holy Ghost, that shall not be forgiven unto men*"
(Matt. xii. 31). And it speaks of being "*guilty of an
eternal sin.*" Read Mark iii. 28, 29 (R.V.): "*But
whosoever shall blaspheme against the Holy Spirit hath
never forgiveness, but is guilty of an eternal sin; because
they said, He hath an unclean spirit.*" It seems to be
generally agreed that this sin consists in resisting the
Holy Ghost and the dictates of conscience, and continuing to refuse Christ, till God's Spirit leaves altogether.
It certainly does not mean that there is any sin so great
that Christ's blood cannot wash it out, for the first part
of this verse says: "*Verily I say unto you, All sins shall
be forgiven unto the sons of men, and blasphemies wherewith soever they shall blaspheme.*"

But if sinners continue to go on in sin, and to resist
the Holy Ghost, and to say, No, no, to the offers of
Christ, God's Spirit sometimes leaves them and ceases
to strive with them, and then there is no hope. They
are guilty of "an eternal sin."

But, reader, if you are yet anxious to be saved, and

are afraid that you have committed this sin, it is clear
that you have not committed it. The Spirit of God
has not given you up, if you are anxious to be saved.
All anxiety about the salvation of the soul comes from
Him. Be thankful that God's Spirit is still striving
with you. The devil very often tries to persuade anxious
inquirers, as he tried to persuade John Bunyan, that
they have committed this sin when they have not
committed it at all, in order to keep them away from
Christ. Be not ignorant of his *devices*. But beware.
You cannot tell the day or the hour when God may
give you a last trial, as He did Pharaoh, and as He did
King Saul, and others. And if you continue to resist,
and to say No, no, to the offers of Christ, and to go on
your way serving the devil, God may give you up, and
then there will be no hope. You will be guilty of this
eternal sin.

Brownlow North thought that this sin consisted in
"saying No to Christ once too often," and that he had
very nearly committed it himself. Take care, then.
This day may be the last day He may strive with you ;
and if you lie down to-night rejecting Christ, God may
say, "You are joined to your idols, I will let you alone."
Then you will lose your anxiety, and grow hardened
and careless, and probably mock at Christians and
laugh at religion. " *Woe unto you when God shall depart
from you.*" But thank God that He has not departed
yet. Be not afraid ; only believe in Christ.

5. I FEAR I AM NOT ELECTED.

This is another temptation of the devil, by which he
has tried to frighten away many earnest souls from
Christ. Now, the Bible does seem to teach clearly that
God does choose His people, otherwise they would
never choose Him. " *Ye have not chosen Me, but I have
chosen you.*" "*According as He hath chosen us in Him
before the foundation of the world, that we should be holy
and without blame before Him in love*" (Eph. i. 4).
Election is true ; but it is a doctrine with which you
have no more to do at present than you have with
making the laws of Japan. It belongs to God's people,

and to them alone. If you would come into my house, and take away some of my goods, you would be taking what did not belong to you. And just so, when you meddle with election, you meddle with what does not at present belong to you.

What you have to discover is, not that you are an elect saint, but that you are a lost sinner. When you have discovered this, and been enabled by divine grace to take Christ as your Saviour, and thus to make your calling sure, your election will be sure also. And there is no other way of making your election sure. To refuse, then, to believe in Christ till you first find out that you are elected, is as foolish as it would be to refuse to enter London, unless you could put your foot on the tower of St. Paul's at the first step. The elect are just those who believe in Christ.

Your rule of duty is not what is written in the Lamb's Book of Life, but what is written in God's Holy Word. The Bible tells you that the mercy of God is infinite, and that the merits of Christ are infinite, and that "*the Holy Ghost saith—To-day.*" Take God at His word, and trust your soul on the merits of Christ ; and you need not fear election. It is a false inference from the doctrine with which Satan is troubling you. If you neglect salvation because of a decree which you do not understand, the sin lies on your own head—you are lost because of your own unbelief. Why should you think that you are not one of the elect? No human being out of hell can ever know that he is not. You have as good a right to believe yourself one of the elect as any unconverted sinner that ever lived.

You are somewhat like a man travelling to a railway station, intending to go by train to a distant town. It occurs to him that perhaps there may not be a vacant seat, and he becomes afraid. But he meets one of the porters, who tells him that there are a great many carriages at the station, and that they will hold a wondrous number ; and his fear is somewhat lessened. A little farther on he meets the chief manager of the railway, whose word he cannot doubt. He informs him

that never once during the many years since the railway
was opened was man, woman, or child left behind for
want of room.   He shows him, moreover, the Act of
Parliament which expressly says that no one who comes
with a ticket shall be left behind.   Now his fear is
altogether gone.   Perhaps you can make your own
application of the story.   When God tells you that His
elect people are no scattered few, but a multitude that
no man can number, and that since the world began no
one ever came to Him through Christ, and was refused;
and when He shows you this in God's law,—"*Him that
cometh to Me, I will in no wise cast out*,"—surely you will
no longer be alarmed by this groundless fear—What if
I am not elected?

Do as John Bunyan did when assaulted by the same
temptation.   " Begin at the beginning of Genesis, and
read to the end of Revelation, and see if you can find
that there was ever one that trusted in the Lord and
was confounded."   Do as the old woman did, who
resolved that if there were only three elect people in the
world, she would strive to be one of them.   " *Be not
afraid, only believe.*"

6. I FEAR THAT THIS WAY OF SALVATION FOR
NOTHING, THROUGH THE DEATH OF CHRIST, IS TOO
GOOD TO BE TRUE.

" I cannot think," you say, "that we get all our sins
forgiven, in a moment, when we believe.   It is too
wholesale, and too easy."   " Too easy !"   Don't say that
again, dear reader !   If you only knew what Jesus
suffered, when He cried, "*My God, My God, why hast
Thou forsaken Me?*" you would never say again that it
was too easy.   Was it easy for Him ?   And if it had
been the least harder for us, not one of us could possibly
have been saved.

One evening, after a meeting, I was talking to an
anxious young man, who prided himself on his orthodoxy, and I was trying to show him the way to be
saved.   As he was on his road home, a companion of
his, who had remained behind and listened to our conversation, said to him, " *John, that is too easy, wholesale*

work." When John told this to me afterwards, I was somewhat vexed; but yet I was glad that the objector had caught hold of the two ideas I wished to teach John: *First,* That when he got Christ and His death, he got a full pardon of all his sins—"*wholesale work."* *Second,* That he got this by simply taking Christ and His death home to himself—"*God's easy way."*

Something like the following conversation took place: "John, you are a Presbyterian?" "Yes." "Tell me what is *justification?*" "Justification is an act of God's free grace, wherein He pardoneth all our sins "— "Now stop, John, for a moment. What is the difference between an act and a work?" "An act, sir, is done in a moment, a work takes time. "Tell me, John, if you threw a stone through this window, would that be an act or a work?" "An act, sir." "If you built this house, would that be an act or a work?" "A work, sir." "Well, is not justification an *act* of God's free grace, wherein He pardoneth all our sins? Does not that question say that God pardons all our sins in a moment?" "Yes, sir." "Is that not *wholesale work?*" "Yes." "Tell me, John, if you had been getting goods for five years from Mr. H., and were now due him ten pounds, and could not pay it, and if I paid it all for you, would not all your debt of ten pounds be blotted out in a moment?" "Yes, sir." "Is not a debt blotted out when it is paid?" "Yes." "Now, tell me again, what is *justification?*" "Justification is an act of God's free grace, wherein He pardoneth all our sins, and accepteth us as righteous in His sight, only for the righteousness of Christ imputed to us, and received by faith alone." "Now, John, mark that last word, '*alone*'—'*faith alone.*' What you need in order to get pardon is *faith alone*— just taking Christ and pardon along with Him. Do you know, John, why that word *alone* is put there?" "No, sir." "Well, Roman Catholics hold that we are justified by faith; but not by faith alone, but by faith and six other things along with it. They teach that all adult persons, before they receive forgiveness or renovation, must be prepared for receiving them by exercising what

they call the seven virtues,—faith, fear, hope, love,
penitence, a purpose to receive the sacrament, and a
purpose to live a better life. Thus they put faith only
as one of seven things, whereas the Bible tells us that
faith is the one thing needed to obtain justification—
faith alone.

"Of course, John, these other six things are all good,
and will all follow faith. Faith will not remain alone.
But the only thing needful in order to get pardon is
taking Christ as our Saviour—*faith alone.* That is the
reason why the words '*faith alone*' are used in your
Catechism. I do think, John, that there are a good
many persons who hold something like this Roman
Catholic doctrine in many of our Protestant churches.
Perhaps they may not hold that we are justified by faith
and these six other things; but they hold that we are
justified by faith and three or four of these other things.
But the Bible and your Catechism agree that we are
justified by *faith alone. This is God's easy, wholesale
plan.*"

7. I FEAR THAT I WOULD FALL AWAY EVEN IF I
WERE A CHRISTIAN, AND THAT I COULD NOT KEEP
MYSELF.

Indeed you could not keep yourself. But you would
not need to keep yourself. The 121st Psalm tells you
(in the Revised Version) six times over that the Lord is
your keeper, and that He will keep you. Read two
verses, 7, 8 : "*The Lord shall keep thee from all evil; He
shall keep thy soul. The Lord shall keep thy going out
and thy coming in from this time forth, and for evermore.*" Believe this because God says it, and trust Him.

Remember this, that when you accept Christ you get
a new power you never had up till that moment—a new
power which no unconverted man ever had. You get
Christ to dwell in you by His Spirit. You get not only
a new power, but a new indweller—a new inhabitant,
who dwells in you for the very purpose of enabling you
to live a holy and a useful life. "*Know ye not your own
selves, how that Jesus Christ is in you, except ye be
hypocrites?*" (2 Cor. xiii. 5).

11

"*Know ye not that ye are the temple of God, and the Spirit of God dwelleth in you?*" (1 Cor. iii. 16). What can Jesus not do, dwelling in you by His Spirit? He promises: "*My grace is sufficient for thee, for My strength is made perfect in weakness*" (2 Cor. xiii. 9). No wonder that John Bunyan wrote: "And oh! methought that every word was a mighty word unto me, as *My*, and *grace*, and *sufficient*, and *for thee*: they were then, and sometimes are still, far bigger than others be."

Yes, even though you were a Christian, you would fall away if you had to keep yourself. But Jesus promises that He "*will keep you from falling*" (Jude 24). He will do it. And is not His name called Jesus, "*for He shall save His people from their sins*"? (Matt. i. 21). A needle put on its point on the table would fall unless it were held up. But if you put your finger on each side, and hold it up, it will stand. Fear not, then, weak believer. God will hold thee up with His two great hands. "*Underneath thee are the everlasting arms.*"

8. THERE IS A FEAR THAT IS NOT GROUNDLESS. YOU FEAR THAT IF YOU GO ON LIVING IN SIN GOD WILL NOT SAVE YOU, AND TAKE YOU TO HEAVEN.

You are right here. It is quite true that you cannot keep yourself from your besetting sins. The best man in the world cannot do so. He must look up to Christ to keep him. Much less can you keep yourself. But God can keep you, and He says He will, if you trust Him. But perhaps there is one sin or more from which you do not want the Lord to keep you. You want to practise them, and yet get to heaven. It may be love of the world, or of a wicked companion, or drink, or lust, or lying, or revenge. It is that thing that you think so often about, that comes into your mind first when you awake in the morning. What is it? You can tell yourself. Perhaps, like Augustine in his early days, your heart's prayer is: "O Lord, convert me—O convert me; but not to-day, Lord, not to-day." Now, if this be the state of your mind, do not imagine, I beseech you, that you want to be saved. *The truth is, you do not want to be saved.* You want to live in sin, and yet escape hell. There is no such salvation with God. Jesus saves His people, not *in* their sins, but *from* their sins. "*Be ye not deceived; God is not mocked; for whatsoever a man soweth, that shall he also reap*" (Gal. vi. 7). "*Rejoice, O young man, in thy youth; and let thy heart cheer thee in the days of thy youth, and walk in the ways of thine heart, and in the sight of thine eyes: but know thou, that for all these things God will bring thee into judgment*" (Eccles. xi. 9).

If you are honestly willing for the Lord to keep you, or willing to be made willing, the Lord can and will keep you. He is waiting and wanting to keep you from your besetting sin. He does not ask you to give up any pleasures except sinful pleasures, and He will give you other pleasures a hundred-fold greater. Very often the battle is fought in one last ditch, about one besetting sin; and when you are willing that God should save you from that, the victory is won, and peace flows into the heart.

How poor and worthless such pleasures are, is seen when one is pardoned and accepted in Christ! There was a gay, thoughtless young man of the world, an ardent frequenter of theatres, ballrooms, card-tables, and the like, the late Mr. Stevenson Blackwood of the London Post Office. Sometimes he met in drawing-rooms with Miss Marsh, authoress of the *Life of Hedley Vicars*, and other works. At a party one evening he said to her, "Oh, I suppose, Miss Marsh, you are at your old work of wanting us to give up dancing and card-playing and all these things?" "No," she answered. "No, Mr. Blackwood, I want you to accept Christ, and everything in Him, and to do it just now; and when you are accepted in Christ, to judge of all these things you speak of from the position of one accepted." It was not long till he was enabled to accept Christ; and without any painful sacrifice whatever, all these things simply dropped off from him of their own accord, and he became a most useful evangelist and writer. My unconverted reader! if you are willing to let Christ take your place, and die in your stead, and come into your heart and make you holy, how little you will value these empty bubbles! And it is not likely that you will ever be willing to part with them till you do get something better. Oh that you were willing to take Miss Marsh's advice!—"No, Mr. Blackwood, I want you to accept Christ, and everything in Him, and to do it just now; and when you are accepted in Christ, to judge of all these things you speak of from the position of one accepted." The Lord enable you so to do; and this will be the most memorable day in all your history— the day when you were born again,

X

The Holy Ghost saith, To-day

A SABBATH school teacher one morning asked each member of his class three questions: *First*, Do you believe that God is able, for Christ's sake, to pardon all your sins? Each scholar answered, Yes. *Second*, Do you believe that God is willing, for Christ's sake, to pardon all your sins? Each answered, Yes. *Third*, Do you believe that God is able and willing, for Christ's sake, to pardon all your sins—*Now*? They all hesitated, and seemed not to be quite sure of this. And this is quite natural to the human heart.

Many people seem to think that they must wait till God the Spirit gets willing to lead them to Christ. They seem to think that God the Father is willing to accept Christ as their substitute now; and that Christ is willing to take their guilt now, and to come into their hearts and make them holy. But, they say, I must wait till God the Spirit gets willing to lead me to Christ; and thus practically they cast the blame of their damnation on the Holy Spirit. Are some of my readers not doing this at present? I know that I did it for many a day. This is horrible profanity. An American preacher has called it "*the Atheism of the Holy Ghost.*" And there is a good deal of this practical atheism. Let us look at a few particulars on this point.

1. *The Holy Ghost delights to lead you to Christ now.*

Does God the Spirit not love you as much as the Father or the Son? Is there a difference in the love of the Godhead? Reader! how long have you been anxious to be saved? A month. Who made you anxious during the past month? None other than God's Spirit. Does not this show that He is willing to save you? Here is a *fact* worth a hundred *feelings*, that God's Spirit has made you anxious, and is far more willing to save you than you are to be saved. Any anxiety you have has come from Him. Does He mean to tantalise you? What have you been doing during the past month? Resisting the Holy Ghost, who wishes to lead you to Christ.

Before Jesus left the earth, He told His disciples: "*It is expedient*"—better—"*for you that I go away; for if I go not away, the Comforter will not come unto you; but if I depart, I will send Him unto you.*" And what was the work that the Spirit was sent to do, which made it better that Jesus should leave? "*And when He (the Spirit) is come, He will convince the world of sin, and of righteousness, and of judgment; of sin, because they believe not on Me*" (John xvi. 7, 8). He will lead sinners to see their sins, and to see Jesus. This is the very work that He was sent to perform,—to show sinners the sin of not believing in Jesus. And sinners never will think this a sin till God's Spirit teaches them. Yet many seem to think that the Spirit is unwilling to do this work, and that they must wait till He gets willing. *Unwilling!* Why, on the day of Pentecost, when He came in power, He converted three thousand in one day, and other thousands soon after; and this is just a specimen of what He delights to do, and a fore-caste of what He will do when we come to believe in the Holy Ghost "One of His chief works is just to convince sinners of the sin of not believing in Jesus. Is He not, then, willing to lead them to Jesus?"

Read also Heb. iii. 7, 8: "*Wherefore, as the Holy Ghost saith, To-day, if ye will hear His voice, harden not your hearts.*" Here the Holy Ghost says that He wants you to accept Christ *to-day*. Three times over in the third and fourth chapters He repeats this "*to-day.*" The Holy Ghost does not want you to lie down to-

night rejecting Christ. If you do, you resist the Holy
Ghost. The whole Bible was written by the Holy
Ghost, and it is He who has recorded for us the
hundreds of sayings we have in the Bible concerning
the love of the Father and of the Son to sinners. But
is it not remarkable that He selects this verse from the
95th Psalm, and quotes it here three times over, as if
specially the mind of the Holy Ghost? "Wherefore,
as the Holy Ghost saith, *To-day, if ye will hear His
voice, harden not your hearts.*" The Holy Ghost is
willing to lead you to Christ now, and does not want
you to rise from your seat rejecting Christ. Ponder
and pray over this verse.

Again, before He finishes the Book of Revelation,
among the last verses in the Bible is Rev. xxii. 17:
"*And the Spirit and the Bride say, Come.*" The Spirit
says, Come to Jesus; and the Bride, the Church, says,
Come to Jesus; and let him that heareth — every
Christian—say, Come to Jesus. "*And whosoever will,
let him take the water of life freely.*" The Spirit ends
the Bible by telling us that He wishes to lead us to
Jesus.

Looking back to the Old Testament, we have the
same lesson taught us in Ezek. xxxvii. 1–10. God
told Ezekiel to preach to the dry bones, and to say to
them, "Hear the word of the Lord." Then He told
him to pray to the Spirit: "*Come from the four winds,
O breath, and breathe upon these slain, that they may
live.*" "And when he did so, they lived, and stood up
upon their feet, an exceeding great army." Is not this
to teach us that if we preach and pray for the Spirit,
God will bless His own means and convert sinners?
How very sinful it is for us not to expect God to bless
His own means in grace as certainly as we do in
nature! When we sow corn or wheat, we do expect
God to send the showers and the sunshine, and we
expect to reap. How wicked to think that He will
not as certainly send His Spirit, and bless His own
means of grace!

Even God's own word is twisted so as to insinuate

the lie that God's Spirit is not willing to convert sinners. Have we not heard scores of times, in prayer especially, " Paul *may* plant, and Apollos *may* water, but God alone can give the increase "? And the meaning evidently designed to be conveyed is, You may preach as much as you like, but God alone can give the increase, and He is not likely to give it. Now Paul's words are (1 Cor. iii. 6, 7): "*I planted, Apollos watered; but God gave the increase.*" Yes, God gave the increase, and was delighted to give the increase. "*So then, neither is he that planteth anything, neither he that watereth; but God that giveth the increase.*" " I believe," writes Charles Spurgeon, "that where Paul plants and Apollos waters, God gives the increase, and I have no patience with those who throw the blame on God when it belongs to themselves." What horrid unbelief there is as to the unwillingness of the Holy Ghost to convert sinners! There does seem to be more hatred to the Holy Spirit in the wicked heart of man than to the other persons of the Godhead. Oh that we saw that we live in the dispensation of the Spirit! Oh that we expected Him to give not mere *drops*, but *floods* of blessing! This would honour the Holy Spirit, and He would honour us.

Whatever you do, then, do not cast the blame of your damnation on God's Spirit. To think that God the Father is willing now to save sinners through Christ, and that Christ is willing now to receive sinners, but that the Holy Ghost is not willing to lead them to Christ, and that sinners must wait until He becomes willing, *is a slander on the Holy Ghost.*

2. *You are responsible, then, for accepting Christ now.*

When the Jews asked Jesus what they should do that they might work the works of God, He answered: "*This is the work of God, that ye believe on Him whom He hath sent.*" When the jailor of Philippi, who knew little of the Bible or of Christ, asked Paul, "*What must I do to be saved?*" Paul answered, "*Believe on the Lord Jesus Christ, and thou shalt be saved, and thy house.*" As regards the time, Paul says, "*Behold, now is the accepted*

time; behold, now is the day of salvation" (2 Cor. vi. 2)
You are bound to accept Christ now, for the Holy Ghost
is here delighted to enable you.   And He says, " *To-day,
if ye will hear His voice, harden not your hearts.*"

There are some persons who seem to think that a
sinner is not responsible for this ; and that he should
not be commanded to believe in Christ, or to repent of
his sins, or to turn to the Lord, or to do other spiritual
duties.   They say that he cannot do these things without
God, and that, therefore, he should not be asked to do
them, but just to do outward acts of religious duty which
he is able to do.   Such persons say to an unconverted
man, " Give up bad company ; go to God's house ; wait
on the Lord : wait on, and some time or other the Lord
will convert you."   Now such things are right and
proper enough in their own place ; but many have
waited on and on in this way till they were in hell.
Besides, there is not a word about Christ in all this.
No, a thousand times no ; this is not the exact thing
that we are commanded to say to an unconverted man.
What we are to say is something like this : " You are a
sinner, and on the road to hell.   Christ died for sinners,
even the chief.   He is here this moment offering to take
all your sins, and to come into your heart, and make
you holy.   You are bound this moment to accept His
offer, and to rest on His atonement ; and the Spirit of
the Lord is here to enable you."   Those who wait and
wait and wait are willing to give God all the glory of
their salvation ; but they are not willing to take to themselves all the blame of their damnation.   They do not
seem to see the sin and shame of rejecting Christ.

There is no uninspired book on this subject at all to
be compared with Andrew Fuller's *Gospel Worthy of all
Acceptation.*   Fuller in early life held these notions himself.   We will quote some sentences from his noble
book : " It is the duty of ministers not only to exhort
their carnal hearers to believe in Jesus Christ for the
salvation of their souls ; but it is at our peril to exhort
them to anything short of it, or which does not involve
or imply it.   We have sunk into such a compromising

way of dealing with the unconverted, as to have well-nigh lost sight of the spirit of the primitive preachers; and hence it is that sinners of every description can sit so quietly as they do in our places of worship. Christ and His apostles without any hesitation called on sinners to repent, and believe the gospel; but we, considering them as poor, impotent, and depraved creatures, have been disposed to drop this part of the Christian ministry. Considering such things as beyond the power of their hearers, they seem to have contented themselves with pressing on them the things they could perform, still continuing enemies of Christ, such as behaving decently in society, reading the Scriptures, and attending the means of grace. Thus it is that hearers of this description sit at ease in our congregations. But as this implies no guilt on their part, they sit unconcerned, conceiving that all that is required of them is to be in the way, and wait the Lord's time.

"But is this the religion of the Scriptures? Where does it appear that the prophets or apostles treated that kind of inability, which is merely the effect of reigning aversion, as affording any excuse? And where have they descended in their exhortations to things which might be done, and the parties still continue enemies to God? Instead of leaving out everything of a spiritual nature, because their hearers could not find it in their hearts to comply with it, it may be safely affirmed that they exhorted to nothing else, treating such inability not only as of no account with regard to the lessening of obligation, but as rendering the subjects of it worthy of the severest rebuke." So writes Andrew Fuller.

Certainly, all the men whom God has used to revive His work in the world have preached the duty of accepting Christ NOW, and the great sin of unbelief. Luther and Calvin did this, and Baxter, and Bunyan, and Wesley, and Whitfield, and Spurgeon. So also did Robert M'Cheyne and William Burns. The last-named, William Burns, tells us that he never came up to this point of demanding sinners on the spot to accept Christ till that day in Kilsyth, in 1839, which was the

commencement of the great awakening. On that day
he was led up by God to command them to accept
Christ now ; and hundreds did so, and from that time
he *commanded* sinners in God's name at once to accept
Jesus.

3. *Your inability is no excuse for not accepting Christ
now.*

Without God's Spirit you cannot, but with Him you
can. Some persons think that Christ was a very inconsistent preacher. They say at one time He commanded
His hearers, " *Come unto Me, and I will give you rest.*"
At another time He laid this to their charge, " *Ye will
not come to Me, that ye might have life.*" At another
time He warned them, "*He that believeth not shall be
damned.*" And yet at another time He told them, " *No
man can come to Me, except the Father which hath sent
Me draw him*" (John vi. 44). "What an inconsistent
preacher !" they say. Yet the preacher was Jesus.
There is no inconsistency. The reason they *could not*
come was because they had *no will* to come. Ye *cannot
come* and *ye will not come* explain each other.

I do not know any clearer illustrations on this subject
than the following, which I have used before :—

In Genesis (xxxvii. 4) we are told that "Joseph's
brethren hated him, and *could not* speak peaceably unto
him." Why could they not speak peaceably unto him?
Simply because they hated him so much, and in this
consisted the greatness of their sin. Peter tells us of
men " *having eyes full of adultery, and that cannot cease
from sin* " (2 Pet. ii. 14). Why *cannot* they cease from
sin ? Because their eyes were full of adultery. And in
this consisted the greatness of their sin. It was a fact
that they *could not* cease from sin; yet this did not
excuse them.

Did ever a drunkard plead as an excuse before a
magistrate, that he had such a love for drink that he
could not pass a public-house without going in and
getting drunk ? Did ever a murderer plead at the bar
of justice, that he hated his victim so much that he
could not go near him without killing him ? Would not

this show *malice prepense*, and make his crime the greater? And the only reason why you *cannot come* to Jesus is because you love sin so much, and hate the Lord so much. *" They hated Me without a cause"* (John xv. 25). *" The carnal mind is enmity against God; for it is not subject to the law of God, neither indeed can be"* (Rom. viii. 7). The reason why you cannot come to Christ is not because you have not hands, or feet, or intellect, or affections, but because you have not a *will* to come. *" Ye will not come to Me."* Your inability is *moral*, not *natural*; and therefore it is inexcusable

Man is a free agent; he does what he pleases. We are all conscious of this, and feel that we are responsible for our acts. But until we are converted we have no desire to will good, and we will only evil. This arises from the depravity of our hearts, resulting from our fall in Adam. Put a stone on your hand. Now take away your hand, and the stone falls to the ground. Why does it fall, and not go upward? Because it is its nature. So with our wills before conversion. We will only evil because our nature is only evil, and that continually. But when our hearts are changed, we will as naturally to do good, while still liable to evil. We are free agents: we do what we like. The only reason why you cannot believe in Christ is because you hate Him, and that without a cause. And in this consists the greatness of your sin.

But, awakened sinner! while you have no excuse for being unable to come to Christ, God has provided a remedy for this. He has sent His Holy Spirit, who is just beside you this moment, delighted to lead you to Christ. God the Father is here, delighted to accept Christ as your substitute, and He says, *Now.* Oh, reader! let your heart respond, *"Now*, Lord, I accept Thy Son as my Saviour." God the Son is here, delighted to take your sins, and to come into your heart, and He says, *Now.* Let your heart answer, *" Now*, Lord Jesus, I take Thee as my Saviour, and I do depend on Thee." God the Holy Ghost is here,

delighted to lead you to Christ, and He says, *Now.*
Let the answer of your heart be, "*Now*, Holy Spirit,
I count upon Thee to enable me, and I will depend
upon Jesus—I do depend upon Jesus."

4. *You are not to wait at the pool, but to accept Christ now.*
Dr. Nettleton, the great American evangelist, who
was believed to have been the means of converting tens
of thousands, and who was a very decided Calvinist,
often said that he was sorely tried by the *injudicious
directions* which some professors of religion were in the
habit of giving to awakened sinners. He said he
apprehended more evil from this source than from all
the opposition of the avowed enemies of religion.
Wherever he preached a series of sermons to the unconverted, he usually occupied one meeting in considering these *injudicious directions.* A sketch of the address
was found among his notes, from which we will give
a few sentences. "*Wait at the pool*, it is said. You
must not be discouraged, for we read of one who
waited thirty-eight years. Now we may accommodate
passages of Scripture for the purpose of illustrating
acknowledged truth; but we must not trace analogies
too far. This use of the passage contradicts many
plain declarations of the Bible—particularly all those
which enjoin the duty of immediate repentance. Suppose a person should address sinners in this manner:
'Behold, now is the acceptable time! behold, now is the
day of salvation!' but *wait at the pool.* 'Choose ye
this day whom ye will serve'; but *wait at the pool.*
'God now commandeth all men everywhere to repent';
but *wait at the pool.* The effect of this direction is to
make the impression on the sinner's mind that he is not
under obligation to obey God immediately.

" The sinner is told that he must not be discouraged,
for the impotent man waited thirty-eight years. This,
however, is not said. It is said that he had an infirmity
thirty-eight years; but it is not said that he waited
a day. Be this, however, as it may, he was not healed
by the pool after all, nor is there any evidence that he
would have been if he had waited all his life."

5. *You are not to be patient and wait God's time, but to accept Christ now.*

Nettleton says: "*Be patient, and wait God's time!* Is the sinner to understand that he is too anxious for the salvation of his soul, and that he ought to wait patiently in his sins till God shall see fit to change his heart? *Patient in his sins!* Rather let him be more and more impatient with himself, and with his deplorable condition. Let him tremble in view of a judgment to come, and weep and howl for the miseries that are coming upon him.

"What is meant when the sinner is directed to wait God's time? Is it meant that God is not now ready to receive the sinner? Is it meant that the sinner is willing to do his part, and that he must wait for God to do His? If so, why not speak plainly, and tell him this? To direct him to wait God's time is directly calculated to release him from his sense of obligation to repent to-day, and to counteract the operations of the Divine Spirit. It is to plead the sinner's cause against God.

"But is it not hard to distress the sinner by pressing him with his obligations? It is painful, but it is necessary. It is painful to the surgeon to probe to the bottom a dangerous wound; but it must be done, or the patient will die. If, through false pity, we console the sinner under these circumstances, there is reason to fear that his blood will be required at our hands. If we direct the sinner to wait, we direct him to run the awful hazard of losing his soul." So wrote Nettleton.

Of course, when we ask God to deliver us out of our difficulties, or to raise up our friends to health, if it be His will, we must wait His time. But this is altogether different from waiting God's time to convert us. God's time to convert us is *Now*.

6. *You are not merely to pray for God's Spirit to enable you to accept Christ, you are bound to accept Christ now.*

It is quite right to pray for God's Spirit to enable you to accept Christ. But you should believe that He is here, delighted to enable you, and you should accept

Christ now. You must not put prayer for the Spirit
in the room of accepting Christ. To do the one duty
does not release you from doing the other also.

The man with the withered hand was ordered to
stretch it forth. He might have said, " Lord, I cannot.
Why bid me stretch out my hand ? " But he believed
that the Lord who gave the command would give the
power; and so he made the attempt, and the power
was given.

God commands you to believe on His Son; you
cannot without God's Spirit. But look away to Jesus,
and believe that the Spirit of God will enable you; and
He will. You have not to feel the Spirit. No one ever
felt the Spirit enabling him to come. But, believing
that He will enable you, come to Christ. You must
come to Christ. True, the Spirit must work, but you
must come. You must make up your mind to take
Jesus. You cannot be saved without this. The Spirit
of God enables you to believe, but He does not believe
for you. If you put off, you make up your mind to
put off, and that is just rejecting Christ. You must
believe in the Lord Jesus; not *try* to believe, but
believe. Not *pray* to believe, but believe. It is right
to pray, but you should pray believingly, and believing
prayer is just the same as believing: it is just, " Lord
Jesus, I take Thee."

Andrew Fuller says on this point: " Repentance
toward God, and faith toward our Lord Jesus Christ,
are allowed to be duties, but not *immediate* duties. The
sinner is considered as unable to comply with them,
and therefore they are not urged upon him; but instead
of them he is directed to pray for the Holy Spirit to
enable him to repent and believe. This, it seems, he
can do, notwithstanding the aversion of his heart from
everything of the kind! But if any man be required
to pray for the Holy Spirit, it must be either sincerely
and in the name of Jesus, or insincerely and in some
other way. The latter, I suppose, will be allowed to be
an abomination in the sight of God. He cannot, therefore, be required to do this. And as to the former, it

is just as difficult and as opposite to the carnal heart as repentance and faith themselves. Indeed, it amounts to the same thing: *for a sincere desire after a spiritual blessing, presented in the name of Jesus, is none other than the prayer of faith."*

7. *Resist, then, the Spirit no longer, but accept Christ now.*

This is the great sin—to refuse Christ. Never think of it or speak of it as a *misfortune.* It is the damning sin. "*Ye will not come to Me, that ye might have life."* All your other sins would be forgiven if you came to Jesus with them, and laid them on Him. You do not believe that Jesus can be so kind and good as to atone for your sins, and give you pardon for nothing. You say, "*I cannot believe,"* which just means, "I cannot believe Christ. I think that He tells lies. It is too good news to be true." And so you "*make God a liar, because you do not believe the record that God gave of His Son"* (1 John v. 10). Is it any wonder that the Lord is angry with you? How do you like to be called a liar yourself, and to be told, I cannot believe you? Oh, reader! will the very goodness of God prevent you being saved? There is nothing on God's side hindering you being pardoned *now.* Why do you put off? More people have gone to hell from this putting off, than from any other reason. "Time enough," whispers the devil; "sure you are not going to die to-night!" and you put off and put off till to-morrow, and to-morrow, and to-morrow. "Go thy way for this time; when I have a convenient season, I will call for thee," said Felix. But the convenient season never came. It is always coming, but it never comes.

James D. was a highly respectable young farmer, sober, moral, and of excellent character. He and his brother had cut down a large tree, and had cut it again into pieces, so as to take it away on a cart. One day he was waiting with his cart for some one to come and help; and, losing patience, he put his back under the tree and tried to carry it to the cart himself. But it was too heavy for him. His spine was injured. For months he lay upon his back. Consumption set in, and not long ago he died. His own minister was in America for a time during his illness, and I was asked to see him. From the first he seemed to see clearly that he was a sinner, deserving hell; and as death stared him in the face, he was downrightly in earnest.

Of course I spoke to him about Jesus dying for the ungodly, and offering to carry his sins, and to come into his heart and make him holy. I dwelt much on Matt. xi. 28: "Come unto Me, all ye that labour and are heavy laden, and I will give you rest"; and I told him that the very moment he came to Jesus, and made his sins over to Him, Jesus took them, and they were off him and on Jesus. He could not see it. I left some little books for him to read.

When I went back, he was as much in the dark as before. "Are you really in earnest?" I asked. "I am." "What have you been doing to get peace? Struggling?" "Yes." "Resolving?" "Yes." "Reading books?" "Yes." "Praying?" "Yes." "Trying to feel sorrow for sin?" "Yes." "Trying to feel love to God?" "Yes." "Looking into your own heart to see if you have got faith?" "Yes." "So I thought, James. You have been doing everything except the one thing that saves—namely, believing that Jesus, who died for the ungodly, is here, willing to take your burden now, and to carry it for you—everything but saying, Yes, Lord Jesus, I take Thy offer. Here are my sins, I make them over to Thee; I come to Thee with them, and Thou dost give me rest." "I cannot understand it," he said.

When I went back, he was as blind as ever, but even more in earnest. I told him of a tract I had been reading, called "The Engaged Ring." "A widow lady was talking to a young girl, who, like you, was anxious to be saved; and, like you, was thinking that Jesus was not willing to save her. She said to the young girl, 'Do you see that ring?' 'Yes.' 'Well, let me tell you its history. My late husband loved me when I was a young girl, and asked me to marry him. But I did not care for him, and did not want to be engaged

12

so soon. I wished to be free to talk to other young men. I did not refuse him. I neither said yes nor no, but just put him off. He might have left me, but he did not. He came back again and asked me to marry him; and again I put him off, saying neither yes nor no. He came back again; and now I saw that he really loved me, and I began to have some love to him, and when he asked me, I said yes, and he put that ring on my finger. Now tell me,' said the widow to the young girl, 'had I to wait for him, or had he to wait for me?' 'Of course he had to wait for you,' said the young girl. 'He wanted you to say yes. You had not to wait for him at all.' 'Well, it is just so with you. Jesus is waiting for you, wanting you to say yes to Him, and the moment you honestly say yes, all your sins become His, and all His riches become yours. It would just delight the Lord to take your sins this moment, and save you.'" I told James all this at greater length, but he could not see it.

The next time I went back, he was as dark as ever. "Tell me, James," I said, "is there anything in your life—are you doing anything that would prevent God from giving you peace?" "Not that I am aware of," he said. "What, then, is hindering you from being saved and getting peace?" I asked. "I do not know," he replied. "Well, I will tell you. You will not come down low enough and take salvation on God's terms. He offers it as a gift—for nothing. He will not sell it. He gives it. 'Eternal life is the *gift* of God through Jesus Christ our Lord.' Now you do not *work* for a gift, or *buy* a gift. You just *take* it. But you are too proud to take salvation for nothing. You are not willing to be a beggar, entirely depending upon the Lord. And so you want to work for it, and struggle for it, and pay something for it, and prepare yourself for it. You will never be saved *till* you *come down*, and are willing just to take it for nothing, and be a poor beggar depending on the Lord. It is pride —the pride of your wicked nature—that is hindering you from being saved, though you do not think so.

You are putting your struggles and efforts and prayers in the place of Christ. If you were willing to let the Lord carry your sins this moment, and tell Him so, this moment He would take them away. Oh that you were willing to take salvation *as a gift*!" He could not see it, and I left him.

Soon after this his own minister came home, and I did not like to go back. But I was greatly interested in James, because he was so like myself when I was anxious to be saved. One Sabbath evening I heard that he was dying, and that if I wished to see him alive, I must go over soon. I went on Monday about four o'clock, and he died the same evening about seven. His brother told me that about a week before he had heard him praying, and saying, "I thank Thee, Lord Jesus, that I can trust Thee now." On the Sabbath before he died—the day before I saw him—he sent for a Christian woman, a neighbour who had been sent home from the Belfast Hospital as incurable. He asked her to come and see him if she were at all able. She managed to do so with the help of her husband. As soon as she was seated, he asked, "Tell me, are you resting upon Christ?" "I am," she said. "Are you, James?" "I am," he replied. "I see all about Jesus plainly now."

When I went on Monday, he was evidently dying, and I did not like to talk much to him. "Well, James," I said, "do you see more clearly about Jesus now?" "Yes, I see it all clearly." "Are you trusting Christ?" "Yes, I am." "Is it long since?" "Two or three weeks ago." And he died. And we laid him in the grave in the hope of a glorious resurrection to eternal life. Oh, reader! tell me *are you resting upon Christ?* "Yes or no?" Or are you struggling, and trying, and endeavouring, and putting your own exertions in the place of the finished work of Jesus? Do what Jesus bids you: "*Come unto Me, all ye that labour and are heavy laden, and I will give you rest.*"

XI

𝔚𝔥𝔞𝔱 𝔴𝔢 𝔤𝔢𝔱 𝔴𝔥𝔢𝔫 𝔴𝔢 𝔱𝔞𝔨𝔢 𝔠𝔥𝔯𝔦𝔰𝔱

I WANT you to know what you get when you take
Christ. I do not mean what you get a month
after, or a year after, or ten years after; but what you
get, quick as a flash of lightning, in the moment when,
by God's Spirit, you take Jesus to be your Saviour. I
will mention briefly *twelve* things that you get—get in
a second, get to commence life with, get to carry you
on your journey to heaven. And there are many more
than twelve. I heard an excellent minister say not
long since, that the reason why Christians do not live
more holy and useful lives is because they do not know
the capital they have got to trade on.

1. *You get a full pardon of all your sins.* Read Acts
xiii. 38, 39: "*Be it known unto you, therefore, men and
brethren, that through this Man is preached unto you the
forgiveness of sins; and by Him all that believe are
justified from all things.*" Please think over and pray
over this verse. There are few lovelier ones in the
Bible. "*By Him*"—by Christ—"*all that believe*"—not
some, but *all* that believe—"*are justified*"—not *will be*
or *can be*, but "*are justified*"—"*from all things.*" This
means that all your sins are pardoned the moment you
believe. And it means more.

Read also John iii. 18: "*He that believeth on
Him is not condemned.*" That is, he is pardoned.
Who is pardoned? He that believeth on Christ.
Does Christ say here that he *will be* pardoned? No,
but that he *is* pardoned. When? The moment that

he believes. How foolish, then, it is for any one to say he believes in Christ, but is not sure whether he is pardoned or not! He is just saying he does not know whether Christ's word is true or not.

Read also Mark xi. 28: "*Come unto Me, all ye that labour and are heavy laden, and I will give you rest.*" Christ here says that when you come to Him with the burden of your sins, and lay it on Him, He takes it, and gives you rest. "*I will give you rest.*" Does Christ ever break His word?

If you do honestly trust Christ, though it may be feebly, God says that your sins are forgiven; and you should believe this simply because God says it. No one ever saw God blotting his sins out of His book. No thrill passes through you at the moment when God blots out your sins. Nothing of the kind. You simply believe that they are blotted out, because God says that at the moment when you trust Christ He does blot them out. You take His word for it. And when you believe on His bare word that they are blotted out, this makes you thankful, and joyful, and happy. "Luther, do you *feel* that your sins are forgiven?" some one asked the Reformer. "No; but *I am sure* they are. Get thee behind me, Satan." If you are a real believer in Christ, however feeble, your sins are forgiven, whether you know it or not. But you will never love the Lord much, or serve Him well, till you do know it. That is a certainty.

And what a pardon it is that you get—a *full* pardon, a *free* pardon, and an *everlasting* pardon! God says that your "*sins are cast behind His back,*" where He does not see them (Isa. xxxviii. 17). He says: "*As far as the east is from the west, so far hath He removed our transgressions from us*" (Ps. ciii. 12). How far away from us is the great nebula of Orion? So far hath He removed our transgressions from us. He says He has "*cast all their sins into the depths of the sea.*" Not into a *river*, but into the *sea*. Not into the *shallows*, but into the *depths* of the sea. Again He says: "*Their sins and their iniquities will I remember no more*" (Heb.

x. 17). They are not merely *forgiven*, but *forgotten.*
Men say, " I forgive, but I cannot forget." God
says that when you believe, *He remembers your sins
no more.* Not one of the sins of the Old Testament
saints is mentioned in the New. God says that when
you believe, you are " whiter than snow " (Ps. li. 7).
You are " clean every whit " (John xiii. 10, and xv. 3).

I have heard ministers preach that at the moment
we believe, all our sins—past, present, and to come—are
blotted out. Somehow this does not look like Scripture.
It always reminds me of Tetzel's speech when selling
indulgences—when he told the people that his *indulgences*
would blot out even the sins that they intended to
commit. Dr. Charles Hodge says it is more scriptural
to say that all our past sins are blotted out in the
moment of our justification, and that our future ones
will not be imputed. Reader! think for a little what a
blessing this is, and praise God for it! The world says
Blessed is the man who is rich, who is powerful, whose
family is prospering in the world. But God says:
" *Blessed is the man whose transgression is forgiven, and
whose sin is covered; blessed is the man unto whom the
Lord imputeth not iniquity, and in whose spirit there is
no guile* " (Ps. xxxii. 1, 2).

2. You not only get pardon; *you are brought
into God's favour, and are accepted as righteous in
His sight.* God's anger is turned away, and you are
" *accepted in the Beloved* " (Eph. i. 6). Yes,—" *accepted
in the Beloved.*" It is one thing to be pardoned, and
another and better thing still, to be brought into
God's favour. An emperor of Russia condemned one
of his nobles to death. The other nobles interceded
for him. " For your sakes," said the emperor, " I
will spare his life, but he shall never come into my
favour." But God never pardons any one without also
bringing him into His favour. " *O Lord, I will praise
Thee: though Thou wast angry with me, Thine anger
is turned away, and Thou comfortedst me. Behold,
God is my salvation; I will trust, and not be afraid*"
(Isa. xii. 1, 2).

The moment that we believe in Christ, all our sins are made over to Him, and all His "obedience unto death" is made over to us, and we are "*made the righteousness of God in Him*" (2 Cor. v. 21). God reckons us as having lived Christ's righteous life, and died Christ's atoning death; and thus we commence our Christian life with a perfect righteousness. Thus we get from under the curse: "*Cursed is every one that continueth not in all things which are written in the book of the law to do them.*" Thus God can reckon us not only free from guilt, but righteous; and can pronounce us "*righteous in His sight, only for the righteousness of Christ imputed to us, and received by faith alone.*"

This is the discovery that Alexander Anderson, Free Church minister of Aberdeen, made, as recorded in his *Life*, written by Rev. Norman Walker. "I was pardoned; I felt sin was taken 'out of the way'; but I had not yet apprehended the glorious *righteousness* which God has to *give away*, and clothed in which we appear to Him '*altogether lovely.*' The Father had embraced me; but I was not yet at home, nor did I feel at home. This, however, was the subject of a distinct revelation, which the Lord was pleased to vouchsafe to me, at Banff. It came to me at once, and truly I had good matter for a song. . . . When God justifies, He does so, not with His essential righteousness, but with a righteousness *that is communicable.* To think and know that there is an unseen, yet real something, called a perfect righteousness, which, as a robe, hides our unrighteousness when it is drawn over it! And oh, what a mercy actually to know, and to be able to do what is needful to be done with it,—namely, to pull it over the deformity! The Lord has a righteousness! The Lord has a righteousness! The greatest blessing we could receive is the gift of a perfect righteousness."

This is also what John Bunyan saw. "One day. as I was passing into the field, fearing lest yet all was not right, suddenly this sentence fell upon my soul—

Thy righteousness is in heaven. And, methought, withal I saw with the eyes of my soul, Jesus Christ at God's right hand; there, I say, was my righteousness; so that, wherever I was, or whatever I was doing, God could not say of me, 'He wants My righteousness,' for that was just before Him. I also saw, moreover, that it was not my good frame of heart that made my right-eousness better, nor yet my bad frame that made my righteousness worse; for my righteousness was Jesus Christ Himself, 'the same yesterday, and to-day, and for ever.' Now did my chains fall off my legs indeed, I was loosened from my afflictions and my irons; my temptations also fled away; so that from that time those dreadful scriptures of God left off to trouble me. Now went I also home, rejoicing for the grace and love of God. Now Christ was all; all my righteousness, all my sanctification, and all my redemption" (1 Cor. i. 30).

This seems to be quite scriptural; and no wonder that the poet wrote, when he saw it:

> " Had I an angel's holiness,
> I'd tear aside that wondrous dress
> And wrap me up in Christ."

These two blessings—*pardon and acceptance as righteous*—constitute what is called, in the New Testament, *justification.* This is a word very often used in Romans and Galatians. *To justify* is a law term, and signifies to pronounce righteous, or just. When a judge pronounces a prisoner, who has been tried, not guilty of the charge, he justifies him. The word does not mean, anywhere in the New Testament, to *make holy*, in a moral sense, but always to *pronounce righteous*, or just, in a legal sense. Take, for instance, Rom. viii. 33, 34: "*It is God that justifieth; who is he that condemneth?*" Here it is evident that to *justify* is the opposite of to *condemn*. In Isa. v. 23, woe is pronounced on those "*who justify the wicked for reward.*" Now, it never could be sinful to make the wicked holy. There is scarcely a word in the Bible, the meaning of which is less open to doubt. It never means, **to *make*** a person holy in a moral sense, but always, as a judge, to *pronounce* a person righteous or just. In this sense it is used throughout the New Testament: "*Knowing that a man is not justified by the works of the law, but by the faith of Jesus Christ, even we have believed in Jesus Christ, that we might be justified by the faith of Christ, and not by the works of the law ; for by the works of the law shall no flesh be justified*" (Gal. ii. 16).

It is of great importance to see the exact meaning of the word, *to justify*, and to see the exact grounds on which God can pronounce a wicked man justified or righteous. When Luther saw this, his heart rejoiced. "I felt immediately," he wrote, "as if I was wholly born anew, and had found an open door into Paradise itself." And when he made it clear to others by his preaching and writings, tens of thousands leaped for joy. What Luther saw on the subject is nowhere more clearly defined than in the Larger Catechism of the Westminster Assembly : "Justification is an act of God's free grace unto sinners, in which He pardoneth all their sins, accepteth and accounteth their persons righteous in His sight ; not for anything wrought in them, or done by them, but only for the perfect obedience and full satisfaction of Christ, by God imputed to them, and received by faith alone."

The word *imputed* is perhaps not easily understood. I remember once getting a clearer view of its meaning, from Philemon, 18th verse, where Paul writes to Philemon about Onesimus : "*If he hath wronged thee, or oweth thee aught, put that to mine account.*" It is the very same word that is translated in Rom. v. 13, *impute*, that is translated here—*put that to mine account.* Impute it to me, just means, *put it to mine account.* The moment that we believe, God puts to Christ's account the guilt of all our sins, and He puts to our account Christ's whole obedience unto death—all His righteous life and atoning death, not a part of His work, but His whole work, and we are *pronounced righteous* (justified), "*not having our own righteousness, which is of the law, but that which is through the faith of Christ, the righteousness which is of God by faith*" (Phil. iii. 9).

God, as our judge, deals with us, on account of our

sins, once for all in the moment that we believe. Our sins are no more remembered against us. It is quite true that, after we are justified, we need our daily and hourly sins forgiven. We get into a new relationship to God, and become His children, and have Him as our Father; and we need, *as children*, to come to Him, *as our Father*, and confess our daily and hourly sins. This was what Christ meant when He said to Peter, "*He that is bathed needeth not save to wash his feet, but is clean every whit*" (John xiii. 10, R.V.). You have got the great bath; you are justified and regenerated. You don't need to get these again. You may ask for a sense of these. But you cannot be justified and regenerated twice. You do not need to get your head and hands and whole body into the bath again. But you do need to get your feet washed. You go into the world and contract new guilt, and you need to come to God as your kind Father, and confess your daily and hourly sins; and *as a Father*, He has promised, for Christ's sake, to forgive you. "*If we confess our sins, He is faithful and just to forgive us our sins, and to cleanse us from all unrighteousness*" (1 John i. 9).

Let us, then, believers, keep short accounts with God; and as soon as we sin, confess our sins, one by one, to our heavenly Father, and ask Him to forgive us for the sake of Jesus. And let us believe His word—that He does forgive us. Mr. Hewitson, Free Church minister of Dirleton, in Scotland, said: "I can testify to the glory of God's grace, that no night do I confess my sin without absolute confidence that it is forgiven. I know it to be so. If any one ask me how I know it, I just answer, '*If we confess our sins, He is faithful and just to forgive us our sins, and to cleanse us from all unrighteousness.*' I believe in God's truthfulness, that is all." There are many real Christians who have no peace or assurance, simply because they do not confess their daily and hourly sins to God.

But even when we are unconscious of our sins, as we often are, and cannot, therefore, confess them individually, "*the blood of Jesus Christ, His Son, cleanseth us from all sin.*" Miss Frances Ridley Havergal thought that she got a great blessing from seeing this taught in 1 John i. 7, by the word *cleanseth* (present tense)—not *cleansed*, but *cleanseth.* She knew very well that she was a child of God, and that God, as a judge, had forgiven her sins. But she knew also that, as a child, she needed daily and hourly forgiveness ; and here she was taught that the blood of Christ *cleanseth* her, day by day—*cleanseth* her, hour by hour—keeps *dropping, dropping* on her sins, and keeps *cleansing* her. This text was to her, therefore, unspeakably precious, and it is engraved on her tomb at Astley : "*The blood of Jesus Christ, His Son, cleanseth us from all sin.*"

3. *You become God's child, and get God for your Father.* It is a good thing to get pardon, and a still better thing to get God's favour; but it is better still to become a child of God. And every one who believes in Christ, becomes that instant a child of God. How do you know this ? Read John i. 12 : "*As many as received Him, to them gave He power to become the sons of God, even to them that believe on His name.*"

This, then, is how you know that you are a child of God : not by feeling, but by believing on His name. "*Ye are all the children of God by faith in Christ Jesus*" (Gal. iii. 26).

If you really trust Christ, even feebly, you are a child of God, and God loves you, for the sake of Christ, as He loves Christ. And He is delighted to guide you and to protect you, and to provide for you, and to be to you everything that a loving father is to his child. Jesus prays, John xvii. 27 : "*That the world may know that Thou hast sent Me, and hast loved them as Thou hast loved Me.*" You have not to make God love you : you have to know and believe the love that the Father hath to you. A child has not to make his mother love him : he has to believe in her love. It is not presumption to believe in her love. I wish we could cease from our efforts to make God love us, and our efforts to *feel* His love, and just *believe* in His love to us.

A little boy walks with his father along the street. The boy has no money. But the father says, "Now, Tom, whatever you see that you would like, ask me for it; and if it would be good for you, I will be delighted to get it for you." The boy asks for this, and for this, and for this, and gets it. See how a little boy who has no money can get everything he needs from his kind father. So it is with us. "*Behold what manner of love the Father hath bestowed upon us, that we should be called the sons of God*" (1 John iii. 1).

4. *You are married to Christ, and get Christ for your husband.* "*I am married unto you, saith the Lord*" (Jer. iii. 14). "*That ye should be married to another, even to Him who is raised from the dead, that we should bring forth fruit unto God*" (Rom. vii. 4). I know no illustration which shows more clearly what we get when we take Christ, than marriage. There is a poor girl, having no money, and nothing lovely about her. But a rich duke sets his love on her, and asks her to marry him, and she says yes; and they are married. On the day before, no one would credit her a pound. On the day after, she would get credit for ten thousand pounds. Why? Because she said yes, and was married to her rich husband.

And, reader! the moment that with your heart you say yes to Jesus, and accept Him as your Saviour, you are married to Him, and all His riches become yours. And now, though you are poor in yourself, you have the richest husband in heaven or earth. He is ever beside you; and it just delights Him to supply all your need, and it honours Him to supply all your need, and He is bound to supply all your need. Go to Him, therefore, with the utmost confidence for everything that you require.

5. *You get God's Holy Spirit to dwell in you, and to enable you to live a holy life.* It is God's Spirit who comes into you, and enables you to believe; but when He comes in, He remains in you, and

never leaves: "*I will put My Spirit within you, and cause you to walk in My statutes, and ye shall keep My judgments, and do them*" (Ezek. xxxvi. 27).

The living God dwells in believers for the very purpose of enabling them to live a holy life! Oh, weakest believer, God the Father dwelleth in you! "*Ye are the temple of the living God; as God hath said, I will dwell in them, and walk in them*" (2 Cor. vi. 16). God the Son dwelleth in you! "*Know ye not your own selves, how that Jesus Christ is in you, except ye be counterfeits?*" (2 Cor. xiii. 5). God the Holy Ghost dwelleth in you! "*Know ye not that ye are the temple of God, and that the Spirit of God dwelleth in you?*" (1 Cor. iii. 16). When you don't know, or when you forget that God dwelleth in you, then you try your own wisdom and strength, and you fail. When you remember that God dwelleth in you, and make use of Him, then you succeed.

My unconverted reader! Do you know this, that when you believe in Christ, you get a new power in you —God's Spirit—that you never had before, and that no unconverted person ever had. Not long since I was in a waiting-room at a railway station on my way to preach that evening. A young man came in, and we were alone. I told him where I was going, and that I meant to tell the people that, however bad they had been, they could get pardon through Christ, and God's Spirit to dwell in them to enable them to live a holy life ; and I asked him had he got Christ. He said, No. I told him that Christ was here in this room, willing to save him now. "You don't know who I am," he said. "I have lived a wicked life." "I am sorry to hear it ; but Christ died for wicked people, and He is willing to take all your sins and pardon them now." "But what about living right in the future?" he asked. "When you accept Him as your Saviour, you get God's Spirit to dwell in you and work in you—you get a new power to overcome sin." Do you see this?

6. *You get a new heart, and a new nature.* "*A new heart also will I give you, and a new spirit*

will I put within you" (Ezek. xxxvi. 26). When the Holy Spirit comes in, He creates in you a new heart. Again, He says: *"I will put My laws into their hearts, and in their minds will I write them"* (Heb. x. 18). And again: *"It is God who worketh in you, both to will and to do for His good pleasure"* (Phil. ii. 12-13). He will make you *know* His will, and *love* His will, and *do* His will. And now, " *Work you out what God works in.*" Surely, when you get God's Spirit to dwell in you, and a new nature, you could do many things that you cannot do without them.

7. *You get repentance and godly sorrow for sin.* When you come to Christ as you are, wicked, hard-hearted, and unfeeling, He takes your sins, and gives you with one hand repentance, and with the other, remission of sins. Ponder over this text, Acts v. 31: *"Him hath God exalted with His right hand to be a Prince and a Saviour, for to give repentance to Israel, and forgiveness of sins."* " *To give* repentance." It is a gift which we get when we come to Him without it. " *They shall look upon Me whom they have pierced, and shall mourn for Him as one mourneth for his only son"* (Zech. xii. 10). When you see the love of Christ to you, you will mourn for grieving Him and crucifying Him. It is after sinners come to Christ that they get real grief and sorrow for sin. What a striking verse this is! " *That thou mayest remember, and be confounded, and never open thy mouth any more because of thy shame, when I have forgiven thee all that thou hast done, saith the Lord God"* (Ezek. xvi. 63).

Halyburton tells us in his Autobiography: " Another remarkable effect of this discovery was the exercise of evangelical repentance, which was very different, in many respects, from that sorrow with which I was before acquainted. It differed in its rise. Sorrow before flowed from the discovery of sin as it brings on wrath ; now it flowed from a sense of sin as containing wretched unkindness to *One* who was Himself astonishingly kind to an unworthy wretch. I looked on Him whom I had pierced, and did mourn. The sorrow I had before, I

looked on as a burden : it was nothing but selfish concern for my own safety, and a fear of the righteous
resentment of God. But this sorrow was sweet and
pleasant, as being the exercise of filial gratitude. Besides, it wrought carefulness to avoid sin, anxiety to
please God, indignation against sin, and fear of offending
God again."

8. *You get power to love Christ.* *" We love Him
because He first loved us "* (1 John iv. 19). Love begets
love. No one ever loved Christ until he first believed in
Christ's love to him. The way to get any kind of feeling
is not by direct efforts to feel, but by thinking about
those objects that are fitted to excite that feeling. If I
told you to hate Claverhouse, and you had never heard
anything about him, you could not do so. But if I gave
you a sketch of his bloody history, and entered into all
the details of the murder of poor John Brown of Priest-
hill, your heart would at once swell with indignation
against him. Or, if I asked you to love Mackay of
Uganda, you could not do so till you knew something
of his history. But if I told you of his twelve lonely
years in Central Africa, during which his life was in
constant danger, and yet how he lived and laboured
away, and suffered and died for the good of the Africans,
you could not help loving him. Just in the same manner
you cannot love Christ till you know and believe His
wondrous love to you. And the more you see of His
love to you, the more you will love Him. Like the
woman who was a sinner, being forgiven much, you will
love Him much.

9. *You get power to pray in the name of Jesus.* When
you accept Christ, your sins are made over to Christ, and
His righteousness and death are made over to you, and
are reckoned as yours just as much as if you had done
them yourself. You have a right, then, to ask God for
anything and everything that Christ's righteousness
merited, and that God has promised. And what is there
that three-and-thirty years of obedience, crowned by His
death, does not merit? You may come to God with as
much confidence as if you had lived a perfectly righteous

life, come just as Jesus Himself would come, for you are
one with Jesus. What wonderful promises are given in
the Bible to the prayers of Christians in the name of
Jesus! " *Whatsoever ye shall ask in My name, that will
I do, that the Father may be glorified in the Son. If ye
shall ask anything in My name, I will do it*" (John xiv.
13, 14). And again : " *Verily, verily, I say unto you,
Whatsoever ye shall ask the Father in My name, He will
give it you. Hitherto have ye asked nothing in My name.
Ask, and ye shall receive, that your joy may be full*" (John
xvi. 23, 24). There are Christian women lying bed-
ridden for years in garrets, who have been taught how
to pray in the name of Jesus, and in the day of judgment
it will be seen that they did more for God and the
world than some whose names are blazoned abroad as
the world's greatest benefactors. What a power it is to
pray in the name of Jesus !

10. *You get power to do good works, and to please God.*
The first thing you do that really pleases God is saying
yes to Jesus, and accepting Him as your Saviour. Then
God and you are friends. After that your works and
services are pleasing to Him.

Remember that, as long as you live, you must depend
entirely on the righteousness and death of Christ for
pardon, and acceptance, and heaven. But when you
depend on Him, and then, with some measure of faith
and love, do things to please God, He is pleased; He
writes them down in His book ; He never forgets them ;
He will give you a reward for them,—not of debt, but
of grace,—and you will have a higher place in heaven
than if you had not done them. " Cornelius, thy prayers
and thine alms *are come up for a memorial before God*"
(Acts x. 4). Or, as it is explained in verse 31 : " Thy
prayer is heard, and *thine alms are had in remembrance*
in the sight of God." God promised to remember them.
And what a wonderful verse is Heb. vi. 10 : " For God
is not unrighteous to forget your work and labour of
love, which ye have showed towards His name, in that
ye have ministered to the saints, and do minister" !
God says. He would be unrighteous if He forgot their

kindness and gifts to His people. And read Matt. x.
40–42 : "He that receiveth you, receiveth Me ; and He
that receiveth Me, receiveth Him that sent Me. He that
receiveth a prophet, in the name of a prophet, shall
receive a prophet's reward ; and he that receiveth a
righteous man, in the name of a righteous man, shall
receive a righteous man's reward."

How blessed to know that even here we can please
God! I remember very well that for years after I
trusted Christ I thought I did nothing that pleased God,
because I did not do it perfectly. I do suppose we do
nothing perfectly. But we can do it honestly and up-
rightly, anxious to please Him. And I remember yet
how delighted I was when the discovery dawned upon
me that if I did some work from some degree of love to
God,—even though it came far short, even though there
was not enough of faith and love in it,—God, for Christ's
sake, would pardon whatever was wrong in it, and God,
for Christ's sake, would accept, and be pleased with
whatever was right in it; and that even here, like Enoch,
we "might have this testimony that we pleased God."
I do believe it is far easier to please God than to please
many of our fellow-men, even fellow-Christians.

What a difference, then, there is in works done before
conversion and works done after conversion! Works
done before conversion go for nothing. "Apart from
Me, ye can do nothing" (John xv. 5). Works done
after conversion, with any degree of love to God, bring a
gracious reward. Look at that board! See the upper
line !

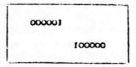

There is the figure 1. Put o before it. How much is
it? Just 1. Put five o's before it. How much is it?
Just 1. Put five hundred o's before it. How much is
it? Just 1. Now look at the lower line. There is the

13

figure 1. Put 0 after it. How much is it? 10. Put five 0's after it. How much is it? 100,000. Put ten 0's after it. How much is it? Ten thousand millions. The first line represents works done before conversion ; the second line represents works done after conversion.

Won't we then, dear readers, seek to do good works from love to Him? Won't we ask God for grace to scatter good thoughts about us, and good words about us, and good prayers about us, and good deeds about us, and good money about us, and seek to be like Christ here, and near Christ in heaven? I am sure that God has no fault to find with ambition after this fashion.

11. *You get the precious promises of the Bible as yours.* " *All the promises of God* IN HIM *are yea, and in Him Amen, unto the glory of God by us*" (2 Cor. i. 20). And what riches are in these promises ! They are promissory notes, signed with Christ's own name, for everything you need. Take them to God, and ask Him in the name of Jesus to cash them, and you will get all that is promised in them. Remember that a note with Rothschild's name to it will be paid as certainly as if Rothschild himself presented it.

12. *And you get everlasting life.* Not life for a day, or a month, or a year, but everlasting life. " *Verily, verily, I say unto you, He that believeth on Me hath everlasting life*" (John vi. 47). What a priceless treasure— " life that shall never end" ! There is a wonderful promise in John v. 24, which, I believe, was the means of giving peace to Mr. Moody : " *Verily, verily, I say unto you, He that heareth My word, and believeth on Him that sent Me, hath everlasting life, and shall not come into condemnation, but is passed from death unto life.*" What precious links are in this verse ! What promises to him that just trusts Christ ! " *Hath everlasting life.*" " *And shall not come into condemnation.*" "*But is passed from death unto life.*" And who has all these things ? The man, or woman, or child who believes in Jesus. " *Everlasting life !*" Who can tell all that it means ? " *My sheep hear My voice, and I know them, and they follow Me ; and I give unto them eternal life, and they*

*shall never perish, neither shall any man pluck them
out of My hand"* (John x. 27, 28). Praise the Lord!
" Everlasting life."

All these twelve blessings you get, and many more,
not in a month or a year after conversion, but in the
very moment that you trust Christ. You get them to
start life with. Paul speaks of the " unsearchable riches
of Christ." What riches of colour, and smell, and beauty
lie hidden in a rosebud, to be unfolded in due time !
And what unsearchable riches there are in Christ !

> " Lord, without Thee we are poor, have what we may ;
> And with Thee we are rich, take what Thou wilt away."

And now, unconverted reader! Christ is just beside
you this moment, willing to take your sins, and to
come into your heart and to make you holy, and give
you all these riches. You are like Hagar, perishing
with thirst, while a well of water is just beside you.
The river Amazon, in South America, is the largest
river in the world. At its mouth, where it flows into the
ocean, it is some miles wide, and ships sometimes are
floating in its fresh water when they think they are out
upon the salt sea. One day a vessel was in this condition. The water in the casks was exhausted, and the
sailors were suffering from thirst. And yet they were
floating in fresh water. By and by another vessel came
in sight. The signal was run up, " Water ! water ! We
are dying for want of water." As the strange vessel
drew near, the captain of it put the speaking-trumpet
to his mouth, and shouted, " Let down your buckets and
drink. There is fresh water all round you. You are in
the Amazon." And so, dear reader! you are in danger
of dying for ever, and yet the loving Jesus is near you,
just beside you, able to save you, and delighted to save
you. Oh that this moment you would talk to Him, and
tell Him out your sins, and say, " Lord Jesus, here and
now, I do take Thee to be my Saviour, and Thy death
to atone for my sins. Lord, I believe ; help Thou mine
unbelief."

XII

Assurance of Salvation

THERE are few subjects more interesting to young and old than assurance. Can a Christian be fully assured of his salvation? Can anyone be a Christian who is not assured? How is assurance to be got? Will Christians be better Christians with assurance or without it? Such is our subject. May God the Holy Ghost guide our thoughts. Lift up your hearts to God and pray for this before reading another line. After a person is converted, the next best thing for him is *to know* that he is converted.

M'Cheyne wrote to a young friend: "Do remember the words of Peter, ' *Give diligence to make your calling and election sure* ' (2 Pet. i. 10). Never rest till you can say what John says, ' *We know that we are of God* ' (1 John v. 19). Men of the world always love to believe that it is impossible to know that we are converted. If you ask them, they will say, ' I am not sure, I cannot tell.' But the whole Bible declares that we may receive, and know that we have received, the forgiveness of sins (Ps. xxxii. 1, and 1 John ii. 12). Seek this blessedness —the joy of having forgiveness. It is sweeter than honey and the honeycomb."

Bishop Ryle says: "I heartily wish that assurance was more sought after than it is. Too many among those who believe begin doubting, and go on doubting, live doubting, and die doubting, and go to heaven in a kind of mist. It would ill become me to speak in a slighting way of ' hopes ' and ' trusts '; but I fear many of us sit down content with them, and go no further. I should like to see fewer 'peradventurers' in the Lord's family, and more who could say, 'I know and am persuaded.'"

Spurgeon says : "Rest not, any one of you, till you know of a surety that Jesus is yours. Do not be content with a hope; struggle after the full assurance of faith. This is to be had, and you ought not to be content without it. It may be our lifelong song, 'My Beloved is mine, and I am His.' Away with the idea that we cannot know whether we are condemned or forgiven, in Christ or out of Him ! We may know, we must know; and as we appreciate our Lord we shall know. Either Jesus is ours, or He is not. If He is, let us rejoice in the priceless possession. If He is not ours, let us at once lay hold upon Him by faith; for, the moment we trust Him, He is ours. The enjoyment of religion lies in assurance; a mere hope is scant diet."

Some persons have, unfortunately, been taught to believe that all assurance is enthusiasm, and that the moment men are sure of escape from hell they will begin to live wicked lives, and that there can be no holiness except from fear of the lash. Such was the case with the great Dr. Samuel Johnson. He was certainly sincere in his endeavours after salvation ; but, while fasting often, and constantly lamenting over sin, he never seemed to get a sense of pardon. His diary is a melancholy record. Here is an extract from it on his fifty-sixth birthday, Sept. 18, 1764: "I have now spent fifty-five years in resolving; having, from the earliest time almost that I can remember, been forming schemes of a better life. I have done nothing." There is good reason to believe that before he died he got clearer views of God and His salvation. But his error about assurance is the error of thousands.

QUESTION I.—*Can any one, while in this life, be sure that he is in a state of grace, and will finally be saved?*

The Roman Catholic Church is the only one in the world that teaches that no one can possibly be sure, while he lives, without a special revelation from God, that he is in a state of grace. That Church holds that a person may have a "conjectural probability," "a good hope," but that he cannot have assurance. The Council of Trent declares that "a believer's assurance of the pardon of his sins is a vain and ungodly confidence"; and Cardinal Bellarmine calls it "a prime error of heretics."

Are there not many Protestants who hold very much the same views on this point, and tell you candidly they do not believe that any one can be sure of pardon and heaven till he dies? This is the purest Romanism, though held by many ignorant Protestants. Certainly the Shorter Catechism of the Westminster Assembly is very clear on the point, when it puts "assurance of God's love" foremost as one of the blessings flowing from justification, adoption, and sanctification. Tell me, reader, do you really think that the way to heaven is so exactly like the way to hell, that no one can possibly tell whether he is on the one or on the other till he dies? Even if you do believe this, the Bible plainly teaches the opposite.

HEAR JOB:

" I know that my Redeemer liveth, and that He shall stand at the latter day upon the earth ; and though after my skin worms destroy this body, yet in my flesh shall I see God " (Job xix. 25, 26). Yet Job lived about two thousand years before Christ, and had very little light compared with what we have.

HEAR DAVID:

"Goodness and mercy all my life
Shall surely follow me ;
And in God's house for evermore,
My dwelling place shall be."—(Ps. xxlii. 6.)

How absurd it is for persons to sing these lines, and then in a minute or two calmly tell you they do not believe that any one can be sure of getting to heaven till he dies !

HEAR ASAPH:

"Thou shalt guide me with Thy counsel, and afterwards receive me to glory " (Ps. lxxiii. 24).

HEAR CHRIST'S OWN WORDS:

" At that day ye shall know that I am in My Father,
and ye in Me, and I in you" (John xiv. 20). He here
tells us that when the Spirit comes, we shall know that
we are in Christ, and that Christ is in us. We shall
know it.

HEAR PAUL:

" We know that if our earthly house of this tabernacle
were dissolved, we have a building of God, an house not
made with hands, eternal in the heavens" (2 Cor. v. 1).
Again, what a lovely verse is this: " I know whom I
have believed, and am persuaded that He is able to
keep that which I have committed to Him against that
day" (2 Tim. i. 12). Please remember that Paul was
" a pattern to them that should hereafter believe."

Hear another verse written by Paul, which has given
comfort to thousands of Christians. Old Fleming thus
describes the death-bed of Robert Bruce of Edinburgh,
the famous Scotch divine: " His sight failed him, whereupon he called for his Bible: but finding his sight gone,
he said, ' Cast up to me the eighth chapter of Romans,
and set my finger on these words: *I am persuaded that
neither death, nor life, nor angels, nor principalities, nor
powers, nor things present, nor things to come, nor height,
nor depth, nor any other creature, shall be able to separate
me from the love of God, which is in Christ Jesus our
Lord.* Now,' said he, ' is my finger upon them?' When
they told him it was, he said, ' Now God be with you,
my children; I have breakfasted with you, and shall
sup with my Lord Jesus Christ this night'; and so gave
up the ghost."

HEAR JOHN:

" We know that we are of God, and the whole world
lieth in wickedness" (1 John v. 19).

We could give scores of such texts. It is quite clear
that the great majority of the primitive Christians had
assurance. No doubt there were a few who had not,
but these were such exceptions to the general rule, that

the apostles wrote to the Churches as if they were all
assured of salvation. Take the brief Epistle to the
Colossians as a specimen :
  " *Who hath delivered us* from the power of darkness,
and *hath translated us* into the kingdom of His dear
Son : in whom we *have redemption* through His blood,
even the forgiveness of sins " (i. 13, 14).
  "As *ye have therefore received* Christ Jesus the Lord,
so walk ye in Him " (ii. 6).
  "Even *as Christ forgave you*, so also do ye " (iii. 13).
  Some people do not go quite as far as the Romanists, but still very near it. They think that no one can
be sure of salvation till he has lived, perhaps, forty
years a Christian life, and is just about to die, and
then God, in great kindness, opens his eyes to see he
is safe, and gives him assurance. Meanwhile, poor
man, he must, "all his life, through fear of death, be
subject to bondage," to free him from which very
bondage, Paul says that Christ died (Heb. ii. 15).
Certainly this is entirely different from what the Bible
teaches, and it differs very little from the Romanist
view of the subject. There is not more than a paper
wall between them. But it is very pleasing to the
carnal mind, and unconverted men would like to believe
it. They say, " I do not know that my sins are forgiven ;
but very few, if any, can tell whether they are or not,
till they die ; and perhaps mine are forgiven, though I
do not know it. I'll just hope for the best, and take
chance like the rest, and make a leap in the dark at
the end." How very unlike this is to the Bible ! Rev.
William Guthrie of Fenwick, who wrote one of the
best books ever written on assurance,—*The Trial of a
Saving Interest in Christ*,—says : "Not only may a
godly man come to a sure knowledge of His gracious
state, but it is more easily attainable than many
apprehend."
  QUESTION II.—*Can any one be a real Christian if he
be not sure that he is pardoned and in a state of grace ?*
  Without any hesitation we answer, Yes. They would
break many a bruised reed, and quench many a smoking

flax, who hold that no one can be a Christian unless he is sure of it at all times. Some of the best Christians I have ever known have, at times, doubted their salvation. When they were weak and delicate, perhaps spitting blood, or nervous, they have said, "I fear I never was converted; it was all formality; I had no real love to God." Yet no one had a doubt of their religion except themselves. Let us fall into the hands of God, for His mercies are great, rather than into the hands of those who would give over to Satan all who could not answer "yes" to the question, Are you born again? Let us see what the Bible says on this point.

HEAR ISAIAH:

"Who is among you that feareth the Lord, that obeyeth the voice of His servant, that walketh in darkness, and hath no light? Let him trust in the name of the Lord, and stay upon his God" (l. 10). Here were persons who feared the Lord, and obeyed Him, and yet walked in darkness, and had no light.

HEAR ASAPH:

"Will the Lord cast off for ever? and will He be favourable no more? Is His mercy clean gone for ever? Doth His promise fail for evermore? Hath God forgotten to be gracious? hath He in anger shut up His tender mercies?" What is his reply to these doubts and lamentations? "And I said, This is my infirmity: but I will remember the years of the right hand of the Most High." I will think of the time when God's face shone on me (Ps. lxxvii. 7–10).

HEAR JOHN:

"These things have I written unto you that believe on the name of the Son of God, that ye may know that ye have eternal life" (1 John v. 13). Here is stated the object for which John wrote the epistle, that those who believed might know that they had eternal life. Does not this clearly prove that some of them did not know it, and that John was anxious that they should know it?

HEAR PAUL:

"Believe on the Lord Jesus Christ, and thou shalt be saved" (Acts xvi. 31). He does not say, If you believe that you believe, you shall be saved. To believe that you believe, is another and different thing. Paul says if you believe on Christ you shall be saved, even though you may not believe that you believe.

HEAR PETER:

"Wherefore the rather, brethren, give diligence to make your calling and election sure" (2 Pet. i. 10). Three lessons are taught in this verse. *First*, That the way to make your election sure is to make your calling sure. When you are sure that you are called, you ought to be sure that you are elected. *Second*, That it needs diligence for Christians, who are here called "brethren," to make their calling and election sure. Lazy living will not lead to assurance. Plainly this implies that there were some "brethren" who were not sure. *Third*, That God wants you to be sure, and commands you to give diligence to make your calling and election sure. Mark, reader, here is a *command* as clear and specific as "Remember the Sabbath day, to keep it holy"—to "give *diligence* to make your calling and election sure." If you are satisfied without assurance and not diligently seeking it, you are breaking a command of God.

I think I hear some reader ask, Do you really mean to say that a person may be born again, without knowing that a great change has passed over him? No, I do not. He will know that *a* great change has taken place, but he may not be sure that it is *the great change*. Is not that plain enough? Probably this is what is meant by 1 John v. 10: "*He that believeth on the Son of God hath the witness in himself.*" Guthrie of Fenwick says it means: "He hath somewhat of the sanctifying work of God's Spirit in him, which is a sure, although not always a clear and perfect, witness." Rev. Harington Evans, however, thought, from the preceding context, that this verse meant: "He that believeth on the Son of God hath the witness in himself that the Bible is true—not that he himself is a believer, but that the Bible is a revelation from God " (*Sermons*, i. 383). Probably Guthrie is right regarding the meaning.

Again, you ask, Could a real Christian be satisfied without knowing whether he is a child of God or of the devil; whether he is on the road to heaven or to hell? No; I do not think he could. If he be satisfied without it, just let him take for granted that he is no Christian at all. Certainly God's command is clear: " Give diligence to make your calling and election sure." Mark, reader, this is *a command*.

QUESTION III. — *What is the scriptural view of assurance?*

That Christians *may have* assurance, and *ought to have* assurance; but that it is possible to be a Christian without having assurance. This is the doctrine of the Westminster Confession also. Except the Bible, there is nothing clearer on assurance than the 18th chapter of the Confession. It teaches that Christians "may, in this life, be certainly assured that they are in the state of grace"; and this certainty "is not a bare conjectural and probable persuasion, grounded upon a fallible hope, but an infallible assurance of faith"; yet that it " *doth not so belong to the essence of faith*, but that a true believer may wait long, and conflict with many difficulties, before he be partaker of it." The words, "doth not so belong," show that the Westminster divines considered *faith* and *assurance* to be very close to each other, though distinct.

It is well known that the Reformers taught that assurance is of the essence of faith, and therefore that all believers have assurance. Luther and Melanchthon and Calvin taught this. It is taught also in the Augsburg Confession, and in the Heidelberg Catechism. It is not taught in any other of the Reformed Confessions. This is now generally believed by Protestants to be an untenable position. There were two reasons which led the Reformers generally to take up this position:

First, They were very godly men themselves, con-

stantly abounding in the work of the Lord, and God
seems to have given them constant assurance of their
salvation.

Second, They were contending with Romanists, who
taught that no one could possibly know that he was a
believer, without a special revelation from God, and
they were naturally led to go to the opposite extreme,
and to hold that no one could be a believer without
knowing it. But almost all Protestants now agree that
this position is an extreme and an untenable one, and
that the doctrine taught in the Bible is that believers
may be, and *should be* assured of their salvation, but that
persons may be believers without being assured of it.

This does not mean that every one who says he is
sure of salvation has a well-grounded assurance, or is
a Christian at all. There is a hope of the hypocrite
which shall perish. The Laodiceans thought they were
"rich, and increased with goods, and had need of
nothing, and knew not that they were wretched, and
miserable, and poor, and blind, and naked."

Nor does it mean that all Christians have the same
degree of assurance. Some are able to say, like Paul,
" I have fought a good fight, I have finished my course,
I have kept the faith." While others are able just to
say, "Lord, I believe ; help Thou mine unbelief."

Nor does it mean that a Christian has the same
degree of assurance at all times. A man went to
Charles Simeon one day, and found him so full of joy
and happiness in Christ, that he left, wondering if he
himself could be a Christian at all. The next time he
met him, he found him sad and downcast. The truth
is, that some people have far more assurance than they
think, while others have far less than they imagine.
Some seem to suppose that they cannot have assurance
unless they have always warm, happy feelings, and are
rolling on the top of a wave of religious emotion. If
such were the case, few Christians would have assurance.
But this is not the case at all. God never meant us to
be always rolling in waves of religious emotion. It
would not be good for us. We could not sleep. Our

poor bodies could not stand it. Here we must often
walk by faith, and not by sight.

Nor does it mean that Christians can always tell the
time and place when and where they were brought to
Christ. Some are able to do so. The three thousand
at Pentecost could do so. So also could Saul of Tarsus,
and the jailor of Philippi. And so can many in the
present day.

But there are not a few, the children of pious parents,
who never remember a time when they did not, in some
measure, trust Christ and love Him, and who seem, like
John the Baptist, to have been born again in their
mother's womb.

Others seem to be led on gradually. They get a
little light now, and a little more light again. They
know that now they do trust Christ, and they know
that a month or a year ago they did not trust Christ.
But as to the day and hour when they passed from
death into life, they cannot tell. They can say, however,
" *One thing I know, that whereas I was blind, now I see.*"

Halyburton says: "I cannot be very positive about
the day or the hour of this deliverance; nor can I
satisfy many other questions about the way and manner
of it. It was towards the close of January, or the beginning of February 1698, that this seasonable relief came."

Dr. Nettleton, the American preacher, had great
terror of mind. Soon after he "felt a calmness for
which he knew not how to account." He thought at
first that he had lost his convictions, and was going
back to stupidity. This alarmed him; but still he
could not recall his former feelings; a sweet peace
pervaded his soul. He did not, however, for several
days suppose that he had experienced a change of
heart; but, finding at length that his views and feelings
accorded with those expressed by others whom he
regarded as friends of Christ, he began to think it
possible that he might have passed from death unto life.

The more he examined himself, the more evidence
he found that "old things had passed away, and all
things had become new."

Jonathan Edwards wrote about the converts at Northampton in New England: "It has more frequently been so among us, that persons have had the gospel-ground of relief for lost sinners discovered to them, and have been entertaining their minds with the sweet prospect, while they have thought nothing at that time of their being converted. There is wrought in them a holy repose of soul in God through Christ, and a sweet disposition to fear and love Him, and to hope for blessings from Him in this way ; and yet they have no imagination that they are now converted ; it does not so much as come into their minds."

On this point we will give an extract from the sermons of Dr. Archibald Alexander of Princeton, one of the most experienced and judicious Christians that ever lived. He says:

"One circumstance, which will appear strange to those who have not learned it by experience, is, that in the first exercises of the new convert there is frequently no thought or question whether these are the genuine exercises of one born of God. There is no room, at present, for such reflex acts ; the mind is completely occupied with the objects of its contemplation ; and often, when these views are clear, forgets itself, and is absorbed in beholding the glory of God in the Mediator, or the wonders of redemption as set forth in the gospel, or the beauty of holiness as manifested both in the law and the gospel. Thus often Christ is received, true faith is exercised, the heart is humbled in penitence, and exercises sincere love to God, without knowing or even asking what the nature of these exercises may be ; and these views and exercises come on so gradually, in many cases, that their origin cannot be traced.

"So far is it, then, from being true that every regenerated man knows the precise time of his renovation, that it is a thing exceedingly difficult to be ascertained. It is not difficult to know, that on such a day our minds were thus and thus exercised, but whether these were the exercises of genuine piety, is quite another question ;

or whether, if they were, they were the first of the kind, is still a different question. Some who speak confidently of the day and the hour of their conversion, never were truly converted, but were imposed on by a mere counterfeit. Others who have the same confidence of knowing the precise time of their conversion, though true Christians, are mistaken as to this matter. They were enabled obscurely to view the truth, and feebly to believe, long before the period at which they date their conversion. Some attain a full assurance of hope who do not pretend to know when their spiritual life commenced. All they can say is, with the blind man in the Gospel, 'One thing I know, that whereas I was blind, now I see.'

" As in the dawning of the natural day, we often can know assuredly that the day has commenced because the objects around us are distinctly visible, when we could not tell the precise moment when the day dawned. Sincere souls, who have the scriptural evidences of piety, need not be distressed because of their ignorance of the day and hour of their vivification. But let not those who have never experienced any change take comfort from this, as though it were possible that they also may have experienced regeneration, while they know nothing about it. In regard to such we may truly say, You cannot be converted without knowing something about it ; you cannot be the subjects of a series of new views and feelings without being conscious of those spiritual exercises." So writes Dr. Archibald Alexander.

Readers ! "*give diligence then to make your calling and election sure.*" Yes, make it sure ; let there be no mistake about it. This is very necessary, for there are many people who think they are on the road to heaven when they are not. Do you ask how I know this ? Because Jesus said it. In the Sermon on the Mount He said :

" *Many shall say to Me in that day, Lord, Lord, have we not prophesied in Thy name? and in Thy name have cast out devils? and in Thy name done many wonderful works? And then will I profess unto them, I never*

knew you: depart from Me, ye that work iniquity"
(Matt. vii. 22, 23). "*Many*"—mark, "*many*"—shall thus
deceive themselves. Would it not be dreadful if you,
reader, were one of the number?

John Wesley tells us that for many years he was
really in earnest, reading his Bible regularly, praying
at stated seasons, fasting, going about holding meetings,
etc. ; and yet that, till he was thirty-five years of age,
when he met Peter Bohler, the Moravian, he had not
been depending upon the Lord Jesus Christ and His
atonement. He had just been an earnest Ritualist, depending for salvation on going through a round of forms
and ceremonies and good works. So he himself thought.

Alexander Anderson of Aberdeen, a Free Church
minister, whose life has been written by the Rev.
Norman Walker, tells us that he was kind, and gentle,
and amiable, and moral, and a good neighbour, etc.,
and that he expected on account of these things to get
to heaven. But one day, when preparing a sermon on
the death of Christ, he came to see that he had not
been depending on the death of Christ—on the blood
of Christ at all, and that he had been deceiving himself.

In the parable of the Sower, Jesus tells us that some
seeds fell on rocky ground,—that is, on a rock covered
over with a little earth,—"*and forthwith they sprang up
because they had no deepness of earth, and when the sun
was up they were scorched, and because they had no root
they withered away.*" And He explains the meaning
of this : "*He that receiveth the seed upon rocky places,
the same is he that heareth the word, and anon with
joy receiveth it, yet hath he not root in himself, but
dureth for a while; but when tribulation or persecution ariseth because of the word, by and by he is offended.*"
It is to be feared there are many of these rocky-
ground hearers. They have been attending meetings
or perhaps reading some good book ; God's Spirit is
striving with them, and they become in earnest ; they
experience some new sensation, and have some kind
of joy and lightness of feeling ; and they think that
this is conversion when it is not, and, of course, they

soon fall away. It is no real conversion till they come
to the Lord Jesus Christ, and depend upon Him and
His finished work. That is the real, genuine article.
There is no mistake about that.

There is a very striking passage in Hebrews vi. 4–6,
which seems to say that a man may go a long way and
not be saved at all. "*For it is impossible for those
who were once enlightened*,"—that is, instructed in the
principles of the Christian religion,—"*and have tasted
of the heavenly gift*,"—mark the word "*tasted*," not fully
enjoyed, but merely *tasted*, that is, have experienced
some pleasure from the tidings of the heavenly gift of
Jesus Christ,—"*and were made partakers of the Holy
Ghost*,"—that is, of His ordinary operations, or of His
miraculous powers,—"*and have tasted the good word of
God*,"—that is, have experienced some degree of comfort from the good and gracious promises of Jehovah,
—"*and the powers of the world to come*,"—that is, the
terrors of a future state,—"*and then fell away*"; so that
it seems to be possible for persons having all these to
fall away, and to show that they had not the root of
the matter in them. Balaam seems to have had all
these things.

It is to be observed that there is nothing said here
respecting their love to God, or their faith in Christ, or
their repentance for sin, or their keeping God's commandments, which are the common evidences of
regeneration. But this difficult passage shows that it
is hard to say how far a man may go and not be a
Christian at all. It is very hard to say also how far a
man may fall, and yet have the root of the matter in him.

Now, would it not be sad if any of us, readers, were
depending on our feelings, or on being good neighbours,
or on going through a round of forms, and so deceiving
ourselves? Would it not be awful if we expected to
get to heaven, and found, like *Ignorance* in the *Pilgrim's
Progress*, when he knocked at the gate of heaven, " Then
I saw that there was a way to hell, even from the gates
of heaven"? "*Let us then give diligence to make our
calling and election sure.*"

14

XIII

How Assurance is to be got

ASSURANCE is the work of God's Spirit. "The Spirit Himself beareth witness with our spirit, that we are the children of God" (Rom. viii. 16). We do not know how He operates, nor is it necessary that we should know. We may be assured on good grounds, without being able to explain *how* we are assured. We may see a landscape clearly, and not be able to explain how we see it. Surely God's Spirit is able to make it clear to us, in His own way, that we are the children of God. Certainly it is not by dreams, or visions, or voices from heaven. These might deceive. If we depended on these, Satan might tell us, when we came to die, that it was he who sent these dreams and visions. One verse of God's word is a far better foundation to rest on than any number of dreams and visions, though God may make use of these at times. How, then, do we get assurance? It seems to me there are four ways in which God's Spirit gives assurance; sometimes in one way, sometimes in another, sometimes in several ways combined. He works as He pleases, and we must not limit the Holy One. But whether we agree about the way of getting assurance or not, let us keep our eye upon the cross of Christ, and let us have the assurance. "*Lord, I don't want to dispute,*" wrote the poet Crabbe in his diary ; "*I want to be saved.*"

1. *The first and best way to get assurance is by looking directly at Jesus, as seen in the word.* Dr. Andrew Bonar, the companion of M'Cheyne, calls this "*the direct or short way.*" God's Spirit causes faith to rise into assurance while simply continuing to behold Jesus.

This direct look at Jesus was the way in which
Duncan Matheson got assurance. After spending
months in strugglings, and efforts, and prayers, and
resolutions, and doing everything that earnestness could
do to get pardon and peace, he says: "I was standing,
on the 10th December 1846, at the end of my father's
house, and meditating on that precious word which has
brought peace to endless weary ones, 'God so loved the
world, that He gave His only-begotten Son, that whosoever believeth in Him should not perish, but have
everlasting life.' I saw that God loved me, for I was
one of the world. I saw the proof of His love in the
giving of His Son Jesus. I saw that *whosoever* meant
anybody and everybody, and therefore *me*, even me.
I saw the result of believing—that I would not perish,
but have everlasting life. I was enabled to take God
at His word. I saw no one but Jesus only, all in all
in redemption. My burden fell from my back, and I
was saved. Yes, saved! That hour angels rejoiced
over one more sinner brought to the Saviour. Bunyan
describes his pilgrim as giving three leaps for joy as
his burden rolled into the open sepulchre of Christ. I
could not contain myself for joy. I sang the new song,
salvation through the blood of the Lamb. The very
heavens appeared as if covered with glory. I felt the
calm of a pardoned sinner; yet I had no thought about
my safety. I saw only the person of Jesus. I wept
for my sin that had nailed Him to the cross, and they
were tears of true repentance. Formerly I had set up
repentance as a toll between me and the cross; now it
came freely as the tear that faith wept. I felt that I
had passed from death unto life."

This direct look at Jesus was the way in which
Charlotte Elizabeth also got assurance. When very
young, she felt a strong desire after salvation. In hope
of finding peace, she read the word and prayed three
times a day; but no peace. Then in a note-book she
wrote down every sin she committed, as far as she
knew them, in order to avoid them in future; but no
peace. Then she had texts of Scripture hung round

her bedroom to fix her thoughts on divine things, and to aid her in keeping God's commandments; but still no peace. She was almost in despair; she thought herself eternally lost. One day she opened a little book as she lay on the drawing-room sofa. It told of a boy under deep sense of sin. The case was like her own. She read on. The boy began to speak of One who was "wounded for our transgressions, and bruised for our iniquities." "I see it now," she cried. "From that moment," she adds, "I never had a doubt Christ *would* save me. I never had a doubt He *had* saved me." She rang the bell for the servant, and said, "I have found Christ."

This direct look at Jesus is the way in which the three thousand at Pentecost got assurance, and the jailor at Philippi, and hundreds of thousands since, specially in times of awakening, without looking at their faith, or waiting for weeks or months to see fruits of their faith. Surely the Spirit of God can do this.

Dr. Andrew A. Bonar dwells very much on this point, and says that, while other ways are scriptural and confirmatory, this is the *best*, and *shortest*, and *direct* way. He says, if there were no way of getting assurance except by looking at our own faith and fruits, "farewell to gospel-joy — except in the rarest cases. For the more a soul grows in grace, the more the believing man rests in Christ, and drinks in of His Spirit, just the more dissatisfied does he become with all his fruits; his holiness does not please him; he finds defects in it; he finds it mixed and impure; and the longer he lives the life of faith, he gets more and more keen-sighted in detecting blemishes in his graces."

Dr. Bonar adds: "Thus faith, as it gazes on its object, passes on to full assurance, and if any one now seek to disturb your calm rest by asking, 'Are you quite sure that you do really believe what is giving you such rest?' what other reply could you give but this: 'As well ask me, when I am enjoying and revelling in the glories of the setting sun, Are you sure your eye really sees the sun which you so admire?'"

Regarding those who think that assurance is to be got

alone by looking at their own faith and fruits, or *better* than by looking directly at Christ, Dr. Bonar says: " *You are, by this method, taking off your eye from Christ to a great degree.* For you try to believe, and then you look to yourselves to see if you have believed. You look up to the brazen serpent, and then you take off your eye to examine your wound, and to see if the bites are really healing, so that you may be sure you have looked aright! You are like a gardener who, after planting a flower in a rich soil, might be foolish enough to uncover the soil in order to see if the root had struck. Surely better to let the root alone, having once ascertained the richness of the soil, and allow the plant to spread out its leaves to the warmth of the sun. Keep looking to Christ, and the effects cannot fail to follow."

Spurgeon says that the way he gets assurance is by coming to God afresh each day as a poor sinner, and taking Christ afresh as his Saviour. He is afraid that if he had to get it by looking alone at his faith and at his fruits, he might often think he was not a Christian at all.

So also thinks Dr. Charles Hodge, who takes very high ground on this point. He says: " There is another view which almost discards assurance, or makes it a rare and almost unattainable gift. This makes hope an inference drawn from promises in a rational way. Here all depends on the clearness of the evidences of regeneration; and as these can seldom or never be so clear as to preclude all doubt, so there can seldom be any scriptural assurance of salvation." Regarding the way in which the Spirit witnesses with our spirit, he says: " It is direct or immediate. The Spirit assures us just as He produces assurance of the truth. Just as the voice of God in the heavens, in conscience, in the law, in the gospel, reveals itself in His word; so, when the Spirit speaks to the soul, it is known to be the Spirit."

2. *A second way in which God's Spirit gives assurance is by making us conscious that we believe, and showing us clearly that " He that believeth on the Son hath everlasting life."*

Take this promise, John iii. 36: " *He that believeth on*

the Son hath everlasting life." Not *will have,* or *may have,* or *can have,* but *hath.* I suppose that no one trusts Christ perfectly. But surely we may know that we do honestly depend on Christ, and therefore that we have God's word for it that we have everlasting life.

Old Guthrie, in his *Trial,* says: "The heart's closing with Jesus Christ is so discernible in itself, that we may well place it among the marks of a gracious state." Not long since we asked a young woman in County Antrim this question: "Do you think that God has pardoned your sins, or do you only hope that He will pardon you some day?" She replied: "I believe that He has pardoned me, but I do not feel that He has pardoned me." "What makes you think that He has pardoned you when you do not feel it?" "Because I know that I depend on Christ in a way I did not do even a week ago. I am sure I do depend on Christ. And the Bible tells me that if I depend on Christ, my sins are pardoned, and that I have everlasting life. And I just take God at His word, and *believe* that He has pardoned me because He says it, and this makes me thankful, and joyful, and happy." Surely this is a scriptural way of getting assurance.

To hear some people talk, who know very little about it, you would think that God's Spirit could not make any one know that he did depend upon Christ. Guthrie says: "We often drive people from their just rest and quiet by making them apprehend faith to be some deep, mysterious thing; and by exciting unnecessary doubts about it, whereby it is needlessly darkened." It is so simple in itself, that if we understand what it is to believe, we must have believed; and no one ever understood what it was to believe till he had believed.

"But," says some one, "I would not be so presumptuous as to say that I depended on Christ." *Presumption, indeed!* What presumption is there in taking what God offers you? If God did not offer you Christ and pardon with Him, then there would be presumption; but not to accept Him when you are commanded to do so, is daring wickedness and unbelief. Samuel Rutherford says he does not see much presumption in a drowning man taking hold of a rock, and holding on. The presumption is in daring to reject Christ. When God offers Him to you, to fling Him back in His Father's face and say, "No"; when Christ offers to carry your sins, to say, "No; I would rather carry them myself to hell than be indebted to You." Oh, this is the presumption! There is an awful amount of *mock humility* in the world, which is only another name for wicked unbelief.

But says some one who does not believe in assurance, "Everything is promised to those who believe, but how do you know that your faith is of the right kind?" We answer: Can God's Spirit not make us know this? Dr. Bonar illustrated it thus: "Suppose a nobleman condemned for high treason, and the day has come when he must die. But that morning a document is put into his hand; it is a pardon from the king, on no other terms than that he accept it. He reads! As he reads, his countenance is flushed, his eye glistens, and in a moment he is full of joy. What think you of any one arresting the current of his joy by the suggestion, 'Are you quite sure you are accepting the pardon? Is your act of acceptance complete and thorough?'"

3. *A third way in which the Spirit of God gives assurance is by letting us see marks of grace in our hearts and lives.*

Faith is one of these marks; but it is so important and distinct in itself, that we have thought it better to make it a separate head as above. But there are other marks which may assure us that we are Christians. Even from the first moment that we believe, God's Spirit may give us assurance. But if we live for a month or a year, we should expect to see changes in our hearts and lives.

This is certainly a scriptural way of getting assurance, and confirms the first and second way. Jesus said: "By their fruits ye shall know them." Paul says: "Our rejoicing is this, the testimony of our conscience, that in simplicity and godly sincerity, not with fleshly wisdom, but by the grace of God, we have had our conversation in the world" (2 Cor. 1. 12). And John writes his first Epistle expressly to teach us how we may know that we have eternal life, and he gives *marks by which to know*. We are to look on these *marks of grace* or *fruits of the Spirit*, however, not to depend on them at all, but as the sailor looks at marks on the land to see if his anchor holds.

We must ask God for His Spirit to enable us to examine ourselves, for there are at least two kinds of people very liable to be deceived. There are godly men and women, real Christians, easily depressed, who are always writing bitter things against themselves, and who can scarce ever see any tokens of good in their hearts or lives. On the other hand, there are ignorant, careless, godless people, who are easily satisfied with little evidence, or without any evidence at all.

I want to lay down some marks of a real Christian, by which we may examine ourselves. But please remember that we must take our natural temperaments into account. Some of God's people are naturally lively and cheerful; others are naturally sad. Some are pretty equally serene day by day; others are some days elevated, and other days depressed. Some are openly communicative; others are naturally silent and retiring. These are natural differences. We must take these constitutional peculiarities into account.

There are six marks of a real Christian, by which we want you to examine yourselves.

(1) *Do you often think about Jesus, and talk to Him?* If you do, this is an evidence that you love Him. "*If any man love not the Lord Jesus, let him be Anathema*" (1 Cor. xvi. 22). But you must not judge of your love by your feelings. Your feelings change with the weather, or with the state of your health. I have met persons whose lives showed that they did not know Christ, and yet they said, "I do love the Lord"; while others, who would have died for Christ, said, "I fear I don't love Him at all. I don't feel I have any love to Jesus." There are two evidences of love that are very plain: *First*, no one ever loved a person without thinking of that person. *Second*, no one ever loved a person without doing things to try and please that person.

Now, do you show your love to Jesus by thinking about Him? I am sure you do not think about Him enough ; but do you think about Him sometimes between morning and night? Is it to you a pleasant thought that Jesus is with you every day, and every hour, and knows your thoughts, even your wicked thoughts? or is it an unpleasant thought? Do you talk to Him at times, saying something like this: "I thank Thee, Jesus, for dying for me, and for watching over me day by day. I do depend on Thee, and I will depend on Thee to guide and keep me"? If you do, who keeps you thus talking to Him? Is it your own wicked heart? No. Is it the devil? No. It is the Spirit of God dwelling in you. So be thankful.

But if you never think of Jesus at all—if with you it is nothing but the world — the world — the world— from morning till night, can you imagine that you love Jesus? If you loved Him, would you not think about Him sometimes?

(2) *Do you show your love to Jesus by keeping from things that would vex Him, and by doing things that would please Him, and by keeping His commandments?* If you really love a person, you will try to please that person. You would rise at twelve o'clock at night to please him, and you would walk twenty miles, if you were able. Would you not? Now, if you love Jesus, you will keep from doing things that you think would vex and grieve Him, and you will do things that you think would please Him. Do you seek thus to keep His commandments? "*If ye love Me, keep My commandments.*" Do you seek to please Jesus? He Himself said: "*My meat is to do the will of Him that sent Me, and to finish His work.*" "*I came from heaven, not to do Mine own will, but the will of Him that sent Me.*" Do you thus seek to do the will of God from day to day? or do you just please yourself? Have you an increasing desire to do the whole will of God?

If you thus think a good deal about Jesus, and seek day by day to please Him, you have better evidence that in some degree you do love Him, than if you heard

an angel from heaven tell you that you loved Him, or
than if you saw your name written in letters of fire
upon the sky.

(3) *Do you like to be in the company of God's people?
or do you prefer to associate with the wicked?* I know
that at times you must be in the company of the wicked;
but with whom do you like to associate? Was there
not a time when you did not like to be in the company
of Christians, or join in their talk? You would rather,
in your heart, have broken stones upon the roadside
for a day, if no one had seen you, than have been for a
day in a room with a few people talking about Jesus
and His love. Is it so now? See how, in a time of
awakening, young Christians run to meet other young
Christians, and see them walking and talking with their
arms round each other. Do you like to be in the
company of Christians? Examine yourselves. A very
excellent minister in America tells that at one time this
was the only clear evidence he had. And if you have this,
thank God for it. "*By this shall all men know that ye are
My disciples, if ye have love one to another*" (John xiii. 35).

(4) *Do sin and sinful thoughts cause you pain?* Now
remember that you cannot prevent the devil from
suggesting wicked thoughts to you. He suggested
them to Christ Himself. It is no proof at all that you
are not a Christian that wicked thoughts come rushing
into your mind. You can suggest wicked thoughts to
another; and the devil can suggest wicked thoughts
to you. And he will do so; you may be sure of that.

But do you love them? Do you dwell on them, and
think over them and over them in your mind? Or are
you grieved and vexed for them? Do you fly to
Jesus, and say: "Lord Jesus, here is the devil suggesting wicked thoughts to me. Lord, I look to Thee.
Hold Thou me up, and I shall be safe. Lord, I depend
on Thee to put them out of my mind"? Do they
cause you pain? And do you grieve for them in a
way you did not do once? I am sure you do not
grieve for them as much as you ought; but do you
grieve for them at all? Examine yourselves.

(5) *Do you find a new delight in the Bible, and in
prayer, at least at times?* I do not mean to say that
all Christians, at all times, have a great delight in the
Bible and in prayer. Unfortunately it is not so. But
if you are a Christian, there will be times when the
Bible will be a new book to you, and prayer will be a
new thing to you.

Do you understand the Bible in a different way from
what you did once? Do you know what believing in
Christ means? Thank God if you do, for there was a
time when you did not. Every minister knows that, in a
Bible class, it is not always the cleverest or best educated
boys or girls who answer best about Christ. Sometimes
it is clear that the half-stupid ones know more about
Christ than the cleverest. I remember one Sabbath that
a young girl in my Bible class began to answer in a way
in which she had never done before. Everything seemed
clear to her now. I said to myself, That girl has got
new light lately on her Bible ; and so she had.

How differently you read a letter from your father
in America and the letter of a stranger! Do you read
the Bible, believing it to be a letter from your Father
in heaven? And do you understand it in a way you
did not once? Examine yourself.

*Again, as regards prayer, are there times when you
pray differently from what you used to do?* When
Saul of Tarsus was converted, Jesus said, " *Behold, he
prayeth.*" Saul had said his prayers before, but now he
prayed. I think it is Dr. James Hamilton of London
who speaks of a man and his dog going up together
to the top of a mountain. Both look at the same
beautiful landscape, but how different the landscape
looks to the man and to his dog! So prayer is a
different thing to the Christian and to the careless one.
Reader! you remember a time when you knelt down,
and got up again ; and if any one had asked you what
you were praying for to God, you could not have told,
for you had really asked Him for nothing. But now,
are there times when you kneel down, and look up to
God as a kind Father, and ask Him for blessing after

blessing, assured that He will give it? If so, thank God.

(6) *Have you any real desire for the salvation of others?* When one sees something of the value of his own soul, he feels anxious for the salvation of others, and specially of his friends and neighbours. "*Andrew first findeth his own brother Simon, and brought him to Jesus.*" "*Philip findeth Nathanael, and saith, We have found Him of whom Moses and the prophets did write, Jesus of Nazareth.*" Robert M'Cheyne was brought to Jesus by his brother, and Henry Martyn by his sister. Have you any desire, and are you making any effort, to bring any others to Jesus? Examine yourself.

Now, please remember that you may not have all these evidences in active operation at one and the same time. Sometimes you will have one, and sometimes another. One day you may take pleasure in reading the Bible, another day in prayer, another day in work. If you have any of these evidences, be thankful, for if you have one, you must have all in some measure. But I am sure you will not have any of them in as large a measure as you could wish.

Remember, also, that when examining yourself in this way, "We must do it," as old Guthrie says, "at a convenient time, when we are in good case; for the flesh and spirit do lust and fight against each other (Gal. v. 17); and sometimes the one, and sometimes the other, doth prevail. Now, I say, we must choose a convenient time, when the spiritual part is not by some temptation worsted and overpowered by the flesh."

4. *There is a fourth way of getting assurance. When God's people love Him, and serve Him, and seek to walk closely with Him, sometimes He sheds abroad His love in their hearts by His Holy Spirit in such a way that they have no more doubt that they are His children than that they are alive.*

This is what Jesus speaks of in John xiv. 21-23: "If a man love Me, he will keep My words, and My Father will love him, and We will come unto him and make Our abode with him." Again Christ says: "I will

manifest Myself to him." But no one need expect this
unless he is walking very closely with God, and seeking
to do His will. Some people won't believe in this,
because they have had no experience of it. How like
to the King of Siam ordering the head of the French
ambassador to be cut off, because he said that in his
country persons walked on the top of the water in
winter! The king had had no experience of ice.

"I speak with the experience of many saints," says
old Guthrie, "and I hope according to Scripture, if I
say there is a communication of the Spirit of God,
which is sometimes vouchsafed to His people, that is
somewhat besides, if not beyond, that witnessing spoken
of before"; and he goes on to describe it. If you want
to know about it, read the account of Mrs. Jonathan
Edwards, written by her husband; or the account
written by himself of those sweet hours he spent on the
banks of the Hudson, "when the glory of Christ
appeared ineffably excellent, with an excellency great
enough to swallow up all thought and conception,
which kept me the greater part of the time in a flood
of tears, weeping aloud. I had an ardency of soul to
be, what I know not otherwise how to express, emptied
and annihilated, to lie in the dust and be filled with
Christ alone, to love Him with a holy and pure love, to
trust in Him, to live upon Him, and to be perfectly sanctified and made pure with a divine and heavenly purity."

Or read *Rutherford's Letters*, specially those written
from Aberdeen. We give one extract:—

"How many a sweet, sweet, soft kiss, many per-
fumed, well-smelled kisses and embracements have I
received of my Royal Master; He and I have had
much love together. I have for the present a sick,
dwining life, with much pain and much love-sickness
for Christ. Oh, what I would give to have a bed
made to my wearied soul in His bosom! I would frist
heaven for many years to have my fill of Jesus in this
life, and to have occasion to offer Christ to my people,
and to woo many people to Christ. I cannot tell you
what sweet pain and delightsome torments are in

Christ's love! I often challenge Him that holdeth us
sundry. I profess to you I have no rest, I have no
ease, while I be over head and ears in love's ocean.
"Oh, when will we meet! Oh, how long is it to the
dawning of the marriage day! O sweet Lord Jesus,
take wide steps! O my Lord, come over mountains at
one stride! O my Beloved, flee like a roe or young
hart upon the mountains of separation! Oh! if He
would fold the heavens together like an old cloak, and
shovel time and days out of the way, and make ready
in haste the Lamb's wife for her Husband. Since He
looked upon me, my heart is not mine own; He hath
run away to heaven with it. I know it was not for
nothing that I spoke so meekly good of Christ to you in
public. Oh! if the heaven and the heaven of heavens
were paper, and the sea ink, and the multitude of
mountains pens of brass, and I were able to write
that paper, within and without, full of the praises of
my fairest, my dearest, my loveliest, my sweetest, my
matchless, and my most marvellous Well - Beloved!
Woe is me, I cannot set Him out to men and angels!"

These are some of the ways in which the Spirit of
God gives assurance to the believer. Do you really
believe that you are trusting Christ, even feebly, and
that you have any of these marks of grace? Then
thank God. Do thank God. "*Flesh and blood hath not
revealed it unto you, but your Father in heaven.*" We
don't thank God nearly enough for the grace He has
given us. Often say, "*Bless the Lord, O my soul; and
all that is within me, bless His holy name; who forgiveth
all thine iniquities; who healeth all thy diseases; who
redeemeth thy life from destruction; who crowneth thee
with loving-kindness and tender mercies.*" When we
praise God, it pleases Him much, and it is a means
of grace. How can we expect God to give us more
grace, if we do not thank Him for what He has given?
Praise God then much, reader! Let us join in praising
Him for His mercies, temporal and spiritual.
Of that seraphic Christian, Joseph Alleine, it was

written: "Love and joy and a heavenly mind were the
internal part of his religion, and the large and fervent
praises of God, and thanksgiving for His mercies,
especially for Christ, and *the Spirit*, and *heaven*, were the
external exercises of it. He was not negligent in confessing sin, but praise and thanksgiving were his natural
strains; his longest, most fervent, and hearty services."

John Livingstone wrote: "Alas! for that capital
crime of the Lord's people—*barrenness in praises.* Oh,
how fully I am persuaded that a line of praises is worth
a leaf of prayer, and an hour of praises is worth a day
of fasting and mourning."

" Loved with everlasting love,
 Led by grace that love to know;
Spirit breathing from above,
 Thou hast taught me it is so!
Oh, this full and perfect peace!
 Oh, this transport all divine!
In a love, which cannot cease,
 I am His, and He is mine.

Heaven above is softer blue,
 Earth around is sweeter green!
Something lives in every hue
 Christless eyes have never seen;
Birds with gladder songs o'erflow,
 Flowers with deeper beauties shine,
Since I know, as now I know,
 I am His, and He is mine.

Things that once were wild alarms
 Cannot now disturb my rest;
Closed in everlasting arms,
 Pillowed on the loving breast.
Oh, to lie for ever here,
 Doubt, and care, and self resign,
While He whispers in my ear—
 I am His, and He is mine.

His for ever, only His;
 Who the Lord and me shall part?
Ah, with what a rest of bliss
 Christ can fill the loving heart!
Heaven and earth may fade and flee,
 Firstborn light in gloom decline;
But while God and I shall be,
 I am His, and He is mine."

XIV

Assurance Promotes Holiness

SOME people seem to think that if they were assured of their salvation, they would become proud ; and so they make their doubts no small part of their religion, and pride themselves on their humility, because they never had assurance. This " pride that apes humility is the worst of all pride." If every one is humble who lacks assurance, what a superabundance of humility we must have in this world! Old Traill says: " They are quite mistaken who think faith and humility are inconsistent. They not only agree well together, but they cannot be parted."

The Bible *commands* us to give diligence to make our calling sure, and therefore assurance *must be* favourable to holiness. And the Westminster Confession, following the Bible, says: " It is the duty of every one to give all diligence to make his calling and election sure ; that thereby his heart may be enlarged in peace and joy in the Holy Ghost, in love and thankfulness to God, and in strength and cheerfulness in the duties of obedience—the proper fruits of this assurance : so far is it from inclining men to looseness." And is not the Confession right in this ?

(1) *Peace and joy.* Here are two men, both of them Christians; but the one is assured of his salvation, the other is not. Which of them will have more joy and peace ? How can a man have joy and peace, when he does not know but that he may be in hell before the morning ? How can he " *rejoice in the Lord alway*," as he is commanded to do in Phil. iv. 4 ? The thing is simply impossible. But when he knows that his sins

are forgiven, and that the Lord loves him, then he can
"*be glad in the Lord and rejoice.*"

(2) *Love and thankfulness to God.* How can a man
love God much, when he does not know whether the
Lord loves him or not? "*We love Him because He first
loved us,*" and the more we see of His love to us, the
more we love Him. Here are two men of your acquaintance. The one, you are sure, loves you; the
other you are very uncertain about; sometimes you
think he loves you; at other times you think he does
not; at this present moment you could not say whether
he loves you or not—Which of these men will you love
most? Certainly, the one that you are sure loves you.
And so the man who is sure that God loves him, will
love God much more than the man who does not know
whether God loves him or not. Can there be much love
and thankfulness to God without assurance? I think not.

(3) *Courage and cheerfulness in working for God.*
Bishop Latimer wrote to Ridley: "When I live in a
settled and steadfast assurance about the state of my
soul, methinks then I am as bold as a lion. I can
laugh at all trouble; no affliction daunts me. But
when I am eclipsed in my comforts, I am of so fearful a
spirit that I could run into a very mouse-hole." And so
it is with every Christian. He works far better when he
knows God loves him. The doubters are generally do-
nothings and drones. David was right when he prayed:
" Restore unto me the joy of Thy salvation; then will I
teach transgressors Thy ways, and sinners shall be
converted unto Thee " (Ps. li. 12).

(4) *Strength to live a holy life.* We have no strength
in ourselves to serve God, and must go to God for it.
Whether will we go to God with more confidence if we
are sure He loves us, or if we are not sure? Certainly,
if we are sure. " The joy of the Lord is our strength."
Oneness with Christ is the source of all holiness and
usefulness. But if we do not know that we are one with
Christ, we cannot go to Him with as much confidence,
and bear as much fruit, as if we do.

We will take this opportunity of dwelling somewhat

15

at length on the way in which we are to live a holy life. There are three ways in which really earnest people seek to overcome sin, and to live a holy life:

1. The plan of earnest Roman Catholics.
2. The plan of ignorant Protestants.
3. The Bible plan.

1. *The plan of earnest Roman Catholics.* They try to do it by *ascetic austerities.* They starve themselves; they climb up sharp rocks on their bare knees till the blood flows freely; they sleep in rough, hairy garments; they plunge naked into cold, freezing water; they get up out of their warm beds, and lie down naked in winter on the cold floor, till they bring on rheumatism or pleurisy, and sometimes death. Some have lain down and slept in their coffins, which they kept in their rooms. Even the great Pascal wore an iron girdle round him with sharp spikes, which he drove into his flesh when wicked thoughts came into his mind.

Now it is true we are to keep the body under, and to deny self. But this is not at all what the Bible means by denying self. The Bible means us to deny ourselves whatever is sinful; but this is denying ourselves what is not sinful, and seeking to atone for our sins by doing things hateful to our nature, as if that pleased God. It is really melancholy to think that any human being could imagine that our kind, loving Father would be pleased by some of these things, which would tend even to shorten our lives. "The Sixth Commandment requireth all lawful endeavours to preserve our own life and the life of others." This is just old heathenism over again. It injures the body, while it does not crucify sin. We are to use the world, but not to abuse it. God says, " I desired mercy, and not sacrifice." God's religion does not consist in crossing every desire of our nature, but in giving us new hearts and new desires, so that it becomes a pleasure to serve God. We give up our old sins not by crossing our nature, but by getting a new nature and new pleasures.

This is the Bible way of overcoming sin, and not the plan of *ascetic austerities.* There is nothing in these

which can put down sin. They have never done it.
Luther fasted and prayed, lay on the cold stones, for
four days ate nothing, and for seven weeks scarcely
slept. But he tells us he found that he carried his sinful
heart with him to the cell, and that, though he could
shut out his friends, he could not shut out his wicked
thoughts. He said afterwards that he never had more
wicked thoughts than when alone in his cell. We
cannot but admire the earnestness of some of these
men, but this plan never accomplished its purpose. Oh
that we were as earnest, but on the Bible plan! How
rapidly we would grow in grace!

2. *The plan of earnest, but ignorant Protestants.* By
the word "ignorant," I do not mean ignorant of
grammar, or history, or literature, or even theology, but
of the Bible plan of overcoming sin. Here is the plan
which almost every earnest Protestant Christian at first
adopts. He says: "I will overcome my sins; I will
read my Bible more; I will pray more; I will strive
against sin more; I will work more; I will do it." Now
these things are all excellent things in their own place,
as I shall show after a little. But they are the streams,
not the fountain. They are the means of grace, and
not the source of grace. Mark, there is not a word
about *Christ*, or the *Spirit*, in all this. "I will read my
Bible more; I will pray more; I will strive against
sin more; I will work more; I will do it—I, I, I."

Now, Christian, don't you remember a time when you
tried to get pardon by this very plan? You struggled,
and resolved, and prayed, and tried, and worked; but
you never got pardon till you got above and beyond all
these things to Christ—till one day you saw that Jesus
was able and willing to carry all your guilt, and to save
you, and you said, "Lord Jesus, here and now, I do
depend on Thee"; and that moment you passed from
death to life. Now you are just doing over again, on a
higher level, what you did then on a lower. Oh that we
saw the truth of this verse: "*Apart from Me ye can do
nothing*" (John xv. 5). And of this verse: "*Not that
we are sufficient of ourselves to think anything as of our-*

selves, but our sufficiency is of God" (2 Cor. iii. 5). And of this verse: *"He giveth power to the faint, and to them that have no might He increaseth strength"* (Isa. xl. 29).

I do think that the hardest thing in the world is for a Christian to give up depending on his own wisdom and his own strength, and to depend entirely upon Christ to keep him from falling, and to enable him to live a holy life. Hervey, the author of *Theron and Aspasio*, was once ordered by his doctor to follow the plough for the benefit of his health. There was an old Christian ploughman near him, who belonged to Dr. Doddridge's congregation, and Hervey often walked up and down the field with him. One day he asked the old plough-man what he thought was the hardest thing in religion. The old man replied that Mr. Hervey was a learned man and a clergyman, and he would wish to know what he thought was the hardest thing in religion. " I think it is to deny sinful self," said Hervey. "Well,' said the old Christian, ." I think there is a harder thing still—to deny righteous self—to deny ourselves a proud dependence upon our own works, and struggles, and efforts, and prayers, for justification before God." Hervey afterwards said that at the time he thought the ploughman an old fool; but, said he, " I have since learned who was the fool—not the pious ploughman, but the proud James Hervey."

Now I believe there is a harder thing still; namely, for a Christian man, washed in the blood of the Lamb, to give up depending on his own wisdom and his own strength to keep him from falling, and to depend entirely upon Christ. I do believe that this is the hardest thing in the universe. Of course God's Spirit alone can enable us to do the one or the other. But usually a much longer time is spent in teaching us that we have no wisdom of our own or strength of our own to live a holy life, than in teaching us that we cannot depend on our own righteousness to obtain pardon. Oh to be able honestly to say:

> "I'm a poor sinner, and nothing at all;
> But Jesus Christ is my all in all."

A good many years ago I heard a lady tell the following about her own mother:—Her mother was a Christian, but had a hot, fiery temper, which sorely troubled her. One night it burst forth into a perfect passion, and she resolved that she would get the victory over it. So she rose next morning at six o'clock, and spent two hours over her Bible with prayer, and then came down to breakfast. But somehow that morning everything was wrong. The husband was cross, and the servant was cross, and in a few minutes she lost her temper, and burst into tears. Up she went to her bedroom for another hour; but when she appeared on the stairs, the servant, cross as ever, was waiting for her, and soon she lost her temper again, and came into the parlour in tears. " Am I never to get the victory over this bad temper? " she said. " I could tell you what is wrong," said her daughter, "but you would not listen to me." " I will listen to any one who will tell me how I can get the victory over this temper."

" Well," said her daughter, "you went upstairs, and you asked God to enable you to overcome your temper, and you came down the stairs depending on yourself, because you had prayed — depending on your own prayers, and not depending on God to whom you prayed. Mother, there is the greatest difference in the world between depending on your own prayers, or depending on yourself because you have prayed, and depending on God to whom you have prayed. Do this: go upstairs for a few minutes, tell the Lord you cannot keep yourself, though you have prayed, and that you are going to depend entirely upon Him to keep you; and come down the stairs remembering that Jesus is beside you, and tell Him, 'Lord, I am depending on Thee to keep me. Thou wilt keep me from falling. Thou wilt save me from my sins. Now, Lord, I am depending on Thee,' and just see if that will not do." And her daughter testified that it was the means of making a wonderful change in her life.

This is what the Apostle Paul teaches in the seventh chapter of Romans. He is giving his own experience when a Christian man, and he says that as often as he depended on himself and on his new nature to overcome the old nature, he was beaten, beaten every time. But as often as he looked up to Jesus Christ and trusted Him, he was enabled to overcome. And this is just the experience of every Christian as well as of Paul. He does not at all mean that up to a certain moment he was always beaten, and after that moment he was always victorious—nothing of the kind. But that to the end of life, as often as he, Paul, depended on himself—" me," " me "—and his efforts and struggles, he was beaten ; and that to the end of life, as often as he, Paul, depended on Christ, he was enabled to overcome. " O wretched man that I am, who shall deliver me from the body of this death? I thank God, through Jesus Christ our Lord."

3. *The Bible plan of sanctification.* It is the work of God's Spirit dwelling in the heart. But how does God's Spirit operate? By turning the eye of the believer to the living, loving Saviour. "*I thank God, through Jesus Christ our Lord.*" You remember, Christian, how you were converted. It was the work of God's Spirit. But He turned your eye to Jesus dying upon the cross for sinners, and showed you how willing He was to save you. And at the moment when you were converted, you were thinking about Christ. And just so, when the Spirit of God sanctifies, He turns our eyes to Jesus. *Who* shall deliver me from the body of this death? He does not ask *what* shall deliver me? There is no *what* can deliver us ; but there is a *who*—a living, loving Saviour who can: "*I thank God, through Jesus Christ our Lord.*"

The same truth is taught in 1 Cor. i. 30: "Of Him are ye in Christ Jesus, who of God is made unto us wisdom, and righteousness, and sanctification, and redemption." We are in Christ, and Christ is in us— and God has made Christ unto us wisdom. We have no wisdom—but Christ is our wisdom, and is free to us as the air. We have no righteousness of our own that can recommend us to God—but Christ's righteousness is as free to us as the sunshine. We have no source of

holiness in ourselves—but Christ is our sanctification
and strength, and He is delighted to give us His
strength every day and every hour, for our every need.
We have nothing, then, in ourselves to glory of, but we
should glory in the Lord.

(1) *Believer in Christ! you know that at the moment
when you were enabled to accept Christ, you were made
one with Christ.* Oh that we knew more, remembered
more, about this oneness with Christ! *"In that day
ye shall know that I am in My Father, and ye in Me,
and I in you"* (John xiv. 20).

Dr. Vaughan, on the Epistle to the Romans, writes:
" Although justification by faith may be, to a super-
ficial reader, or in certain agonies of the Church's history,
the salient point in St. Paul's doctrine, it is not more so,
in reality, than any other. Equally (at least equally)
characteristic of St. Paul is that ideal of the Christian
life which some call mysticism, enthusiasm, fanaticism
—which some men pass over as not meant for them,
but which he evidently found omnipotent to lift a man
above sin—the present living union with Christ, the
Crucified and the Risen. Instead of saying to the earth-
bound, sensual, selfish being, *Sin must be encountered,
in a sense of duty, that you may be accepted, that you may
win heaven, he says, Christ died, and you with Him;
Christ lives, and you in Him. Reckon yourself dead and
risen. Put on Christ. Let Him live in you. Commune
with Him, love Him, abide in Him, and sin will fall off
from you. The vessel filled with good has no room for evil;
the soul which has Christ in it is emancipated, is free."*

Christ is the vine, and you are the branch. It just
delights the vine to give juice and sap to the branch.
The branch does not grow, and bear leaves and fruit,
by prodigious efforts and struggles. It just abides in
the vine, and draws strength and nourishment from the
root. So Christ delights to give us grace and strength
every moment. What a beautiful text is this!—Isa.
xxvii. 3. The Lord is speaking of His vineyard : *"I the
Lord do keep it (thee); I will water thee every moment:
lest any hurt thee, I will keep thee night and day."*

Christ is the head, and you are "a member of His
body and flesh and bones," and He has promised to
"nourish and cherish you as the Lord the Church"
(Eph. v. 29, 30). It just delights the Head to guide
and direct and invigorate the members. And it delights
Christ to fill you every moment with His Spirit. The
reason we do not live holier lives is because we do not
look up to our Head, and depend on Him. Dean
Goulbourn says: "Many are the seekers after holiness,
the secret of whose failure lies wrapped up in those
four words, '*not holding the Head.*'" "*In Him dwelleth
all the fulness of the Godhead bodily, and ye are complete
in Him who is the Head*" (Col. ii. 9, 10). What we
have to do is to receive from Him day by day, and
moment by moment, and not to attempt to give out
until we have received first. "*Of His fulness have all
we received, and grace for grace*" (John i. 16). Oh that
we were willing to receive, and receive, and receive, and
then to give out what we have received! How strange
that we attempt so many things without looking up to
our Head, and forget Him so much!

Christ is your Husband, and you are His Bride. At
the moment when you were enabled to say to Him,
"Yes, Lord Jesus, I take Thee as my Saviour," you
were married to Him. "*I am married unto you, saith
the Lord.*" There never was a more real marriage.
You have not to be married. You are married. It is
a past transaction—an accomplished fact. You have
the wisest, and mightiest, and loveliest, and greatest
Being in the universe as your Husband. He loves you
a thousand times more than Adam ever loved Eve.
Now, it just *delights* a husband to give to his wife
everything that she needs. And it *honours* him to give
her everything she needs. And he is *bound* to give her
everything she needs. So it just delights Christ, our
loving Husband, to supply all our wants, and to fill us
with His Spirit every day, and every hour, and every
moment. What a sin and shame to doubt this after
He has given His life for us when we were enemies!
"*If, when we were enemies, we were reconciled to God by*

the death of His Son, much more, being reconciled, we shall be saved by His life" (Rom. v. 10).

I happen to be the member of a clerical society which meets sometimes in Belfast. One day we were met there, and were about to go out to a public meeting. Just before rising to go, one of the members said something like the following: Friends, we have been praying for one another each Saturday evening and oftener, that we might be filled with the Spirit. Is it not time that we believed that God has answered our prayers? *" What things soever ye desire when ye pray, believe that ye receive them, and ye shall have them."* We are all in the habit of addressing the unconverted, and we tell them Jesus is here, and He offers this moment to make over His death to you, and to take your sins upon Him ; and you are bound here and now to accept Him, and God's Spirit is here to enable you. And if any one says, *" But I don't feel,"* we almost get angry, and say, Feel! feel! how can you feel till you first believe? Now, friends, Jesus is here in this room now, and He has purchased the fulness of the Spirit for each of us, and it just delights Him to fill us every moment, and He commands us, *" Be filled with the Spirit,"* and He wants to fill us now. Should we not then say, " Yes, Lord Jesus, I take Thy Spirit in His fulness"? And should we not believe, feeling or no feeling, that He does fill us? And should we not go down the stairs, and to our meeting, believing that He is filling us? If we would act thus, it would not be long till God would give us experiences far beyond anything we now enjoy.

Now, is not this the right thing? Is not the Lord delighted to fill us? Are not His commands promises? Is it not an awful sin to refuse to let the Lord into every corner of our hearts? Is not this refusal more wicked than refusing to take Christ at first? But let us remember that God will never fill us except to do His will, and to make us holy and useful. *" If any man thirst, let him come unto Me and drink. He that believeth on Me, as the scripture hath said, out of his belly shall flow rivers of living water"* (John vii. 37, 38).

(2) *But, believer, not only are you in Christ, but Christ liveth in you.* He gives two commands in that verse, "*Abide in Me, and I in you.*" He means, Keep up an abiding sense, *first,* that you are one with Me up in heaven ; and *second,* that I abide in you down upon earth to enable you to live a holy life. Yes, believer, Christ liveth in you. "I will come in to him," Christ promises in Rev. iii. 20. You can say with Paul, "*I live, yet not I, but Christ liveth in me.*"

You will pardon me for dwelling a little on a verse from which I think I have got good. It is 2 Cor. xiii. 5. There are two parts in it. *First,* "*Examine yourselves whether ye be in the faith; prove your own selves.*" Make sure that you are in the faith. Have that point definitely settled. *Second,* "*Know ye not your own selves, how that Jesus Christ is in you,* except ye be counterfeits, or hypocrites, or unbelievers?" If you are in Christ, Christ is in you, whether you know it or not; but I want you to know it. If you do not know it, you will not make use of Him, and you will struggle, and try, and resolve in your own strength—and you will fail. But if you know that Christ is in you, you will never think of depending on your own strength or wisdom when you have Christ in you. I think I hear some reader say, "Well, I do believe that I am in Christ, and that if I died, I would go to heaven; but I cannot think that Christ is in me, otherwise I would live a holier life." Now, reader, look again at this verse. Paul tells you that if you are in Christ, Christ is in you, whether you know it or not. And the reason why you do not live a holier life is because you do not know this—"*Know ye not.*" The emphasis is on "*Know ye not.*" He wants you to know it. If you do not know it, you will just go on with your old efforts in your own strength. But if you know it, you will look up to Jesus, and He will enable you to live a holy life. But you say, I do not *feel* Christ dwelling in me. No, you do not. The blood is circling through your body this moment, but you do not feel it. Your lungs are full of air, but you do not feel it. But God tells you that

If you trust Christ, even feebly, Jesus Christ is in you. "*Know ye not your own selves, how that Jesus Christ is in you, except ye be counterfeits, or unbelievers?*" This, then, is the power to overcome sin, and to live a holy life. "*Not I, but Christ liveth in me.*" We have the *pure One* in us to make us pure, the *patient One* in us to make us patient, the *loving One* in us to make us loving. He wants to work out His own life on earth again in us. The question is not what I can do, but what Christ can do. "He can do exceeding abundantly above all that we ask or think, *according to the power that worketh in us*" (Eph. iii. 20). "*God is able to make* ALL *grace abound towards you ; that ye,* ALWAYS *having all* sufficiency in *all* things, may *abound* to every good work*" (2 Cor. ix. 8). The master of a factory orders a workman to weave so much linen in an hour. The workman could not possibly do it in his own strength, but he has the power of the steam-engine to enable him, and he does it easily. Probably most of my readers know the difference between a slip-carriage on a railway—a carriage which goes a certain distance by the impetus already given to it, and then stops—and a carriage having an engine attached to it. Thank God we have an engine attached to us, nay, dwelling in us, for the very purpose of enabling us to do what God bids us. We should not, then, think of Christ as being merely away up yonder in heaven, or away far from us on earth, but as being one with us, and dwelling in us. "*Christ liveth in me.*"

And we should *expect* Him to work out His pleasure in us. He dwells in us for this very purpose. What has He promised to do for us, and in us? "*Thou shalt call His name Jesus, for He shall save His people from their sins*" (Matt. i. 21). Surely we should expect Him to do this for us. "*Sin shall not have dominion over you*" (Rom. vi. 14). "*My God shall supply all your need, according to His riches in glory in Christ Jesus*" (Phil. iv. 19). "*My grace is sufficient for thee, for My strength is made perfect in weakness*" (2 Cor. xii. 9). Do we honestly believe these promises, and that Jesus is in us, and with us, to do what He has said? Oh that we "knew the exceeding greatness of His power to usward wh o believe!"—not to us who *fear* and *doubt.*

Dr. Robert S. Candlish, in his commentary on 1 John ii. 1, writes thus: "But not only would I have you to make this your aim; I would have your aim accomplished and realised. And, therefore, '*I write these things unto you, that ye sin not.*'

"We are to proceed upon the anticipation, not of failure, but of success in all holy walking, and in every holy duty; not of our sinning, but of our not sinning And we are to do so, because the things which John 'writes unto us' make the anticipation no wild dream, but a possible attainment.

"We must assume it to be possible not to sin, when we walk in the open fellowship of God, and in His pure, translucent light; especially not to sin in this or that particular way in which we have sinned before, and in which we are apt to be afraid of sinning again. For practical purposes this is all that is really needed. But this is needed." So writes Dr. Candlish.

We speak often of the sin of those old Israelites who perished in the wilderness. What was it? They looked at their own weakness; they looked at the strength of their enemies, and they did not reckon upon God, who had promised that He would give them the land. Therefore the Lord was very angry, and sware in His wrath that not one of them should enter into the land. Are we, Christians, not committing the same sin almost every day? We look at our own weakness; we look at the strength of the world, and the flesh, and the devil; and we forget to reckon upon God. Lord, show us more than ever our weakness, and more than ever the strength of our enemies, but show us that the Lord of hosts is with us; that the God of Jacob is our refuge: and then we shall say with the Psalmist, "*Through God we shall do valiantly, for He it is that doth tread down our enemies*" (Psalm lx. 12). Whenever we learn to go to God for His Spirit and for grace with as much confidence of getting them as ever we went to our mother for our breakfast when we were hungry, then we shall be enabled to live holy lives; and not, I think, till then.

I remember reading, years ago, a very brief account of an address given by the Rev. Andrew Murray of Cape Town, at the Pan-Presbyterian Council in Edinburgh. He was speaking on Eph. ii. 10: " *We are His workmanship, created in Christ Jesus for good works.*" He said something like this: When God creates anything for a certain purpose, He makes it easy for it to perform that purpose. He has made the birds to fly, and He has given them wings, and He has made it easy for them to fly. He has made the fishes to swim, and He has given them fins, and He has made it easy for the fishes to swim. And if He has created Christians for good works, I cannot but think that He has made it easy for Christians to do good works. And the reason why so many Christians find it so difficult, is because they forget the words in the middle of the verse, "Created *in Christ Jesus* for good works." If they remembered that they were in Christ Jesus, and that Christ Jesus was in them, they would find it much easier to do the good works.

(3) *But while depending entirely on Christ to enable us to live a holy life, we must set about doing, day by day, and hour by hour, whatever the Lord bids us.* A boy once went to cross a river, and when he came to it, he saw the waters rolling on, and he sat down to wait till they would all pass by, so that he would get over easily. Now we must not be like that boy. We must not sit down and wait till we *feel* that we are holy, and till we *feel* that we have power to live a holy life. We never shall feel that we are holy. Till the day of death we shall feel that we are unholy. We never shall feel that we have power. Till the day of death we shall feel that we have no power. But we will know that we have Christ with us, and in us: Christ — embodied power and wisdom—" *Christ the power of God, and the wisdom of God.*" And we must set about doing whatever the Lord bids us, assured that the Lord Himself

will enable us. We must "*work out our own salvation with fear and trembling—believing that the Lord works in us to will and to do of His good pleasure.*" The man with the withered hand had no power to stretch it forth; but he believed that Jesus, who gave the command, would give the power, and he made the attempt, and the power was given. God commands us to do twenty things that we have no power to do in ourselves; but all His commands are promises; and He never gives a command, but along with it He promises to give the power to obey, if we look to Him for it.

You remember the Israelites crossing the Jordan. God told the priests to take up the ark of the Covenant, and go across the Jordan. I think I see them marching down—tramp, tramp—towards the river. There it rolls and overspreads its banks. But onwards they march at God's command, and at last the foremost of them put down their feet on the water; and then, and not till then, a way is opened up, and they went over Jordan dry-shod. So, feeling or no feeling, we must, day by day, and hour by hour, do what the Lord bids us, and the Lord Himself will open up the way.

Yes, we must do what the Lord bids us, whether we like it or not. We must honestly seek to do the whole will of God. We read about fifty times concerning Moses, "*Whatsoever the Lord commanded Moses, that did he.*" He did many a thing he did not like to do. Saul did not like to slay Agag, and because he disobeyed, the Spirit of the Lord left him, and an evil spirit from the Lord troubled him. Jonah did not like to go and preach against Nineveh, and off he went towards Tarshish; but the Lord sent the storm, and the whale, and in the rough school of affliction he was made willing to go to Nineveh.

Tell me, Christian, is there not something you are doing that you know God wants you not to do? and are you going to continue doing it when Christ died to redeem you from that iniquity? Is there not something you are refusing to do, because you do not like it? Take care: the Lord may have to send affliction upon you to make you willing to do it. What would you think of your servant if she said, "I am not going to do this that you bid me—I don't like it"? or of a sailor if he would refuse to go up the shrouds in a storm, and say, "I don't like it"? or of a soldier who would refuse to attack the enemy when ordered to do so, and say, "I don't like it"? Our duty is to be like Christ, who said, "*My meat is to do the will of Him that sent Me, and to finish His work.*" "*I came down from heaven, not to do Mine own will, but the will of Him that sent Me.*" Oh, if we saw God's love to us, we would see that God's will for us is always our greatest good, and always our highest happiness!

The responsibility lies upon us to obey whatever God commands, believing that we have Christ in us to enable us. "*Work out your own salvation with fear and trembling, for it is God who worketh in you both to will and to do of His good pleasure.*" We must work it out. "*Having, therefore, these promises, dearly beloved, let us cleanse ourselves from all filthiness of the flesh and spirit, perfecting holiness in the fear of God*" (2 Cor. vii. 1). "Let us cleanse ourselves." "*If a man therefore purge himself from these, he shall be a vessel unto honour, sanctified, and meet for the Master's use*" (2 Tim. ii. 21). Yes, the responsibility lies upon us to purge ourselves from these. We have Christ in us to enable us.

When God's still, small voice tells us to go and do anything, let us pray to be guided, and at once proceed to do it. We must not continue praying till *we feel* we have the power to do it. We never *will have* the power, and never, therefore, *can feel* that we have the power. But, believing that God who commands us to do it will put forth His power, let us commence and *do* it. "*And the Lord said to Moses, Wherefore criest thou unto Me? Speak unto the children of Israel, that they go forward*" (Ex. xiv. 15). "Moses! thou hast prayed, and I have heard thee. Now, rise and go forward." "*And the Lord said unto Joshua, Get thee up; wherefore liest thou thus upon thy face? Israel hath sinned, . . . neither will I be with thee any more, except*

ye destroy the accursed from among you" (Josh. vii.
10–12). Having prayed for guidance and grace, and
believing that Christ is in us, we must begin and do
whatever God bids us. It is a far easier thing to
remain on our knees in unbelieving prayer, than to
believe that God has heard us, and to rise and step out
boldly on His promise, and begin to do His work,
assured that He will enable us!

(4) *Here comes in the use of means. We must get
above the means, and depend upon Christ alone. But we
shall never be kept depending on Christ day by day, and
hour by hour, unless we use the means of grace.* We
should connect ourselves with some evangelical church
where God's gospel is faithfully preached, attend its
services regularly, and take part in its Christian work.
It is not a good thing to be gadding about from church
to church, and doing really nothing for God. And we
should go forward to the Lord's Table as often as we have
the opportunity. And we must not run into places of
temptation where the Lord does not send us, nor make
companions of those whose company does us harm. What
is the use of praying, "Lead us not into temptation,"
and then running into places where we know we will be
tempted? If we go into temptation where the Lord does
not send us, He will just let us fall—remember that.

And we must regularly read our Bible with prayer,
may I add, *especially in the morning.* I do believe that
fifteen minutes spent over the Bible with prayer in the
morning is worth five times fifteen minutes spent at
night, when we are sleepy, and when a hundred things
have come into our minds during the day. George
Müller, in every address he gives, tries to impress upon
his hearers the great importance of reading the Bible
with prayer. In fact, we cannot grow in grace without
it. If we do not spend some time alone with God over
our Bibles in the morning, it is almost impossible to
have Christ much in our minds during the day. But if
we thus begin the day with God, Christ will be often in
our thoughts all day long.

Readers of this book! will you promise, by the grace

of God, to spend some time alone with God each morning over your Bible with prayer? I venture to say, if you do, it will not be long till Christ will be much more in your thoughts than He is. You will not depend upon the means, but the means will keep Christ before you all the day.

This, then, is the secret of holiness—*a lifelong look at Jesus*. Mark Guy Pearse says that he likes to spell holiness with five letters—J E S U S. He says that he has often found himself so busy consecrating himself that he has forgotten Jesus, and has come no speed. If we look at Jesus much, we will sin little; if we look at Jesus little, we will sin much. No one ever did, day by day, and hour by hour, look up to Jesus, and depend on Him as much as he ought. But that is our sin and shame. That is our fault, and not God's fault. We must not cast the blame of our wickedness upon God. I know very well that there is no such thing as sinless perfection in the world. "*If we say that we have no sin, we deceive ourselves, and the truth is not in us*" (1 John i. 8). Yes, we deceive *ourselves*, but very seldom do we deceive *others*.

Let us remember, however, that the same God who made Enoch and Moses, and Elijah and Daniel, and John and Paul, and Jonathan Edwards and Robert M'Cheyne what they were, is still alive, and is as willing and able to make us holy. The same treasures of grace are as free to us as to them. There is not one of us who may not be far, far holier than we are.

And let us remember the importance of that little word—*now*. "Behold, *now* is the accepted time; behold, *now* is the day of salvation." "The Holy Ghost saith, *To-day*, if ye will hear His voice, harden not your hearts." We cannot trust Christ unless we mean to trust Him *now*. The greatest enemy of God and man is this demon of delay—this convenient season, which is always coming, but which never comes. Dear Christian readers! Jesus dwells in us now, and dwells in us for the purpose of working all His pleasure in us. Let us believe this now, accept this as a fact now, and

16

commence this moment to do the will of God, whatever it may cost.

We have dwelt thus at length on the Bible way of living a holy life, not only with the view of showing that assurance promotes holiness, but also on account of the importance of the subject itself. Surely, reader, you must see that assurance promotes holiness. How can you look up to God with confidence for His Spirit, if you do not know whether He loves you or not? No one can possibly understand the sixth chapter of Romans, and believe that assurance is not favourable to holiness. Why, here you are commanded, in verse 11: "Likewise reckon ye also yourselves to be dead indeed unto sin, but alive unto God in Christ Jesus." This is a command—a command to Christians to be assured of their salvation. Really there is great ignorance and something radically wrong in the religious views of those who do not see that holiness is promoted by assurance. No doubt, it is true that assurance is promoted by holiness; but it is equally true and equally important, that holiness is promoted by assurance. "Every man that hath this hope in him, purifieth himself, even as He is pure."

Even when Christians do work, with what motive do they work when they have not assurance? Just in order to get pardon or assurance. They are always working from selfish motives, and thinking of themselves, whereas, when they know that God loves them, they have both hands free to serve God, and to do good to men. The eleventh chapter of Hebrews never would have been written if the worthies there spoken of had not known that God was their loving friend. Dr. Cunningham of Edinburgh says very wisely: "We believe that the prevailing practical disregard of the privilege and the duty of having assurance is, to no inconsiderable extent, at once the cause and the effect of the low state of vital religion amongst us—one main reason why there is so little of real communion with God as our reconciled Father, and so little of real, hearty devotedness to His cause and service."

XV

𝔚𝔥𝔶 𝔰𝔬𝔪𝔢 ℜ𝔢𝔞𝔩 ℭ𝔥𝔯𝔦𝔰𝔱𝔦𝔞𝔫𝔰 𝔥𝔞𝔳𝔢 𝔫𝔬𝔱 𝔄𝔰𝔰𝔲𝔯𝔞𝔫𝔠𝔢

THERE are various reasons, and they differ in different cases.

1. *Want of health.* I have known a good many earnest Christians who had no doubt of their salvation when they were in health, and whose godliness was not doubted by others, yet, when they became weak in body, believed that they were not Christians at all. The poor weak body acts on the mind; and it is sometimes very difficult for persons with lung or liver disease, or heart or nervous disease, to have assurance. Old Dr. Archibald Alexander of Princeton was once asked if he had always assurance. "Nearly always," he replied, "except when there is an east wind." I remember well meeting one day on the road a young man, one of the most godly and useful young men I ever knew. He was spitting blood at the time, and he told me he thought that he had never been converted at all, that all his past religion was a piece of formality. He thought that God had forgotten him, and completely forsaken him. Poor fellow! No one ever doubted his conversion but himself. I told him that God had neither forgotten nor forsaken him, that it was just want of health, and that God loved him as much as ever. Oh, my Christian reader, who once had God's face shining upon you, but are now in delicate health, and think that God has forgotten you, remember His promise, "*I will never leave thee, nor forsake thee*"

(Heb. xiii. 5). "Who is among you that feareth the Lord, that obeyeth the voice of His servant, that walketh in darkness, and hath no light? let him trust in the name of the Lord, and stay upon his God" (Isa. l. 10).

2. *Some duty omitted or sin committed.* There is a verse in Isa. lix. 2, which explains much of the want of assurance. *" Your iniquities have separated between you and your God, and your sins have hid His face from you, that He will not hear."* When *Christian* in *The Pilgrim's Progress* fell into the hands of *Giant Despair,* and was confined in *Doubting Castle,* he had left the right road, and had gone over a stile into *Bypath Meadow,* where he ought not to have been. This means that when we leave the path of God's commandments, and go where we ought not, we shall find ourselves soon in Doubting Castle. John Angell James, shortly before he died, said that many of the Christians whom he knew lived in Doubting Castle, and that, from the careless manner of their lives, he would have been much surprised to find them living anywhere else than in Doubting Castle. God cannot give assurance to people living in sin. John Newton says: "I would not give a straw for that assurance that sin will not damp. If David had come from his adultery, and had talked of his assurance at that time, I should have despised his speech."

Perhaps, Christian reader, your want of assurance arises from *some duty omitted.*

Is it neglect of the Bible and of prayer? I remember meeting one day on the road a minister, with whom I had formerly been intimate, and he said, "I don't know how it is, but I have not as much assurance now as when I used to meet you." I said, "Do you read your Bible and pray as much now as you did then?" "I do not think I do," he replied. "Well, that is the reason. There is no mystery about it." Reader, you will soon lose assurance if you do not feed on the milk of the word, and if you do not pray.

Is it fear of confessing Christ before men? Perhaps you are afraid of somebody calling you a saint, and

sneering at you, and so you do not want to be thought
a Christian. God will not give you assurance if you are
ashamed of Christ, and wish your neighbours to think
that you are not acquainted with Him. Remember,
that if you really believe in Jesus, however feebly, you
are bound to confess it quietly, humbly, but decidedly.
*"With the heart man believeth unto righteousness, and
with the mouth confession is made unto salvation"* (Rom.
x. 10). Now, I have heard people confess Christ in a
way that I think He did not like at all, telling everybody in a loud, boasting way, in every place and at
every time, that they were Christians, and that they
knew they were born again, and asking, Are you born
again? Nevertheless, remember that if you are a
Christian, you are bound to confess Christ; you are
bound to go to the Lord's Table and confess Him
there. You are bound also to tell the members of
your own family, and your intimate friends, that you do
believe you have found Christ, and to write the same to
those of them living at a distance. The more gently,
humbly, and unostentatiously you do this the better, if
you do it decidedly. But you must take up a decided
position as a friend of Christ.

I know very well that the devil will tell you when
you are converted: "Keep quiet, for if you fall away,
it would be dreadful, and if you say nothing about it,
it would not be nearly so bad." He knows very well
that you are ten times more likely to fall away if you
keep it hidden. He knows that the very day you
quietly and humbly make it known, you will get rid of
all your wicked companions; and that on the same day
you will get new companions who will do you good;
and that God will be greatly pleased with you for confessing Him, and will give you more grace. Is the
Lord going to give you more grace, when you are
ashamed of the grace He has given you already?
Indeed, He is not. And this is the reason why so
many Christian people have no assurance. They are
ashamed of the Lord, and the Lord cannot afford to
give them assurance. This is the reason why so many

people who you had hoped were converted, and were going to be useful, turn out useless drones. They bottle it up, and hide it, and conceal it through fear of men. Oh, my readers! you will never be of any use as Christians if you are ashamed of Jesus.

Is it that you are doing nothing for God — using no means to bring sinners to Christ? You see persons all around you who are not Christians, and you know they are on the road to hell. God commands you: "Let him that heareth say, Come," and you never in any way say to sinners, Come to Jesus. There you sit. in your easy-chair, and wonder that you have not assurance. Perhaps you are like the old woman who had been seeking for fifty years, and had not got peace. She was asked, " Have you been trying to do anything for the good of others?" "No, I have no taste for that; but they say doubts and fears are good for people, so I'll just have to try and bear them." Reader, every word that you speak for Jesus will come back to your own heart with double power.

Let me ask you a few questions. Do you pray for your children, by name, one by one, each day? Do you pray for any persons, by name, outside your own family circle? Do you ask them to come with you to the house of God and the prayer meeting, and pray for them? Is there any easier way of doing good? A minister told me of a woman who brings about a dozen people each Sabbath to his church. Now, Christian, you say you want to be useful, and you lament that you have not more opportunities of being so. Do you ask your neighbours to come with you to church on Sabbath and on week days? Do you, or do you not? Could you not do this? Will you do it—Yes or No? What is the use of whining about want of usefulness if you will not take even that trouble?

Do you ever speak to a neighbour, when you meet him alone, about Christ, as Jesus did to the woman of Samaria at the well? Do you ever write a letter with prayer to a person to whom you cannot speak? Such a letter has many a time been the means of saving a soul. Do you lend books with prayer, or give tracts with prayer? I saw, the other day, that the Rev. Webb Peploe was converted by a tract given at the Derby races, where he had gone to get rid of his convictions of conscience. A tract given with prayer has oftentimes been the means of saving a soul. Perhaps you could, by a little living sacrifice, visit among the sick, or teach in a Sabbath school, or hold a cottage meeting—could you not? Do you give to the Lord of your money, as He wants you to do? Or are you not turning penurious? If you have large means given you, and you cannot do active work for God, surely the Lord wants you to give largely and to pray much.

If you do not do any of these things, this is the reason probably, Christian reader, why you have not assurance.

Or perhaps it is some sin committed. Is there no one who you think has done you an injury, and you mean to give him as good as you got, the first opportunity? That is the reason you have not assurance. Or perhaps it is love of the world that is eating the heart out of you. Or perhaps you are keeping godless company, and will not give it up. Or perhaps you get drunk now and again. Or perhaps you are not thoroughly honest in your sayings and dealings. Or perhaps you are self-seeking and proud. What is it that you think about first in the morning, and last at night, and often during the day? Probably it is that. Would you want to know the shortest way to get assurance? Lift up your heart to God, and honestly pray, "Search me, O God, and know my heart: try me, and know my thoughts: and see if there be any wicked way in me, and lead me in the way everlasting"; and when God has shown you your sin, confess it, and ask Him for Christ's sake to forgive it, and to keep you from it, and in His strength, *put it away.* Yes, *you must put it away;* and then, and not till then, will you have assurance.

3. *Want of clear views of the gospel, and mixing up your own work with the finished work of Christ.*

Old Brooks, the Puritan, tells of a minister who had great joy in Christ. Speaking, on his death-bed, regarding his peace and quietness of soul, he said that he enjoyed these, not from having a greater measure of grace than other Christians had, but because he had *more clear understanding of the Covenant of Grace.* Lord! give us all this clear understanding.

It is really wonderful what ignorance of the very elements of the gospel there is among professing Christians. Some of them do not seem to know that "Christ died for the ungodly," and seem rather to think that it was for good people that He died. Or they do not see that He *finished the work*, and that when they accept Him they get a finished atonement for their sins, and do not need to atone for their own sins at all, but simply to go on their way rejoicing, and thank Him, and love Him, and please Him who has done so much for them. Or they do not see that Christ's death is as free to them as the air, or as the rain from heaven, and that any one who comes to Him, He will in no wise cast out. Or they do not see that "Now is the accepted time; behold, now is the day of salvation"; and rather think that He wants them to wait till to-morrow. Or they do not see that the moment they are enabled to accept Christ, God pardons all their sins, and they become His children. They have no clear views at all. Perhaps they say that this way of salvation is too easy. *Too easy!* Was it too easy for Christ, who paid their debt? Did Christ not suffer enough when He cried, "My God, My God, why hast Thou forsaken Me?" *Too easy!* Was it too easy for Christ? And if it were a particle more difficult for us than it is, not one of us could ever possibly be saved. Lord! forgive people who talk about Thy plan of salvation being too easy, for they know not what they say!

4. *Not thinking often enough about Christ, and not dealing personally with Him.* Even though we may have clear ideas in our minds, if we do not often think about Jesus, and thank Him, and depend on Him, we shall not have much assurance. But, on the other hand,

If at our work in the house, or in the mill, or in the field, or along the road, we thank Him because He died for us, and is delighted to keep us from falling, and to fill us with His Spirit ; and if we honestly and often look up to Him, and depend on Him, and tell Him that we do mean, by His grace, to follow Him fully ; He will shine on us with the light of His countenance, and will say, "Thou hast ravished My heart, My sister, My spouse."

> "A little talk with Jesus—
> How it smooths the rugged road ;
> How it seems to help me onward
> When I faint beneath my load."

5. *Looking too much in at your own heart, and too little out to Christ and His finished work.* If you keep constantly looking at your own heart, you will find things there not likely to give you assurance. You will find the *flesh* lusting against the *spirit*. David said : "Iniquities prevail against me ; as for our transgressions, Thou shalt purge them away" (Ps. lxv. 3). Paul said : "O wretched man that I am ! who shall deliver me from the body of this death ?" (Rom. vii. 24). But immediately he added, verse 25 : "I thank God, through Jesus Christ our Lord." These two verses should never be separated. God has joined them together, and no man should put them asunder. Read also Gal. v. 16, 17. The Revised Version brings out the meaning clearly. It tells us that as long as we live, the flesh in us will lust against the Spirit, and the Spirit against the flesh, but that the Spirit is much stronger than the flesh, and that therefore we should not be beaten, but should overcome. "*Walk by the Spirit, and ye shall not fulfil the lust of the flesh. For the flesh lusteth against the Spirit, and the Spirit against the flesh ; for these are contrary the one to the other ; that ye may not do the things that ye would.*"

Christian reader ! you have the *flesh* still in you ; but you have one stronger than the flesh or the devil *in you*, and *with you*—even Christ Jesus. He is with you, and in you, by His Spirit, every day and hour ; and He dwells in you for the very purpose of enabling you to overcome sin, and live a holy life. Thank God that you have a power working in you able to overcome the world, and the flesh, and the devil. If you forget Him, and do not make use of Him, you will certainly be beaten, and fall. If you depend on Him, He will enable you to stand. John Owen says: "Never any person did or shall perish by the power of any lust, sin, or corruption, who could raise his soul by faith *to an expectation of relief* from Jesus Christ." Whenever, then, you take one look at yourself, take immediately ten looks at Christ. That is the way to have assurance, and holiness as well. Have you not found this, that on the day when you kept looking at your own heart, and did not look at Christ, you had no assurance, whereas on the day when you kept "looking off unto Jesus," your peace flowed as a river? So it will be while you live.

6. *Not distinguishing between the temptations of Satan and your sins.* The devil will tempt you, even though you are a Christian, yea, because you are a Christian. He tempted Christ Himself, and you cannot prevent his suggesting wicked thoughts to your mind. Spurgeon says you cannot prevent the crows from flying over your head, but you can prevent them from building nests in your hair.

Let us ever keep in mind that we have a wicked nature in us, which makes these temptations most dangerous. If our hearts go out towards the temptation, and we love the wickedness suggested, and think over it, and dwell on it, it becomes sin; and this is too often the case. Then we need to confess our sin, and to ask God for Christ's sake to forgive us, and to keep us from it in future; and we should believe that blessed promise: "If we confess our sins, He is faithful and just to forgive us our sins, and to cleanse us from all unrighteousness" (1 John i. 9). Yes; we should believe that we are forgiven, because God says it, and walk before Him as a forgiven child. Let us take care, however, not to abuse this blessed promise, and use it as an encouragement to go on in sin, and thus make a false use of the blood of sprinkling. We shall soon lose assurance if we do.

But if our souls hate the wicked thoughts suggested, and we fly away to Christ, and trust Him to deliver us from the evil, He will do it, and the *temptation* will not be followed by *sin*. One of the most godly young men I ever knew told me that he believed a hundred wicked, blasphemous thoughts came into his mind one day in an hour, that his soul hated them, and he went to the corner of a field, and lay down and called upon Jesus to deliver him from them. Now these "fiery darts" came from the Wicked One; and yet the devil suggested to this young man: "You a Christian, and these thoughts coming into your mind! You are no Christian." And the young man was almost persuaded that he was not.

Again, the devil sometimes tries to make Christians believe that God is a dreadfully hard taskmaster, and that He demands things which He does not demand at all, and when they do not do these things, they think that they are not Christians. He tries to make them think that if they are Christians, they must never smile, nor wear a decent bit of dress, and that they must speak to every human being they meet about Christ, and that unless they have Christ in their mind every moment, they cannot be Christians. He does like to discourage them, and to take away their peace and joy. Let us not be ignorant of his devices.

7. *Living upon frames and feelings instead of upon the person and promises of Christ.* Happy feelings are precious as fruits, but not good as grounds of confidence. We all like to have them. But some persons seem to think that they cannot be Christians except they are always warm in prayer, and rolling in waves of religious emotion. Now, this is not the case at all. "The Lord cannot always be trindling apples with me," said Samuel Rutherford. "Blessed are they that have not seen, and yet have believed" (John xx. 29). Here we must often walk by *faith*, and not by *sight*. Faith is believing what God says without seeing or feeling, simply because He says it. "Just a moment ago I

looked out of the window, and expected to see Slieve Cruib mountain, but I could not see it, because it was covered with a cloud. Still I am sure it is there, though I do not see it. This is walking by *faith*. At other times I look and see it there. This is walking by *sight*." Once I heard a good man say: "This is what I am going to do—feeling or no feeling, joy or no joy, peace or no peace—I am going to depend upon Jesus and His finished work." That is the way to have both feelings and assurance; not to think about feelings or assurance, but about Jesus.

There are two texts that have done me good a hundred times, and I like them because they are true whether I feel or not. If the devil suggests that we are not Christians, let us not argue the matter with him, but come with these two texts to Jesus, and say, "Lord Jesus, I read that 'Christ died for the ungodly' (Rom. v. 6). That is what I am—ungodly—and Thou hast promised, 'Him that cometh to Me, I will in no wise cast out' (John vi. 37). Lord, if I never came before, I come now; and Thou art bound and delighted to receive me; and if I never was converted before, I am now." I think that is the short and easy way of dealing with the devil.

8. *But the most common reason why people have not assurance is because they are not Christians at all.* It would be very difficult for me to be sure that I have ten thousand pounds in the Belfast Bank, because I have not. And it is very difficult for people to have assurance that they are Christians when they are not Christians at all. Now, my unconverted reader, why should you not be saved? When "Christ Jesus came into the world to save sinners," why not you as well as poor Joseph?

Spurgeon often tells the story of his conversion. He had been anxious for months, struggling, and resolving, and praying, and going to meetings, and yet had no peace. In a sermon preached on Sabbath morning, January 6, 1856, he says: "Six years ago to-day, as near as possible at this very hour of the day, I was in the gall of bitterness and in the bond of iniquity, but had yet, by divine grace, been led to feel the bitterness of that bondage. Seeking rest and finding none, I stepped within the house of God, and sat there afraid to look upward, lest I should be utterly cut off, and lest His fierce wrath should consume me. The preacher rose in his pulpit, and, as I have done this morning, read this text: 'Look unto ME, and be ye saved, all ye ends of the earth, for I am God, and there is none else' (Isa. xlv. 22). I looked that moment; the grace of faith was vouchsafed to me in the selfsame instant; and now I think I can say with truth:

> " 'E'er since by faith I saw the stream
> His flowing wounds supply;
> Redeeming love has been my theme,
> And shall be till I die.'"

In another sermon he gives more particulars. "Just setting his eyes on me, as if he knew all my heart, the preacher said, 'Young man, are you in trouble?' Well, I was, sure enough. Said he, 'You will never get out of it unless you look to Christ.' And then, lifting up his hand, he cried out, as only, I think, a Primitive Methodist could do, 'Look! look! look!! It is only look!' I saw at once the way of salvation. Oh, how I did leap for joy at that moment! I know not what else the preacher said. I did not take much notice of it, I was so possessed with that one thought. Like as when the brazen serpent was lifted up, they only looked and were healed. I had been waiting to do fifty things, but when I heard this word 'Look!' what a charming word it seemed to me! Oh, I looked, until I could almost have looked my eyes away; and in heaven I will look on still in my joy unutterable."

May God enable you, dear reader! to look to Jesus, and this instant you become a child of God by faith in Jesus Christ.

Before ending this book, I would like to say a few words to parents and to children.

Parents! do you make it one of your chief objects in

life to bring your children to Jesus, and to train them
for God? I remember well being in a gentleman's
drawing-room one night. Johnny, at that time his only
child, was toddling about. I made some remark about
Johnny, and about his evident love for him. After a
pause, the father said, "Mr. P., there is Johnny, and I
don't know what kind of a boy he will be. He may grow
up wicked, and bring down my hairs with sorrow to the
grave. But one thing I am sure of—*he will never be in
hell.* For many a time before he was born his mother
and I knelt down and committed him to Jesus. And
many a time since he was born, we have done the same.
And I am sure that Jesus is just the same now as when He
was upon the earth, and that He is as willing to bless
our Johnny as He was the children who were brought
to Him of old; and that some time before he dies God
will convert him and take him to heaven."

I think I see yet the earnestness in his face, and the
tears in his eyes, as he said this.

Some time after, I met a Chinese missionary, to
whom I told the above incident. "Well," he said, "I
have very much the same feeling, though I never spoke
it out so plainly. And there is one verse in the Bible
that I always quote to the end, while I hear many
persons stopping in the middle of it. They say, 'Believe on the Lord Jesus Christ, and thou shalt be
saved,' and there they stop. I never stop there, I
always go on to the end—' Believe on the Lord Jesus
Christ, and thou shalt be saved, *and thy house'* (Acts
xvi. 31). If the first part of it be true,—that if we
believe on the Lord Jesus Christ for ourselves, we
shall be saved,—the second part is equally true, that
if we believe on the Lord Jesus Christ *for our families,*
they shall be saved also. I always quote it to the end."

Parents! do you pray much for your children? If
you do not, who else may be expected to pray for
them? A young man once said to me, "I am two-
and-twenty years old, and I never yet saw my father
pray, nor heard him pray." What a sin and shame!
Hannah prayed to the Lord for Samuel, and lent him

to the Lord as long as he should live. If there were more Hannahs, there would be more Samuels.

You have heard of Monica, the mother of Augustine. When she went to Ambrose to tell him of her son's sinfulness, and to ask his counsel, he said, "Duly and piously admonish him of his errors." "Alas! that I have long done in vain." "Then let him behold the example of thy holy life." "That also," replied the mother, "have I conscientiously striven to do, but it has failed of success." "If so," said Ambrose, "you have no resource but prayer." "I have prayed for him," was the reply, "till *my knees* are like the knees of a camel." "Go, woman; the child of so many prayers can never perish." The end of the matter was, that God converted Augustine, and made him the most useful man who lived from Paul to Luther. Do you pray thus for your children?

Parents, you should not only pray for your children, but pray *believingly* for them. Read this promise of God, who cannot lie: "The Lord thy God will circumcise thine heart, *and the heart of thy seed*, to love the Lord thy God with all thine heart, and with all thy soul, that thou mayest live" (Deut. xxx. 6). And think often about Jesus when He was upon earth, how much displeased He was at the disciples for trying to keep away the little children from Him, and how much pleased at the mothers for bringing them to Him. Think, also, how He took them up in His arms and blessed them, and said, "Suffer the little children to come unto Me, and forbid them not, for of such is the kingdom of heaven." Assuredly those children were blessed. Is He not the same Jesus now, and as willing to bless your children as those of old? Is He not present with you in your room? Put them into His arms; lay them upon the bed, or sofa, or chair, and ask Him to take them into His keeping, and to give you grace to train them for Him, and He will assuredly do so. "Train up a child in the way he should go; and when he is old he will not depart from it" (Prov. xxii. 6).

But, parents! if you live careless and unconverted, and do not pray for your children, and train them for God, but for the world, and if you and they be lost, they shall torment you for ever. "Father! mother! you never prayed for me, nor taught me to pray. You never told me about Jesus and His death, and how willing He was to save *me*. You never spoke of heaven or hell; and here I must be for ever. No thanks for the money you left me. What good will it do me now? If you had told me about Christ, and prayed for me, I might have been for ever in heaven. On you, father! mother! lies the blame of my damnation. Oh, this eternity of woe!"

Children! would you not be much happier if you knew that your sins were forgiven; and that Jesus was your ever-present Friend; and that when you died you would get to heaven? And why should you not? Did not Jesus die for children, as well as for grown-up people? Does He not love children as well as grown-up people? Did any child ever go to Jesus, asking Him to take his sins, and make him holy, and Jesus said, No?

Bishop Simpson of America said: " I am satisfied that the day is coming when, in all the churches of the world, we shall look chiefly to the conversion of children, and, as a comparatively rare instance, to the conversion of those in maturer years. The strength of the Church will be put in the grand work of bringing the children early to Christ. Then they will grow up beautiful Christians, stable Christians, developed Christians, working Christians, loving Christians." To all of which we say, Amen.

Printed in the United States
219995BV00001B/4/P